# HOW WE WON & LOST THE WAR IN AFGHANISTAN

# HOW WE WON & LOST THE WAR IN AFGHANISTAN

## Two Years in the Pashtun Homeland

DOUGLAS GRINDLE

Potomac Books
*An imprint of the University of Nebraska Press*

All photos by the author.

Library of Congress Cataloging-in-Publication Data
Names: Grindle, Douglas, author.
Title: How we won and lost the war in Afghanistan:
two years in the Pashtun homeland / Douglas Grindle.
Description: Lincoln: Potomac Books, an imprint
of the University of Nebraska Press, 2017. |
Includes bibliographical references and index. |
Identifiers: LCCN 2017017416 (print)
LCCN 2017037656 (ebook)
ISBN 9781612349541 (cloth: alk. paper)
ISBN 9781612349916 (epub)
ISBN 9781612349923 (mobi)
ISBN 9781612349930 (pdf)
Subjects: LCSH: Afghan War, 2001—Personal
narratives, American. | Afghan War,
2001—Journalists. | Grindle, Douglas.
Classification: LCC DS371.413 (ebook) |
LCC DS371.413 .G754 2017 (print) |
DDC 958.104/7—dc23
LC record available at https://lccn.loc
.gov/2017017416

Set in Lyon Text by John Klopping.

To those Afghans, Americans,
and people of allied nations who
gave much of themselves to
make Afghanistan a better place

# CONTENTS

# ILLUSTRATIONS

# ACKNOWLEDGMENTS

This book could not have been written without help from a wide range of people who provided the inspiration and insights needed to bring it to fruition.

In Afghanistan I was incredibly lucky to collaborate with many colleagues in the field who worked in the military, in government, and in private employment. They made it possible for us to understand our options so we could push forward on many fronts and make our corner of Afghanistan a better place. Without their wisdom and hard work, none of this would ever have happened. Sadly, with the continuing instability in Afghanistan, it is best to leave a number of names of these brave Afghans unwritten in the text.

The manuscript owes a great debt to my tireless editor, Laura Taylor, who ensured common sense and good grammar prevailed.

The editors and staff at University of Nebraska Press, to include Tom Swanson, Natalie O'Neal, and Leif Milliken, worked with understanding and professionalism to ensure the best possible book emerged between two covers. They are a first-rate team, and it has been a privilege to work together.

I take sole responsibility for any errors that have crept into the work despite the best efforts of all concerned.

Finally, I appreciate most of all the unending support of my wife, Joy Grindle, who has made the writing of this book an easier task. She was a model of forbearance as I disappeared for nights on end to polish and repolish these words, and she is the best wife anyone could ask for.

# PROLOGUE

In the faded photo a woman stands in bright sunlight in the middle of a poor Afghan village. She gazes confidently into the camera lens. She is in her twenties, with almond skin and black hair tied back. She wears a pleated skirt and a blazer, and she holds a sheaf of papers. Behind her is a mud house. She is a government employee charged with helping villagers stay healthy, and she's clearly proud of her position as a servant of Afghanistan.

The woman was a community health worker. The photo dates from the early 1970s, when she was sent into the villages to improve the health of the women. If she is still alive she would be about seventy. There is a good chance she died many years ago. The average life span for Afghan women is fifty-one years, and forty-eight years for men. More than a million people died during the Soviet war of the 1980s.

The Afghan government no longer sends neatly attired health workers into the villages. The picture is a relic of the past. The government does maintain community health teams inside villages. Often they are husband-and-wife teams. They receive limited training, and they usually keep a low profile to avoid attracting the attention of the Taliban, who would harass or kill them.

Thirty years later a man walks out of Mirwais Hospital in Kandahar City. He is tall, thin, and in his mid-forties. He is dressed neatly, with a worn blazer over his Afghan *shalwar kameez* clothing. But he wears a harried look, as if the day is too short and life too ephemeral to carry the many burdens he bears. He throws his leg over his motorcycle and starts the engine, roaring off.

The man is Dr. Mousa, a full-time physician employed at the government-run hospital. He also works as the government's director of health in Dand District, being responsible for its seventy-five thousand people. He splits his time between the district and the hospital. Because his pay at the hospital is low and he is not paid at all for his work in Dand, he works a third job at a private clinic. His daily pace is frenetic. Dr. Mousa has too many places to go and not enough time. Soon he will lose his job at the private clinic for not putting in enough hours. Dr. Mousa is constantly worried about earning enough money to feed his family.

Even though Dr. Mousa is the health officer for the district, he rarely visits the husband-and-wife teams in the villages. Security threats don't deter him. Unfortunately he cannot afford to go. The government does not pay him, nor does it provide a fuel allowance for his motorcycle. His hospital pay will either feed his family or fund his visits to the community health workers, but not both.

In 2011 Dr. Mousa worked in Dand for nine months without pay. He never received a fuel allowance. He never went to check on the village health teams. Eventually the health ministry shifted Dr. Mousa to another job that offered a salary.

The story of Dr. Mousa and of the old-time community health worker is the story of life in the districts of rural Afghanistan. It is not an unusual one. It is one wherein Afghan officials want to do the job they've been assigned but find it difficult, or impossible, to succeed. It is a story of problems but also one of hope, success, and future promise. But it is offset by sadness and disappointment.

This is the story of a year in Dand District in southern Afghanistan, followed by a year in nearby Maiwand District, and it is also the story of how our U.S. government district team attempted to make things better.

# INTRODUCTION

> Possessing many noble and natural qualities, such as individual courage, hospitality, and generosity, of fine and commanding appearance and presence, good horsemen, capable of enduring, without complaint, much exposure and fatigue, fond of all manly sports, and frank and social in their bearing and manners, there was much calculated to prepossess us in favour of the Affghans as a people on first acquaintance. Further experience, however, proved them to be destitute of all regard to truth, treacherous, revengeful, and bloodthirsty, sensual and avaricious, to a degree not to be comprehended by those who have not lived among them, and thus become intimately acquainted with their character. —**Lt. General George Lawrenc**e, *Reminiscences*, 1875

Ten years after the Americans invaded Afghanistan and ousted the Taliban, the life of an average Afghan had changed in countless ways. More than eight million children attend school, millions of them girls.[1] The bazaars bustle, and a woman can give birth to her baby in the local health clinic. Villagers drive down smooth roads where before they navigated potholed tracks.

Despite this type of progress, much of Afghanistan remains stubbornly and overwhelmingly unchanged. It is a rural land where millions of small farmers eke out a living on two or three acres of thin soil and often give more than half of their harvest to their landlord. Even in 2011 it remained desperately poor, ranking 172 out of 187 in the United Nations' world rankings for human development. With a per capita GDP in 2011 of only $528, Afghanistan remains one of the ten poorest countries in the world. Average life expectancy is 48.1 years, and infant mortality is the highest in the world. Over a third of Afghans live below the poverty line.[2] On top of this, Afghans remain threatened by continuing insecurity. More than twenty-six thousand Afghans have died since the U.S. intervention, and the death toll keeps rising as the Taliban insurgency continues to grow.[3]

Before the current war began Afghanistan was already a shattered country, broken by the Soviet invasion and the subsequent decade of fighting. It is hard to imagine the scale of suffering. By the time that war ended more than a million had died, or roughly one in fifteen Afghans. Seven hundred thousand became widows or orphans. Millions lived as refugees in Pakistan and Iran. Five million to seven million land mines were buried on precious farmland. Fragile irrigation channels that poor farmers had relied upon for centuries lay in ruins.[4]

Into this land came the United States, with high hopes of improving the lot of the Afghans. The U.S. government wanted to build a new and democratic Afghanistan. The logic was simple. To keep out al Qaeda we needed to keep out the Taliban. To keep out the Taliban we needed a strong country capable of defending itself. To defend itself the country needed a government that worked well enough to entice people to support it. To ensure the government was sufficiently effective we needed to help the Afghans create institutions that could help people in urban and rural areas, providing health care, education, roads, electricity, and irrigation. In essence, to accomplish our goals we needed to help build up the nation. That is what we tried to do.

But over time, distracted by Iraq, underresourced, working with allies who routinely broke their promises, using development plans that continually overreached, and having a poor understanding of the society that we endeavored to change, our nation-building efforts faltered. The Taliban used this opportunity to filter back in, and the war started again as a widespread insurgency, helped by corruption, popular disenchantment with the government and its foreign allies, and the missteps of the United States and the international community.

Despite advances in education and health care, what could go wrong did go wrong. Many districts had one medical clinic for fifty thousand people, or none at all. Many of the teachers the government hired were ghost teachers, who taught in ghost schools under trees or who didn't show up at work. Eight million kids were in school, but how many were actually being taught? No one really knew.[5] The Taliban also influenced our progress. They burned down scores of schools and killed thousands of people who supported the government.

Slowly the United States turned away from nation-building. In a speech in late 2009 at West Point President Obama told the cadets that nation-building in Afghanistan was too difficult to achieve. He said, "Indeed, some call for a more dramatic and open-ended escalation of our war effort—one that would commit us to a nation-building project of up to a decade. I reject this course, because it sets goals that are beyond what can be achieved at a reasonable cost, and what we need to achieve to secure our interests."[6] Instead he said America would stay in Afghanistan to clear out al Qaeda and put in place the security forces that would keep them out. (At this time al Qaeda had roughly 150 men in Afghanistan.)

But just saying something doesn't make it true. The original strategic calculus—arrived at by walking the dog backward—still ended with the need for the United States to help the Afghans build their nation to prevent the Taliban from getting back in. So U.S. assistance for nation-building continued after 2009, up from $748 million in fiscal year 2007 to more than $2 billion in FY 2011.[7] Military assistance was vastly higher. The United States pretended to give aid for new and different causes and enterprises. In reality the United States still pursued the same nation-building idea. Simultaneously the surge in military forces ramped up to as many as one hundred thousand fighting men in 2010, when troop strength peaked. We simply doubled down on our effort.

To accompany the military surge the civilian agencies "surged" their people on the ground. Far fewer than the military cohort, the number of these civilians never even approached two thousand. I was one of them, hired by the U.S. Agency for International Development (USAID) in 2011 as a field program officer to help bring projects to villages in rural Afghanistan and to improve health, education, roads, irrigation, and the capabilities of the local Afghan government.

To be truly effective this field position called for paradoxical qualities in its officers. They needed to possess the humility to put the wishes of the Afghans first, paired with the obstinacy to push back against the bureaucracy when it erred.

The U.S. involvement had built in its own limitations. There was inflexibility in the U.S. approach, despite the need to be flexible in an insurgency that was always changing. There existed a willingness to label the Afghans as quarrelsome troublemakers and as the root of many of our problems, even as we expended billions of dollars and hundreds of lives every year to help them take the initiative. Above all a deep-seated distrust toward our Afghan partners prevailed, when only they could win the war and allow us to go home with honor.

This book is the result of the two years I spent in rural Afghanistan, where these paradoxes and limitations came fully into play. It is a tale of hope and success, and of anger and failure.

The story begins at a small coalition military base a short helicopter ride to the south of Kandahar City, the largest city of southern Afghanistan and the heart of the region. There lies a point where four roads radiate out in a crooked cross, surrounded by a patchwork of green wheatfields and brown patches of dirt baked hard by the sun. The landscape is dotted with villages. On either side of this broad stretch of land rise jagged hills, like the teeth of a gigantic dog.

This place named Dand District was where we would work with poor villagers who tilled emerald green fields irrigated by centuries-old canals under blue skies. This story explains how our little group of Afghans, Americans, and Canadians tried to keep out the Taliban and bring hope to the poor farm families who resided in the villages.

Above all it is the tale of the Afghans—of what they tried to do, how we outsiders supported them, and what held them back. It is their story, and I am grateful to have worked among them for two years of my life.

# ABBREVIATIONS

| | |
|---|---|
| ANA | Afghan National Army |
| ANP | Afghan National Police |
| ANSF | Afghan National Security Forces |
| AVIPAUSAID | farm aid program |
| CERP | Commander's Emergency Response Program |
| CHAMP USAID | farm aid program |
| CN | counternarcotics |
| COIN | counterinsurgency |
| COMISAF | Commander of International Security Assistance Force |
| COP | combat outpost |
| DABS | Da Afghanistan Breshna Sherkat (agency in charge of electrical grid) |
| DCOP | district chief of police |
| DDA | district development assembly (of elders) |
| DDC or DC | Dand District Center |
| DDP | District Delivery Program |
| DFID | Department for International Development (United Kingdom) |
| DG | district governor (officially, district sub-governor) |
| DOWA | Department of Women's Affairs |
| DST | district support team |
| FSI | Foreign Service Institute |
| IDLG | Independent Directorate of Local Governance |
| IED | improvised explosive device |
| IRD | International Relief and Development (contractor for USAID) |
| ISAF | International Security Assistance Force |
| ISI | Inter-Service Intelligence Directorate (Pakistan) |

| | |
|---|---|
| KAF | Kandahar Airfield |
| LAV | light armored vehicle |
| MACV | Military Assistance Command Vietnam |
| MASH | mobile army surgical hospital |
| MATV | MRAP all-terrain vehicle |
| MRAP | mine-resistant ambush protected |
| MRRD | Ministry of Reconstruction and Rural Development |
| NDS | National Directorate of Security |
| NGO | nongovernmental organization |
| NSP | National Solidarity Program |
| O&M | operations and maintenance |
| PRT | provincial reconstruction team |
| RP | Regional Platform (South) |
| RRD | reconstruction and rural development |
| RSSA | regional south stability assessment tool |
| SIGAR | Special Inspector General for Afghanistan Reconstruction |
| S-RAD | Southern Regional Agricultural Development Program |
| USAID | U.S. Agency for International Development |

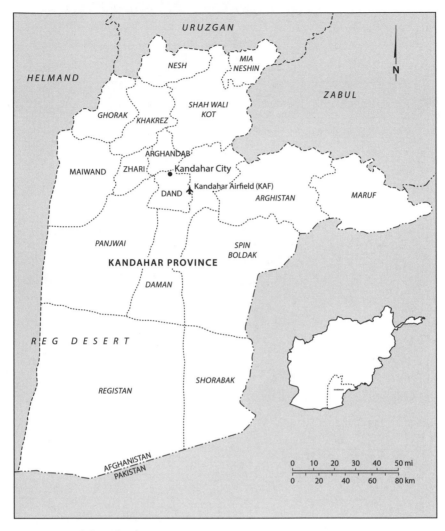

MAP 1. Kandahar Province

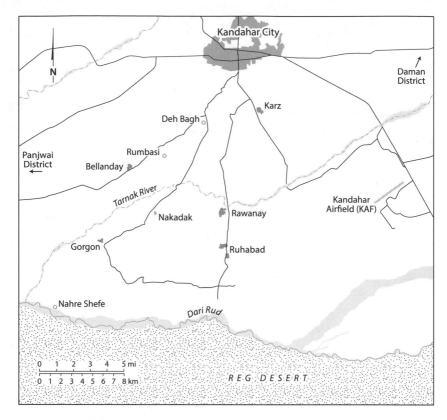

MAP 2. Dand District

# HOW WE WON &
# LOST THE WAR IN
# AFGHANISTAN

# PART ONE

Into Afghanistan

# 1

## The Train-Up

But if you intend to keep India, you must manage to train up men in the spirit of your Malcolms, Elphinstones, and Metcalfes of times past, and of Sir George Clerk in later days;—men who by their character and the confidence the natives have in them, can hold their own without the immediate presence of battalions and big guns.—**Sir Bartle Frere**, *Afghanistan and South Africa*, 1881

I gripped the steering wheel and twisted my head back over my shoulder. The instructor sat beside me, his beefy arm draped loosely across the back of my seat as the speedometer of the old Ford Crown Victoria wound up, passing 25, 35, and 40 as we accelerated down the racetrack in reverse. We bounced tail-first along the speedway. I eased off the gas as we approached the corner. My eyes followed the grass along the edge of the track as I turned the wheel and we circled around the bend and accelerated hard down the next straightaway.

People headed to Afghanistan were expected to know how to drive themselves out of danger in the unlikely event they blundered into an ambush. Reversing at speed and driving through solid objects was designed to give us the confidence to drive ourselves out of dicey situations in the dangerous world we were about to enter.

Despite this danger, most trainees would never actually use these skills. The only driving I would do would be in a minivan on Kandahar Airfield or in the back of an armored military vehicle out on patrol. The high point of the days at the speedway involved ramming through a car that blocked the road, using the heavy Crown Vic as a battering ram. Tips from our burly and brainy instructor included, "Slow down before hitting the blocking vehicle," "leave enough room to accelerate hard through it," and even more to the point, "hit the wheels, which are attached to axles; this the most solid part of the opposing car."

Lots of fun but not very useful for my destination.

It contrasted to our first week of training in Washington DC, where we'd trooped from room to room in USAID headquarters, gathering ID cards, attending security briefings, and completing life insurance forms.

Tedious stuff, but I appreciated being back in the United States. I had just spent sixteen straight months in Afghanistan as a civilian researcher for the Department of Defense working on a human terrain team. I visited villages in the farthest-flung districts in southern Afghanistan and wrote reports for the military. Almost every month I went to a new district, conducted fifty or sixty interviews with the local people, and reported back to the U.S. Army commander on what the people thought about security, how they made a living, what they thought about the Afghan government, and how to improve the situation. My recommendations would end up as projects, in new ways for the soldiers to talk to the people, or new ideas on where best to commit resources.

Three weeks before I arrived in DC I wrapped up my last study in Shamulzai District in Zabul Province near the Pakistan border. I briefed the brigade, delivered a thirty-page paper, stopped at Kandahar Airfield to pick up my transit paperwork, and flew on to Kuwait, Atlanta, Fort Benning, Fort Leavenworth, and finally Boston, where I took a three-week break.

The previous sixteen months in Afghanistan had taught me a lot about what the Afghans thought and how to influence them. I arrived in Washington DC for predeployment training for USAID in late February 2011.

USAID's building was modern and impressive, with a quiet hum of activity and long carpeted hallways lined with hundreds of doors to open-plan offices. It felt good to reconnect with a nine-to-five office environment.

Afghanistan felt a world away when contrasted with healthy-looking Americans dressed in business attire. Yet here we were, part of the expansion of U.S. civilian presence in Afghanistan, our numbers increasing from 320 to almost four times that total in under three years. We trod a well-worn path from office to office, clutching our paperwork. Our in-processing class was tiny, with only six people. All of my fellow classmates were gracious, funny, and smart, and we soon became a happy and close-knit group.

By our second week the flow of in-processing paperwork ceased and we started to really learn in a weeklong seminar. The all-day classes were taught by an experienced Afghanistan hand who had lived and worked there for twenty years and was married to an Afghan man, as well as by a USAID manager who knew the ropes. We learned how to interact with the Afghans, how to identify the most important individual in a house (only lackeys sit beside the door), and how not to insult the Afghans.

We soon moved to formal State Department training, held at the Foreign Service Institute (FSI) in Arlington, Virginia. Here we spent two weeks in large classrooms, crammed in with about fifty people from other agencies. Lecturer after lecturer came in to tell us about the arcane nature of the bureaucracy and our place in it. Unfortunately the lecture material repeated much of the information we had already learned about the culture of Afghanistan, including how the Afghan government worked.

We acquired background information instead of what we wanted: the specifics of what we would be doing. Details were sparse. We asked what we might be doing once we reached Afghanistan. A presenter explained, "One of the most important things we can do is influence the master narrative, especially among the young people." This sounded awfully smart, but did it mean anything?

Training was supposed to prepare us for the next year or two abroad. The previous October, in 2010, a report by the Office of the Special Inspector General for Afghanistan Reconstruction (SIGAR) noted that trainees received "limited information on their roles and responsibilities before arriving at their assigned locations." The State Department assured the inspectors they were working to fix the problem.[1]

Annoyingly the instructors insisted on answering our questions with one correct "book" answer. Despite fifty experienced people in the room, this practice killed any chance for real discussion. Other students had worked in places across the globe and implemented innovative ideas, but they received no encouragement to explain them.

Much of the second week at FSI repeated the first week's lectures with a few variations. In my notes from early April are scrawled the words, "Training hits rock bottom. Seeing the same COMISAF [Commander of

International Security Assistance Force] slide three times today, plus four times previously."

Then one day a dapper-looking man came and spoke to us for about forty-five minutes. He wore the kind of highly polished brown shoes that are seen only in British Parliament or investment banks. Former ambassador Ronald Neumann, who had recently finished leading the U.S. embassy in Kabul for almost three years, said America had simply not devoted the time and effort to winning the war, because it was distracted by Iraq and had let the Taliban back in.

In his experience short-term cycles of three-year plans had failed. And he noted that now, in 2011, America was again embarking on a three-year plan (2011–14) that would probably fail, because American planning was still too focused on the short term. Clearly trying to tell the truth, Ambassador Neumann was a marvel of forthrightness, clarity of vision, and depressing realism.

To finish up our training we flew to Indiana, where the National Guard runs a military-style camp. Here trainees are supposed to learn how to interact with real Afghans in contrived scenarios. Unfortunately the students were ill prepared for the ordeal. Despite our many lectures at FSI, we received no clues on how to deal with Afghans in meetings. Despite our cultural training, we remained ignorant of the cultural and political nuances that would affect our ability to run meetings effectively. The sole advice given to us in the FSI lecture halls was to never promise more than you can deliver or, even better, never promise anything at all.

Indiana was fraught with these unanswered questions. Should we take a hard or soft approach to get Afghans to agree to do the right thing? Which negotiating skills would work best? Indiana would be trial by fire.

The trainees included USAID development people, State Department political officers hired temporarily for Afghanistan, law-enforcement types, and bodies from a bevy of agencies, including the Office of the Inspector General. The training assumed we already knew what made Afghans tick. Most of us had never been to Afghanistan. This wishful thinking broke down almost immediately when the scenarios began.

In Indiana the training kicked off on a somber note. During a video teleconference from the U.S. embassy in Kabul we learned that we would be arriving in an atmosphere of declining resources. One embassy staffer bluntly advised, "We are ramping down our work." And we discovered that most of the development work would be done at the provincial level, not in the districts where a number of us were headed.

We lived in an encampment composed of steel-sided trailers, a large sheet-metal central meal hall, and a similar classroom building. Every day we traveled via military Humvees to an unused mental institution redesignated as the staging area for our meetings. American mentors accompanied us into the rooms where we would meet Afghan Americans pretending to be Afghan government officials. The trainees needed to discern the individual's problem and offer a solution as we fumbled through each forty-five-minute meeting.

Before and after each session the instructors told us to never promise anything to any Afghan, not ever. We were advised to "promise less" and push the Afghans to use money from their own budget. This advice inevitably flew in the face of our real jobs as USAID field officers, which called for us to guide the disbursement of hundreds of thousands of dollars in a single district in a matter of months. It also ignored the reality that the Afghan government had almost no money to fix anything, because its own budgetary funds rarely reached the countryside. No matter; we were to press on within the rules.

As the meetings progressed, the advice given by the American mentors and the Afghan American "players" rarely meshed. The week culminated in a helicopter ride, a traditional Afghan supper and dancing in the old mental institution facility, and a van ride to the airport the next morning. Our little group headed to the bar at the airport and tried to forget the puzzling advice.

We received a course in countersurveillance during which we drove around suburban Washington in a van and tried to learn to detect "terrorists" who were observing us. We managed a detection rate of about 5 percent in spotting lurking watchers, suggesting we had a lot to learn if our eyes and ears were actually needed in our future high-threat environments.

Then it was on to the speedway with high-speed driving in reverse and then firing guns. The weapons instructors, rugged ex-military types, seemed embarrassed by the lack of know-how among the trainees, the majority of whom would be working at the embassy anyway. They advised us that once in Afghanistan we should avoid anything to do with a gun. "Just unload any weapons you happen to see lying around on the ground," they urged soothingly. This was a far cry from my previous U.S. Army job, in which we were issued rifles or handguns and expected to use them.

Four days later our little group of six boarded a packed United Airlines Boeing 777 for a fourteen-hour flight to Dubai. We stayed overnight in a luxury hotel, spent some government cash on beers and chicken wings as we overlooked Dubai's grand canal, and the next day flew to Kabul, where we faced another week of paperwork and lectures while cooped up inside sterile concrete walls. With twelve hundred staff housed in tower blocks and temporary trailers, the embassy boasted all the modern conveniences: an American-style bar, a pool, dining facilities, a shop selling low-priced liquor, a coffee shop, and the same chancery building that had housed the embassy back in the 1970s when the Soviets invaded.

Five days later we scattered, three of us taking a flight to Kandahar. We regretted splitting up our group, but we were glad to be leaving those high embassy walls. I felt bad for the permanent inmates of the U.S. mission, the same relief and regret one feels when leaving a poorly run zoo. The small turboprop roared down the runway in Kabul, bounded into the air, and bounced in turbulence over Kabul's hilltops. The embassy receded behind us, though the hangover caused by our final night's celebrations lingered.

Kabul was past. The Afghan capital represents the strategic and commercial center of the country, and whoever controls Kabul also controls Afghanistan. Ahead of us lay Kandahar, the heart of the Pashtun belt and the center of the insurgency. I'd left Kandahar just fourteen weeks earlier.

# 2

## KAF World

The Quetta Shura Taliban has made Kandahar province and its capital, Kandahar City, primary objectives of their campaign in southern Afghanistan. Kandahar is also the birthplace of the Taliban movement, and the historical powerbase of the family of Afghan President Hamid Karzai.—**Carl Forsberg**, *The Taliban's Campaign for Kandahar*, 2009

The twin-engine turboprop steadily descended out of the flawless blue sky on our approach to Kandahar City. Scattered clouds streaked the sky above. Gradually the mountains of Uruzgan and Zabul Provinces fell behind, and the hills of Kandahar, jagged and wind worn, rose from the flat desert floor. The land reflected infinite shades of brown, dashed with rectangles of green where fields clustered near streambeds and canals.

A large blue lake flashed by. Pooled behind the Dahla Dam, the lake provides water for almost a million people in Kandahar Province. Then Kandahar City slid past the right wing, tiny cars and motorcycles filling the main streets that cut through neighborhoods of compounds, each nestled behind thick walls. The city is flanked to the west by a line of hills that divide the urban area from the rural western districts of the province.

The plane lowered its flaps, dropped its landing gear, and lined up for Kandahar Airfield. Visible beyond the left wing, forty miles to the east, Pakistan lay behind another line of hills jumbled like a mass of waves rolling in from the Himalayas.

We descended the last few thousand feet over green grape vineyards and fallow fields. The plane swept low over a highway that led to Pakistan. We thumped hard onto the runway, the plane braking as we rolled past lines of dusty military helicopters, fighters, and transport planes on adjoining aprons.

Kandahar Airfield, better known as KAF, holds the distinction of being the world's busiest military airfield. A kind of civilization of its own, it lay fifteen kilometers southeast of Kandahar City. It rivaled the Afghan metropolis, being a very American city covered in thick Afghan dust. The airfield was built around Kandahar International Airport, a grand title for a dusty runway and terminal building built in the 1960s as a way station for propeller airliners on the Tehran-to-Delhi route. Even before its completion the airport was obsolete, modern jets passing miles above.

Settling into dusty irrelevance, the airport was resurrected by the American invasion in 2001. During the seven years previous to our team's arrival it had become a metropolis, a boomtown, and testimony to the ever-expanding war effort. KAF was a sprawling monstrosity of modular housing, domed metal workshops, dusty asphalt roads, tents, and the bustle of tens of thousands of people running and servicing the war in southern Afghanistan.

We stepped off the plane and into 85-degree sunshine on a ramp owned by the U.S. embassy. The State Department maintained its own air fleet. Vietnam-era Hueys lined up with rotors pointing crookedly at the sky beside a Russian-built Mil transport helicopter and two old CH-46 Sea Knight twin-rotor helicopters painted in State's special gray-and-blue livery, also Vietnam vintage.

We and our bags were whisked by minivan to the government civilian compound, past military crews laboring over helicopters in various stages of loading and unloading, some with their cowlings open and engines exposed for maintenance. Hundreds of helicopters baked in the sun, most closed up and empty.

At the civilian office we checked in with staff. Regional Platform South, which accommodated civilian government employees who lived and worked in three prefabricated, two-story buildings, was tucked inside a tall wire fence.

The civilian buildings occupied a corner of a sprawling compound that housed the military headquarters. In previous years the embassy staff had worked in a drab, green-painted wooden building closer to the military. Now the hulking white prefabs of RP South represented a step up and a step away from the military's purview, as the enclosure was inside a tall wire fence and sported its own entrance to the rest of KAF. Inside the Platform the linoleum on the floors was clean and free of dust, and the office doors were uniform and trim.

Regional Platform South complemented the military's headquarters, known as Regional Command South. Never mind that the military had something approaching thirty thousand people in the south and the civilians numbered around two hundred sprinkled across the bases in Kandahar and three other provinces. The point was that the civilians were making an "equal" effort, and the military surge troops were being matched by equivalent civilians.

The Platform was organized into functional specialties, some people working on governance, others on agriculture and economics, or infrastructure, health, or education. Oddly the whole setup was almost exactly replicated about twelve miles away in downtown Kandahar City, where civilians and their military counterparts worked at another coalition base. There the Kandahar Provincial Reconstruction Team (PRT) worked with Afghan ministries inside the city, covering the same subject areas and generally feuding with the people assigned to similar jobs at KAF.

Shown to our temporary accommodation trailers, we were released and told to be on hand for the next morning's briefing. Inevitably daily life at KAF revolved around meetings, usually with other Americans and sometimes with other Americans at the PRT. Few KAF personnel, with some exceptions, met regularly with Afghans in the ministries in Kandahar City. Encouragingly the women in charge of health and education interacted with the Afghans—the only way to learn how Afghanistan worked.

Two of us from my training class remained at KAF for a few days to process in before heading to other areas. A third newbie would be based at KAF permanently.

In our downtime we strolled around KAF. The compound was located a short distance from the central quadrangle the Canadians had constructed of wood when they took control of Kandahar five years earlier. Called the boardwalk, it contained shops and fast-food restaurants, with coffee shops, a French-style bakery and deli, a German military exchange, as well as a fully stocked TGI Fridays and a KFC. Off-duty soldiers and a ragtag assortment of civilians in sunglasses and baseball hats strolled the boardwalk at all times of the day and night. Inside the quadrangle the Canadians had built a concrete-floored street hockey rink, complete with professional-looking boards. Matches between teams of sweating soldiers in an assortment of sports clothes were held before cheering crowds.

The surrealism of KAF was enhanced because of its disconnect in space, time, and outlook from the surrounding countryside, as nearby hills loomed over the hockey and volleyball games. A tall wire fence separated KAF from nearby villages, and the feel and flavor of the place was American. Third-country-national staff hired from Manila, Delhi, or one of a dozen other locales ran the dining halls and did most of the basic labor around the base. The atmosphere was determinedly American.

All day and every day jet fighters blasted off from the runway or screamed across the sky, making tight turns at a thousand feet to slow down and line up for landing.

Insurgent rockets occasionally impacted inside the vast base. People queuing for hamburgers in the dining halls might hear an alert and crouch down, waiting for a rocket to land, usually out of earshot. Minutes later they would go back to the buns and Heinz ketchup. The rockets arrived about four times a month but failed to bring the full reality of Afghanistan onto the base itself. Causing a minor trickle of casualties, they seemed like an unwelcome visitation from a war movie rather than an act of war itself.

KAF's boardwalk was a tenacious outcrop of American life, but in the years before our team arrived it almost didn't survive. The previous year the U.S. Army commander, General Stanley McChrystal, and his command sergeant major had taken issue with the "soft" life provided by the fast-food joints and knickknack shops. In his memoir McChrystal said he was disturbed that soldiers in the most forward bases worked without respite while those in the rear at KAF had it easy. He ejected Burger King, Subway, and a few pizza places from the boardwalk.

Six months later the army backpedaled. The "no-fun" policy was scrapped and fast-food joints reopened, with some official mutterings that a tight supply situation on the road from Pakistan had required the shutdown. This reasoning was viewed, widely and correctly, as mealy-mouthed subterfuge. I never met a forward-based soldier who hated the fast-food joints at KAF; they just hated KAF and viewed it as a bastion of rear-echelon people who contributed little to the war effort.

Our stopover in KAF lasted a week. I had been assigned to a half dozen districts by the time I reached KAF. Now I would be going to Dand, a small rural district just south of Kandahar City and just over the rise of hills to the west of KAF. Home to almost seventy-five thousand people, just one American and one Canadian civilian staffed the district. The U.S. guy had already left Dand, heading home, and we overlapped by about forty-eight hours at KAF.

Keith Pratt, a man with a weatherbeaten farmer's face and piercing eyes, resembled a slimmed-down Santa Claus, complete with bushy beard. He blended well with the beard-wearing rural Afghans. The beard disappeared as he transitioned out.

Keith was opinionated and didn't mind making waves. Unpopular in some offices at KAF, he was popular with the Afghans in Dand who saw in Keith someone who would fight for their interests. Keith was running a particularly sharp feud with an adjoining office named the Stabilization Unit, and he related the details with gusto.

Now firmly assigned to Dand, I would fly out the next day. Matthew, from my training class, would be taken to the adjoining district, Panjwai, which was unstable and dangerous.

Our forty-year-old refurbished Sikorsky Sea King helicopter lifted off from KAF and clattered its way fifteen miles west from KAF toward Dand. We flew past the jutting brown hills, looped up past Kandahar City. As we entered Dand we saw scattered villages, each surrounded by fields of yellow wheat and green grapes. Smoke climbed wispily from tall chimney stacks.

The big helicopter circled and descended to a small military base near a road junction. Military tents surrounded by gravel occupied one side of the base; a cluster of white-painted concrete buildings took the other. The base in Dand was home to about one hundred soldiers.

The helicopter circled once, banked harder, and then flared as it crossed a double layer of fortifications to land with a bump on the gravel by the tents. I grabbed my bags and dashed off the helicopter's ramp. The chopper lifted off, sprinkling the base with debris.

A tall guy dressed in short sleeves and old combat pants stepped forward, grabbed a bag, and headed past some shipping containers. We dumped my bags and footlocker in front of a small white "living container" with a big satellite dish on top. A few dusty green tents flapped limply in the breeze. I had arrived at my new home for the next year.

# PART TWO

Into Dand

# 3

## Settling In

We know by painful experience that the Afghans are a people of a totally different character—turbulent—bred from infancy to the use of arms— and with a passion for independence in which they are exceeded by no people in this world. This love of independence is such as to make them intolerant, not only of foreign rule, but almost of any national, tribal or family rule. They are a people among whom every man would be a law unto himself.—**Sir George Campbell**, *The Afghan Frontier*, 1879

The tall helpful guy was a Canadian development official named Antoine Huss. In his early thirties, with sun-bleached hair and a chiseled face that creased easily into a smile, Antoine served as the district political advisor appointed by coalition forces, officially titled the International Security Assistance Force (ISAF). In Dand for almost a year he would depart in about six weeks. While Keith Pratt had concentrated on humanitarian projects and the economy, Antoine tried to improve the performance of the district sub-governor, Hamdullah Nazak, and keep Nazak's relationship with ISAF running smoothly.[1] Antoine spent hours each week teaching English to DG Nazak and advising him on relations with ISAF, villagers, and the provincial government. It helped that Antoine and Nazak were roughly the same age and shared a similar outlook on life.

Although a native of France, Antoine had moved to Canada and worked in a consular office before the tedium of processing passports and writing reports became too much to bear. He envisioned adventure in Afghanistan, obtained a position with the Canadian foreign office, and moved to Kandahar in 2010 after a brief stint in Mali. Wearing a light beard and clothes faded by a year of the blazing desert sun, Antoine was well known to Afghans throughout the district.

The year before Antoine's arrival the Canadians had made a series of mistakes in Dand, the biggest one the appointment of a political advisor who rubbed DG Nazak the wrong way. A political advisor should help the DG to govern better and improve his work habits. The job can be a difficult balance, because the political advisor must implement policies formulated at higher levels of ISAF. Often the local Afghans are unimpressed with these ideas. The political officer then becomes the piggy in the middle.

The solution is for the political officer to make suggestions and to persuade and influence the Afghans but never to pressure them, which would place them in a subservient position from which they instinctively recoil. Antoine realized that cajoling and persuading would work far better than pressuring, and he solved this problem so neatly that DG Nazak consulted Antoine on almost everything of importance in the district.

The political advisor possesses several advantages, the most notable the fact that Afghans regard him as a potent status symbol, like a human Toyota SUV. The advisor's mere presence proves that the governor is important enough to warrant a foreigner assigned solely to him. A political advisor is generally treasured by the DG, even more so if he can access money or development programs (a USAID officer has an automatic step up on this score). The smart advisor builds on this natural advantage.

Antoine's Canadian predecessor had squandered this advantage and alienated DG Nazak with his brusque, dominant manner. Worse yet he pressured DG Nazak and his staff rather than influencing. Nazak complained the advisor wanted to run the district, expecting him as district governor to rubber-stamp ISAF's ideas. DG Nazak felt sidelined within his own district center. "The Canadians told me to do things," Nazak explained about that time. "So then I stayed outside at the clinic for ten days."

Nazak protested by moving from his office inside the Dand District Center (DDC) to a small building outside the front gate that had once been used as a clinic. He refused to return until the advisor left. He also demanded the Canadian battle group strike its tents, which were then only a few yards away from the DDC, and move to a new base that would be built just outside the walls of the compound—which is how the gravel-covered military side of the combined base came into being.

With peace restored DG Nazak moved back into his office. Antoine arrived soon after, becoming DG Nazak's best friend in ISAF and his most trusted advisor.

Nazak learned from this episode that ISAF could be defied if necessary. As security and governance in the district gradually improved and as Nazak gained experience, his leverage over ISAF steadily increased.

Antoine was personable and knowledgeable. He split the daily duties with Keith. Each day Antoine and Keith would walk through the gate separating the ISAF side of the base from the district center compound. Antoine would sit with the governor while Keith mentored the other staff, especially the director of agriculture.

Antoine lived in a white sheet-metal trailer next to mine. His trailer contained a desk and a bed. Mine had two desks, a bed, and a large metal box that housed the satellite receiver equipment. After we lugged in the footlocker filled with USAID-issued gear and my two bags from the helicopter, little space remained. I found that Keith had thoughtfully left a year's supply of coffee, a deluxe brewing machine, and two CDs with files on all his activities.

One desk was mine and the other was used by the Afghan language assistant–cum–political advisor, Mohammad Zahir, who worked for the district support team (DST). A native of Kabul and in his early twenties, he was stocky and intelligent. He had worked for eight years for ISAF, mostly as a U.S. Army interpreter. Now assigned by the State Department to Dand, he kept the foreigners on our district support team out of trouble by advising us on Pashtun customs and etiquette even as he translated complicated Pashtu conversations into English and vice versa. When I arrived in May, Mohammad had been in the district for two months and was trusted by Nazak, which was invaluable as Antoine prepared to leave.

It didn't take long to get settled into my little hooch. The metal container I lived in was located near the perimeter wall of the base and sported a single window. Standing on the wall, which was built of wire-mesh containers filled with dirt and stacked fourteen feet high, I could see every part of the base because the other side was only one hundred yards away. It took less than a minute to walk briskly from one side of the base to the other.

Originally named Strongpoint Edgerton by the Canadians, in memory of one of their soldiers who died in the vicinity, the base was later taken over by the U.S. Army and renamed Combat Outpost (COP) Edgerton. It housed about one hundred people who lived and worked in a dozen green army tents. With a Kuchi nomad camp located just outside in the desert dust, it was a sunnier version of a MASH unit. About a dozen Canadians, who mentored the police and managed projects, worked in the place. They would pull out at the same time Antoine departed.

A headquarters company of U.S. Army soldiers also lived on Edgerton. Three of its soldiers visited the district center daily. The rest of the soldiers, including a platoon of scout-snipers, ran the camp and spent a lot of time in the gym. On many evenings the scouts went out to snatch any Taliban unwary enough to live in Dand. A few stray civilians and military advisors rounded out the personnel.

The base was unlike the embassy and KAF, which were unhappy postings plagued with too many meetings, stifling bureaucracy, and a bar and pool that reminded the inmates of home but did little to cure homesickness. Our base was a small, Spartan prison behind fourteen-foot walls, well away from the pressures and demands of rear-echelon routine. Each day proved different, and being close to the Afghans meant you could see and interact with the people you were assigned to help. It was a happy base. Most people felt physically connected to the war, whether it was catching criminals and the Taliban or working alongside the Afghans. Paradoxically time in Dand slipped by easily with the countryside pressing in and America feeling incredibly remote; the experience at Edgerton felt authentic.

The advantage of living cheek by jowl with the district center became obvious. The morning commute took two minutes, and we could come and go unescorted, spending as much time there as we wanted. That day Antoine walked me over to the district center and showed me through the offices. The DDC was a large, two-story building paid for with Canadian money. It was just over a year old, with a blue stripe painted on the eaves and wire mesh over the windows. Faded red carpets lined the halls and framed photographs hung on the walls, memorializing school openings and VIP visits during the previous eighteen months.

More than twenty Afghan district staff occupied small offices in the building. First introductions felt a little bewildering, but the staff seemed friendly. Keith and Antoine were clearly liked and respected.

The Afghans sat at desks, many of which had computers and printers. I had seen a succession of district centers over the previous sixteen months, and almost none held any staff, let alone people working at desks. In the wilds of Zabul Province, in districts such as Atghar, Daechopan, or Arghandab, the offices stood empty and the district governors remained absent for months at a time. Many of the DGs, when they did appear, did almost no work. Just getting them to show up was an almost impossible task.

One of the most striking district centers was in Arghandab District in Zabul Province. Located in a remote mountain valley, it was a concrete building huddled behind high security walls with a guard tower at each of the four corners. The place resembled the set of an old movie on imperial soldiering, such as *Beau Geste*. The governor's office was a room with a single desk shoved in the corner and a rug and pillows spread across the floor. The DG, Mohammad Afzel, was a well-fed Afghan of about forty-five. He said he wanted to help the people but had no resources. The Taliban had infiltrated the district center, which made it risky for local people to come and see him. Neither could he visit the villages because the Taliban were too strong and the Afghan security forces too weak. He was reluctant to place his life in the hands of his bodyguards from the Afghan National Police, confiding, "They just smoke hash. I don't trust the ANP guys. They are a threat. I tell them to search houses, and they steal everything."

From Arghandab the road to the provincial capital had been cut by the Taliban, so the villagers traveled along a back route through the hills. To get to the district the DG usually hitched a ride with the Afghan National Army soldiers, who made the journey once a month when their supplies ran low and cleared the road of bombs by hand using wooden poles. Consequently he spent most of his time in the provincial capital, Qalat, where he collected his pay and lay low. Governing ranked at the bottom of his list of priorities, and one could hardly blame him.

Here in Dand the staff seemed interested, competent, willing, and cheerful. They sat behind dusty Dell computers, some actually using them. Antoine explained the current priority was to get Internet into the building for the Afghan staff to use—his last goal before his departure, he said.

I met Mohammad Naseem, who held the portfolio for the Ministry of Reconstruction and Rural Development (MRRD). He also coordinated projects. Just getting into middle age and sporting a dyed beard and the stance of a boxer, he laughed a lot and seemed very happy to be there. He attended Kandahar University in his spare time. He had a computer on his desk that he tapped at constantly, producing reports for the provincial MRRD offices.

Naseem was also a former businessman who traveled widely in the region and as far as Greece and Turkey, and he had worked for several medium-sized companies. Now he received the government wage of about $250 a month, plus top-ups paid out by a new USAID program. I suspected he knew more about Afghan trade than most of the American economic advisors brought in at great expense to work at KAF. A colleague in his office, a Mr. Qayum, happily and quietly filled innumerable notebooks, allowing Naseem to take the spotlight and share jokes with ISAF people who came to the office for green tea each day.

The government advisor assigned to the district was Karim Kamin. Only twenty-one, Karim dressed well and spoke polished English. He, too, attended Kandahar University. His father ran the Ministry of Finance section in Kandahar City, so whenever funds failed to clear the bureaucracy in Kandahar, Karim could quickly determine the cause.

Ambitious and smart, Karim had grown up in Kandahar City. Given his pedigree, common sense, and his parents' desire to see him married and following in their footsteps, he would likely spend his life advancing through the Afghan government bureaucracy. Technocrats were slowly coming to the fore in Afghanistan as universities took advantage of the booming economy and stable security in the cities to produce more graduates.

The education director in Dand, Abdul Ahad, had managed to open almost all the district's schools, and he had twelve thousand students enrolled. Tall, unsmiling, reserved, and thin, he was a Barakzai tribal elder. His tribal status trumped that of his job. And while he earned only about $500 a month, his visitors young and old often bowed and kissed his hand.

Finally Antoine took me in to see DG Nazak. Thirty-three years old, Nazak, slender with the beginnings of a paunch, knew some English and had quick, sly eyes and an easy smile. Nazak held the reputation of a young man with a future. After setting up a national youth organization that brought him credibility with the power brokers of the province, he received an appointment as district sub-governor at the tender age of twenty-eight. He possessed obvious shrewdness and willpower. The success of Dand in tamping down the insurgency happened in large part due to his ability to manipulate the villagers and gain their support in the teeth of an armed opposition.

His youthfulness didn't concern the Afghans. The historic father of the Afghan people, Ahmad Shah Durrani, had risen to prominence at a young age. A former chief bodyguard to the Persian shah, Ahmad Shah was twenty-eight years old when the shah was murdered. Under suspicion, young Ahmad fled with the other Afghan bodyguards back to Kandahar, where he became the leader of the southern Afghans in 1747. He ruled with an iron hand that unified the Pashtuns and made them a force to be reckoned with in a region of much stronger neighbors. Nazak's strengths were considerable, and ISAF valued him because he got things done.

By the end of our visit I felt pleased that so many things seemed to be going right. A convivial atmosphere prevailed among the staff, who seemed to care about their responsibilities, and the foreigners appeared to get along well with the Afghans.

Work ceased at midday for lunch. By two o'clock the DDC emptied as people scattered to their homes in Kandahar City. No one lived at the DDC; everyone commuted. I was struck by how similar the place felt to the small-town government offices in central Massachusetts that I had covered as reporter. Dand had a similar combination of coziness, amateurishness, and cheerful competence. An underlying open-mindedness and willingness to learn felt refreshing too.

Back at the base we met the rest of the Americans. The infantry battalion occupied a nearby larger base. One of its companies worked at Edgerton in a tent with offices constructed out of plywood and two-byfours shipped from the United States and nailed together to form cubicles and a few tables. Radios buzzed, two screens showed readouts attached to a camera mounted on a tall pole and focused outside the wire, and a moving map displayed nearby ISAF patrols. The soldiers worked cheek by jowl in a jumble of spare batteries, bullets, a rack of weapons, and old magazines devoted to coverage of hot rods and hunting. A few hand-painted signs from home adorned the walls. It was jumbled, but in its own way it was as cozy as the Afghan setup across the fence.

An officer from battalion headquarters, Captain Matt Kotlarski, ran the projects from the military end. What we couldn't do with USAID money Matt Kotlarski paid for with military money, which the Canadians had already been doing for two years. With the Canadians heading home, Matt would be the only game in town when it came to military-funded projects. Luckily he lived on Edgerton along with a few other battalion headquarters soldiers charged with coordinating the Afghans, the police mentor team, and the battalion scouts.

Matt was dark-haired and fit, a long-distance runner and West Point graduate who hailed from Indiana. His time in the army was scheduled to conclude at the end of his tour, but he wanted to make things better before he rotated out. He saw Dand as a good place to make a mark, and he spent hours in the district center and behind his computer, writing contracts, finding contractors, and consulting with the Afghans and the battalion staff to make sure the details were right.

His boss, the battalion commander of 1-5 Infantry, was Lt. Colonel Brian Payne, a blunt and determined man with an army buzz cut. Medium height and early forties, Payne had an imposing but friendly presence, and with more than twenty years in the U.S. Army he acted as if this posting to a battalion command in a combat zone was the prize of his life. Married with four children, he openly drew parallels between his offspring and the Afghans and his subordinates, as if the rules governing his children back home applied universally. Smart and aggressive in doing whatever it took to improve Dand, he supported the Afghans and Nazak.

A man on a mission, Payne intended to get his soldiers out of Dand, which saw only sporadic insurgent activity, and into the more savage fight next door in the very unstable Panjwai District. He wanted to move his men as quickly as possible, but his five companies in Dand could not leave if the situation deteriorated. So he needed to help the U.S. civilians keep Dand stable while his soldiers left. He directed Matt Kotlarski to work with us to figure out how to keep the insurgents out with ever-fewer resources. He vowed to do whatever it took to make that happen.

That was the vision for Dand laid out at the Platform, where the goal was to begin to turn Dand over to the Afghans. It would be easy to work together, because our basic goals meshed. I had lucked out. No one at USAID had provided a blueprint of how to work with the military. Training provided us even less insight. We'd been told to "be nice and cooperate well." Working closely with the military was key. The civilian plan and the military plan were interdependent, requiring mutual support. If the military and the civilians took off on different tangents while covering exactly the same ground, it could be potentially disastrous, as when DG Nazak moved out of the DDC and then kicked the Canadians off the base.

This lack of preparation for cooperation, or "civ-mil" in the jargon, was puzzling. It was especially so because the previous fall the U.S. government's Office of the Special Inspector General for Afghanistan Reconstruction (known as SIGAR) had issued a report pinpointing several problems with this type of cooperation, noting that ISAF lacked a cohesive structure through which the military and civilians could work together. The report said that, in practice, the civilians and military tended to figure out how to work together once they arrived on the ground, for good or for ill, depending on the personalities involved. It noted that "civilian-military integration relies primarily on individual personalities."[2]

So in this crapshoot we had hit a vein of very good luck with Brian Payne and Matt Kotlarski. Payne would consider anything that might keep Dand stable as he pulled his men out company by company and sent them to Panjwai, and he immediately made me his partner to ensure the Afghan government was supported during the transition. In weekly meetings held at the battalion base, which coordinated the companies, the headquarters, and other elements such as the police training team, he directed that I sit next to him and consulted me often as we considered different courses of action. No-nonsense and results oriented, Brian Payne was willing to back up his convictions with time, cash, and manpower to quickly achieve his long-term results.

By the end of day one in Dand the district looked promising, but the task would obviously be enormous: to improve the performance of the Afghan government and keep insurgents out as security forces departed. The number of civilian programs promised to begin dropping soon, too. At the same time, I faced a steep learning curve. Even while observing how the Afghan government really worked, I needed to develop plans to improve governance and the economy and to reinforce security to make the security gains irreversible, while also ensuring our plans accorded with the plans at the battalion and Platoon.

To do all this we would mentor the Afghans and help them to improve governance by putting in a number of development or stabilization projects. The Afghan staff would learn to govern better the same way a college computer science student might learn to write code: by doing it. We would help them by using American money and then help them as they eventually started to govern using their own Afghan government money (at that time in very short supply). It was a rough blueprint.

Potential problems loomed. Memories of a tension-filled first meeting I had attended at KAF with Keith and two stabilization officials still lingered. They had butted heads over the way forward for Dand's economy, adjourning after an hour in mutual disgust. I wondered when similar obstacles would begin to emerge for me and how long the honeymoon would last.

But first I had other things to worry about. We would need a civilian plan that would improve the Afghans' staff, improve the economy of the district, and shore up security as American soldiers left for Panjwai.

In 2011 Dand experienced only scattered roadside bombs and firefights, but it had been an extremely violent place only a short time earlier and it could easily slide back into the abyss. No one wanted that to happen, least of all the local residents.

# 4

## Ousting the Taliban

The overstretched Canadians began to concentrate on a smaller geographical area around Kandahar City in the spring of 2009. Having pulled out of Panjwai, the Canadian battle group announced in April 2009 its plans to secure a small number of villages in the Dand district, on the southern edge of Kandahar City, where support for the government was stronger, and then to concentrate development aid on these villages.—**Carl Forsberg**, *The Taliban's Campaign for Kandahar*, 2009

The metrics of success aren't how many enemy troops you kill.
—**Fred Kaplan**, *The Insurgents*, 2013

Near the crossroads of two paved roads are about twenty family compounds standing shoulder to shoulder, their high mud walls almost touching. This is the little village of Deh Bagh, a small settlement of a thousand farmers on the southern fringes of Kandahar City, where the urban sprawl gives way to open fields.

Near the crossroads sits an unused high school where one day in May 2011 a group of ragged kids climbed a blue-painted jungle gym and played on the swings. A tiny bazaar of a dozen shops occupies another corner of the crossroads, a bakery sits at the third, and a mosque stands at the fourth.

Next to the high school is the center of government for Dand District. Every American calls the district center the DC or DDC, for Dand District Center. In the military system of acronyms, the district governor becomes the DG and the district chief of police is the DCOP (pronounced D-cop).

The DC is a concrete oasis of modernity amid the somber tans and browns of the mud-walled village. The DC's white paint reflects the sunshine brightly. Next to it stand two slightly shabbier buildings: the old district center, which is hardly used, and the DCOP's poorly maintained police headquarters.

Dand is made up of widely scattered villages where farmers eke out a living by growing grapes, pomegranates, wheat, and vegetables. By the time I arrived in Dand in May 2011 the district had been effectively pacified, except for areas along the fringes to the north and southwest, where soldiers drove cautiously and occasionally hit large bombs. The Taliban skirted the district, infesting the fringes, and it still maintained a hold in Panjwai, the district next door. Dand had not been pacified for long.

In 2009 when the Canadians first redirected resources from across the province into Dand, they concentrated on Deh Bagh village. It became their model village. Stabilizing Deh Bagh was the first step to pacifying the entire district. They commissioned a Canadian NGO to make an agricultural survey of the village, and the consultants suggested improving agriculture and coming up with alternative businesses to boost the farmers' incomes. The Canadians planned to expand that idea over the entire district.[1]

Despite the new resources, security remained poor for a more than a year. A favorite tactic of the insurgents was to use the homemade improvised explosive devices, or IEDs, that would explode when a person or vehicle moved over an electrified switch, detonating a jug of low-tech explosives. That year and the next, patrols regularly ran into IEDs. Canadian and American soldiers drove gingerly along the dirt roads, and they walked warily through fields and along irrigation dikes. The rattle of small-arms fire sounded routinely as security vehicles rolled across the landscape.

Slowly the district improved. In fact 2009 was not the lowest point. In 2007, when DG Nazak arrived, he inherited a district controlled by insurgents. The district center in Deh Bagh had a siege mentality, and the new DG was beleaguered.

"When I first got to Dand, the Taliban were all over the place," Nazak recalled. "Gorgan, Malajat, Nakadak—the Taliban were everywhere. So I asked the people what their problems were and went from there."

The Taliban had come back strongly since the American invasion. In 2001 the Taliban fled from Kandahar Province, heading northward and eastward away from the advancing U.S. Special Forces and the Afghan leaders Hamid Karzai and his local rival, Gul Agha Sherzai, a tribal chief and former governor of Kandahar. People welcomed the change of regime. But over time the Taliban slowly recovered and regrouped, living just over the Pakistani border in the cities of Chaman and Quetta. The Pakistanis helped the Taliban reorganize and push fighters back across the border, often pressing reluctant former Talib commanders back into the fray.

Meanwhile U.S. Special Forces and the Afghan government missed opportunities to recruit onto their own side former Taliban leaders who had given up the war, often persecuting them instead.[2] Corruption set in under Gul Agha Sherzai's rule in Kandahar, and people became disenchanted with the government's inability to bring positive change to many rural villages. As the government and the security forces lost their halo of goodwill in the countryside, slowly the Taliban grew stronger and pushed in from their Pakistani bases, recruiting as they went.

For the first few years after 2001 Kandahar was quiet, NGOs operated freely, and life improved as health care and education ramped up. But then the number of insurgent attacks began to rise in the province and across the south and east.

Across Afghanistan the lengthening casualty lists reflected the rising number of attacks; 57 foreign soldiers had died in 2003, but by 2007 foreign forces had lost 232 service members.[3] Worse, insurgents turned increasingly to laying IEDs, often using techniques learned in Iraq to make the explosions more deadly. The IEDs took an increasing toll. As the years passed the attacks continued to accelerate. In August 2008 the number of attacks per month was under fourteen hundred, but a year later that figure had jumped to twenty-five hundred. A report by DFID, the international development agency for the United Kingdom, noted in late 2008 that across the country "the security situation is rapidly deteriorating."[4]

The American military was also pessimistic. In September 2009 General Stanley McChrystal argued that forty thousand more troops should be sent to Afghanistan to stabilize the worsening situation. Otherwise, he stated bluntly, the war could be lost. According to McChrystal, "Failure to gain the initiative and reverse insurgent momentum in the near-term (next 12 months)—while the Afghan insurgency matures—risks an outcome where defeating the insurgency is no longer possible."[5]

In 2007 DG Nazak stepped into the middle of this rising tide of insurgent violence. He had few police in Dand and less money, and he lived out of a small, shabby district center in the middle of some fields in Deh Bagh.

Many of the villages where the Taliban held sway were in the southern areas of the district and hard to reach. These were the poorest villages in the district and were in a particularly dry area where Keith Pratt had wanted to dig deep wells and grow alfalfa. In 2007 the insurgents relied on these villages for food, accommodations, and information. It was thus vital to get the farmers on the side of the newly arrived governor. But the spread-out nature of the district made it difficult to gain a critical mass of support among these farmers, who rarely ventured far from their villages.

Worse still, Afghan security forces in Dand suffered from divided loyalties between the two rival tribes that lived in the district.

The rising number of attacks of the recent past and the district's historical experience suggested the security forces would not do well. During the Soviet presence insurgents operating in Dand had overrun a Communist base at Deh Bagh village, killing fifty government soldiers. The Soviets had rarely pushed into the heart of Dand, and when they had they had not stayed long.

In one operation in 1985 the Soviets tried to kill a group of mujahidin leaders meeting in the village of Rumbasi, about ten kilometers along the road leading from Deh Bagh to Panjwai. Flights of troop-carrying helicopters and helicopter gunships swooped in to cut off the village, while more Soviets in armored vehicles pushed down from Kandahar City to sweep up the remaining insurgents.

It was a stiff fight. Trapped, the mujahidin skillfully fired on the encircling soldiers, trying to break out. According to an after-action report written by the Soviet commander, as the armored vehicles approached, "the enemy opened up with interlocking, integrated small arms fire which did not let the main body approach the village. . . . Mujahidin who tried to withdraw out of Rumbasi to Ruvabad were cut down by fire from our first lift."[6]

In this encounter one hundred mujahidin died, and they lost thirty weapons. But the Soviet victory was short-lived, as the battalion immediately withdrew to Kandahar City, ceding the ground to the insurgents. Dand would continue to be a sharp thorn in the side of the Communists throughout the Soviet intervention.

So when Nazak arrived as district governor, he faced headwinds that suggested to any farmer the insurgents would be hard to beat. Few farmers would want to align themselves with the side more likely to lose, and this put the wind even more strongly in the sails of the Taliban.

Nazak faced a dilemma. Every day that passed with no progress would diminish the influence of the young and untested governor. His sole previous experience in government was as a simple village elder. It was not immediately obvious whether the appointment of the twenty-eight-year-old as district governor would be a success. So Nazak needed to do something immediately to pull the locals into his orbit. While he could defend the district center, it would be difficult to win people over to his side if he simply remained there and exerted little power in the villages. Yet if he overreached and suffered a defeat, he would lose much of his reputation even before he was established. He needed a plan to maximize his limited influence and resources.

Nazak set about exploiting the few advantages he had. Dand is the historic home of the Karzai family; the family village, Karz, lies in the northeast corner of the district. It is also the base of the Sherzais, an equally influential family whose most prominent son was Gul Agha Sherzai, the local strongman who took the post of provincial governor with the support of U.S. Special Forces in late 2001 after Hamid Karzai was appointed national leader. Sherzai had been governor before the Taliban took over in 1994. More than 60 percent of the people in Dand belong to the tribes of these two prominent government families, a circumstance that offered a natural opposition to the Taliban and was one of the few advantages Nazak held.

Nazak was concerned that the Taliban shadow governor controlled more of the district than he did. In effect Nazak's radius of control around the district center was about as far as a gun would fire.

According to Nazak, he knew the Taliban shadow governor's name was Hekmatullah and that he lived in Nakadak, a village about halfway between the district center and the desert in the south.

Nazak heard that Hekmatullah would go to prayers at a mosque in Nakadak every Friday. One night Nazak gathered up his six bodyguards, drove the six miles toward Nakadak, crossing the wide Tarnak River on the way, and approached the mosque as darkness fell. Coincidentally a wedding party was making its way past Nakadak. Nazak slipped his car into the line of revelers for cover. At the right moment the governor's car slipped away from the wedding convoy and parked near the mosque. Nazak stationed his men near the mosque and walked inside.

Prayers were under way and Hekmatullah was bent over in prayer with the other men. According to Nazak, he, too, bent over and joined the service, kneeling a few feet behind Hekmatullah.

The prayers continued. At last the mullah finished, and Nazak rose quickly. He called out for everyone to stay put, saying, "I am looking for a district governor! The Taliban district governor! Who is that? I am the real district governor! He or I will die!"

Hekmatullah stared at Nazak as he spoke. Nazak relates this tale with gusto, his eyes shining as he speaks. Afghan culture is based on tales of personal power and strength, but even allowing for hyperbole it was a striking thing to do. Nazak's six men were miles from assistance back at the DDC, so it was a high-stakes gamble.

As it happened, no one died that night. Nazak, having made his point, beat a hasty retreat. He and his men, afraid of getting shot in their car on the way back to the district center, elected to walk the two miles north to the Tarnak River, and they didn't stop until they reached the district center four miles beyond the river later that night.

The first roll of the dice in the war to oust the Taliban governor had paid off. Nazak survived and improved his reputation.

Several nights later Nazak repeated his exploit. He took his handful of men and pushed across the Tarnak River again, this time going farther south. They went to a town called Gorgan, where they read out a list of names of the Taliban sympathizers. They announced they knew who these men were, and they would be watching for them. Nazak warned, "Don't ask for projects from me if you support the Taliban." They departed, again reaching the district center safely.

Chancing his luck a third time, Nazak and his men again drove south of the Tarnak River, this time stopping in Chuplanay, a village near Nakadak. Arriving at night, Nazak delivered the same message, calling on people to stop supporting the Taliban. He and his men gave their short speech to the startled residents, who could scarcely believe that the newly installed district governor was pushing into areas far from the district center.

The lightning-strike visits were a clever stratagem. They showed Nazak could get into any village in the district, even in the south. His presence punctured the image of Taliban control. And it cost relatively little. In each village Nazak said the same thing: don't work with the Taliban; work with me and get projects. Supporting the Taliban will lead to nothing. It is time to switch sides. Nazak said the visits took the initiative away from the Taliban, calling into question their control over the district.

More clandestine visits to villages in the south followed. Nazak and his men were never caught. Eventually, as security began to improve and more forces flowed in, Hekmatullah traveled to Pakistan and didn't return.

Nazak had begun the long road to taking the district back, but he needed the support of the Canadians. When they had first arrived in southern Afghanistan in 2005, the Canadians tried to hold a score of districts, an impossible task. Gradually Canadian responsibilities narrowed to three districts: Dand, Panjwai, and Daman. The Americans took over elsewhere.

Change in Dand came slowly. Throughout 2008 and early 2009 the Afghan police waged a back-and-forth fight with the Taliban. Eventually Canadian money began to flow more freely, funding two new mosques and a playground in Deh Bagh, as well as the cleaning of several irrigation ditches in 2008.[7]

In the spring of 2009 the Canadians transformed Deh Bagh into a model village, pouring in resources and sending agricultural experts to visit farmers in their mud compounds. That summer the Taliban counterattacked but were beaten back over two days of fighting. The government, its seat secure, expanded projects into additional villages.

U.S. combat forces strengthened the district, and by September 2010 the tide had turned. Taliban attacks dropped significantly.

People told Nazak they wanted security and projects. Nazak invited them to the district center, and he set about spreading police and projects throughout the district.

Money trickled first into the northern part of the district. It gradually spread south toward the arid zone in the south bordering the Reg Desert. Projects reached the villages where Nazak had pursued the Taliban shadow governor. More people appeared at the district center to ask for projects. The Canadians spent millions of dollars to support those requests.

More than three years after Nazak became governor of Dand, the situation in the villages had been transformed. The district became the most secure in Kandahar Province, with the people firmly on the side of the district governor. As security improved, Nazak's stature grew, with the Taliban reduced to trying to ambush him on the road as he drove past in his armored Toyota. Twelve ambushes at the district center, on the road to Kandahar City, and at his home in the city failed to kill him.

When I arrived in May 2011, Nazak was a young man with influence beyond his years. Elders visited him in the district center every day, one group after another trooping into his office for hours on end, every day.

But on days when the elders filed into his office to sit on cushioned chairs and ask for his judgment about a family fight or a dispute over land with the neighbors, Nazak often got a wistful look in his eye. It was the look of someone enmeshed in routine, who has reached his goals, at least for the moment, and yet cannot help but remember past heroic moments. In their place was a political system Nazak had designed from scratch, one that was built upon the white-bearded elders who appeared at his office each day.

# 5

## Nazak's Grand Bargain

At present, the grand vizier, and almost all the great officers of the state, are Baurikzyes, and they owe their elevation to the courage and attachment of their clan. . . . They are a spirited and warlike clan.
—**Mountstuart Elphinstone**, *An Account of the Kingdom of Caubul and Its Dependencies in Persia, Tartay, and India*, vol. 2, 1842

Each section of a tribe, however small, has its leading man, who is known as Malik, a specially Pathan title. In many, but by no means all, tribes, there is a Khan Khel, usually the oldest branch of the tribe, whose Malik is known as Khan, and acts as chief of the whole tribe. But he is seldom more than their leader in war and their agent in dealings with others; he possesses influence other than power, and the real authority rests with the Jirga, a democratic council composed of all the Maliks.—**Intelligence Branch**, Division of the Chief of Staff, Army Headquarters, India, *Frontier and Overseas Expeditions from India*, vol. 1, 1907

In the fall of 2001 Hamdullah Nazak sat in a jail cell in Kandahar City. He was barefoot because his captors had taken his shoes, and his entire body was battered.

Until that morning his uncle had been with him in the jail, but when the sun rose his uncle was taken from his cell, escorted to the front of a crowd of people in a downtown street of Kandahar City, and hanged from a crane. Nazak knew fear. His Taliban captors had promised twenty-three-year-old Nazak that his turn on the crane would come when the sun rose the next day.

But by a remarkable stroke of good fortune for Nazak, the Taliban ran out of time. The next morning the Taliban fled the city as American and Afghan forces approached. Nazak lived to see his young life almost ended and then suddenly restored.

Nazak was jailed because he was caught spying for the former governor, Gul Agha Sherzai. Four days after the American bombing began, Nazak's uncle, Abdullah Khyal, almost fifteen years Nazak's senior, dispatched Nazak to Sherzai's house in Quetta, Pakistan. There Sherzai gave Nazak a satellite phone, a GPS device, and a small video recorder. Nazak hid them behind the dashboard of his car and drove across the border back to Kandahar.

Nazak, his uncle, and other helpers tracked the movements of the Taliban, plotted their positions, and telephoned the coordinates to Quetta. They eyed the house of the Taliban leader, Mullah Omar, and walked Taliban trenches near the airport. After American bombs struck, they would assess the damage and report back. Sometimes the Americans would strike again if the target was not completely destroyed. Nazak later told a reporter that he hated the Taliban and felt they were an embarrassment to the country.

One day in November Sherzai called on the satellite phone and told Kyal and Nazak to leave immediately. But the Taliban police moved in too quickly, catching them with sketches of Taliban positions, target lists, and a telltale satellite phone number. Nazak was beaten in jail with truncheons and cables across his whole body for weeks on end. His uncle died under the torture before the Taliban took his body to the square to hang before the crowd. They left his corpse there for three days as a warning to others, draping a banner on him that read "Abdullah, son of Habibullah, inhabitant of Salehan, who had a satellite telephone and was giving information to the Americans, and was killing Muslims through the Americans." Nazak learned of his uncle's death only after he was released from jail, and by then Sherzai was in the governor's office in Kandahar City. Nazak was rewarded by Sherzai with temporary command of more than a dozen soldiers.[1]

It was natural that Nazak and his uncle would have sought out Sherzai as a benefactor, and it was his good fortune that he was accepted, though it almost ended his young life and did end his uncle's.

Nazak's uncle was a strong supporter of the monarchy that had been overthrown in the 1970s. Nazak's own family came from a moderately distinguished line of military leaders. His village lay only a few miles from Sherzai's. Nazak was also a member of the same tribe, the Barakzais.

Dand District holds a mix of Barakzai, Popalzai, Achekzai, and various other tribes. Sherzai is not the only powerful figure to come from Dand District; President Karzai, a Popalzai, also hails from the district. The Karzai family seat in the village of Karz, in Dand, is a few short miles from Sherzai's home village. Karzai's Popalzai tribe resides in the northeast of the district, while Sherzai's Barakzai tribal power base occupies the south and southwest.

Competition between the two tribes has lasted for centuries. The Popalzais ruled at the very beginning of modern Afghanistan but were supplanted by the Barakzais; they have tried to claw their way back to dominance ever since. The rivalry exists, in part, courtesy of a common lineage. Both belong to the Zirak Durrani tribal confederation.

This amalgamation of tribes is immensely powerful. The name Durrani originated with Ahmad Shah Abdali, the modern state founder who unified Afghanistan. He was a member of the Sadozai, a minor subtribe of the Popalzai. As a young man, Ahmad Shah was serving as the leader of the bodyguards of a Persian emperor when the latter was suddenly assassinated by unhappy liegemen. Ahmad Shah quickly returned to Kandahar before suspicion could fall on him, as he was carrying part of the Persian state treasure. In 1747, already a noted warrior and suddenly the holder of great wealth, Ahmad Shah was elected leader of all the tribes in a grand *jirga* of tribal elders in Kandahar.

Ahmad Shah quickly took the title Durr-i-Durrani (Pearl of Pearls), and the Durrani name was substituted for his former tribal name, Abdali. Ahmad Shah quickly consolidated the tribes beneath him and embarked on successful military campaigns into India.

Though Ahmad Shah hailed from the Sadozai subclan of the Popalzai tribe, his fame kept alive the claim to Popalzai ascendancy for centuries, even as the Popalzais were overtaken by the Barakzais in power politics. Even in the twenty-first century President Hamid Karzai benefited from his Popalzai heritage.

Tribal splits defined, in part, the fissure between the Taliban and the government. The Taliban have a natural identification with a rival Afghan tribal confederation known as the Ghilzais. And many more Taliban adherents come from another tribal confederation, the Panjpai Durranis.

The very genesis of the Taliban is rooted in this split. According to Peter Tomsen, who worked for years as a U.S. diplomat in the region, the Pakistani intelligence service, known as the Inter-Service Intelligence Directorate or ISI, helped to establish the Taliban in the late 1980s and early 1990s, when the agency promoted young Mullah Mohammad Omar, a Hotak Ghilzai, as a leader. This shrewdly worked the tribal angle. By selecting Omar, they harkened back to the Ghilzai elders, who had led the region before being shunted aside by the Durrani rule centuries earlier.[2]

Popular lore has it that the Taliban arose as a reaction to a single atrocity. The legend goes that a local leader of a gang of gunmen kidnapped, raped, and killed the children of a family of travelers near Kandahar City in 1994. By hanging the leader of that gang from the barrel of a tank gun and then eliminating many other strongmen, the Taliban became a force of popular resistance to the arbitrary disorder then reigning in Kandahar. Other accounts differ on the precise origins of the movement, with the hanging occurring at a different place or time, but most agree that a group of tribal elders and religious figures became disenchanted with the actions of the warlords, who stole, raped, and molested people on the roadways. They banded together to stop the lawless behavior. Mullah Omar, a village religious leader who had fought the Soviets in the Kandahar area, was elected the leader of the group.

Rather than being a popular movement, the reality of how the Taliban grew is murky, according to Tomsen, who says the Pakistani ISI played the tribal card heavily when setting the Taliban in motion, as it had in the 1980s when it supported hard-line party leaders over moderates against the Soviets.

According to Tomsen, "Colonel Imam and ISI's Quetta office had been remolding the Argestan shura into the Taliban for over a year before the apocryphal scene on the road to Kandahar took place. The ancient vendetta between Afghanistan's two largest tribal confederations, the Durrani and the Ghilzai, played an important role in Imam's shrewd construction of the Taliban's hierarchy. He gave overriding preference to anti-Durrani Ghilzais, as Zia had in selecting the seven party leaders. And he placed Ghilzai Hotaks, such as Mullah Omar, in strategic control of the movement."[3]

Though analysts differ on the details, they agree that the centuries-old jostling between the Zirak Durranis and their rivals, the Panjpai Durranis and the Ghilzais, fuels the conflict today.[4] Many ordinary Afghans of the Zirak Durrani, such as Nazak, would have turned naturally against the Taliban. The Taliban's tribalism and radical ideology separates it from Karzai's ethnically mixed government and most of the Afghan people, because banning the education of girls, employment for women, and even music is counter to most of the closely held beliefs of ordinary Afghans.

Given this tribal background, it was natural that Nazak would seek out Sherzai to work against the Taliban. Nazak also wanted to rise. As a teen he'd ping-ponged from job to job, working as a farmer, a carpenter, and in a brickyard, always looking for something better. Even as his father advised him to settle down with a single profession, his mother expressed faith that he would succeed. His home life not always happy; young Nazak had something to prove.

So the arrival of the Americans in Kandahar City proved a double bonus. It saved Nazak's life and installed Sherzai into the provincial governor's office, which he seized at the first opportunity.

In late 2001 Karzai was approaching Kandahar City from the north as Sherzai came from the south. Both enjoyed having American advisors and patronage, but in December Karzai was appointed the head of the interim government. One of Karzai's first moves was to appoint an Alikozai tribal elder and veteran mujahidin commander, Mullah Naqib, as governor of Kandahar Province. Outraged, Sherzai marched to the governor's office and refused to leave. Karzai hastened from Kabul to Kandahar City to see Sherzai, which was probably a mistake, because in a tribal society it made Karzai look weak. When Karzai emerged, Sherzai was still governor, either because Karzai gave in or Naqib acquiesced under pressure.

Naqib retired quietly to a district just north of the city, while Sherzai consolidated his power and began to engage in the massive corruption that marked his tenure as governor. A powerful leader, Sherzai ran Kandahar as his personal fiefdom with little interference from Karzai, taking over business rivals and extorting money by arresting tribal leaders, who could pay the ransom for their release.

Meanwhile a now free Nazak lacked an obvious way forward. Still seeking advancement and progressing steadily in business and local politics, he bounced from Dand to the border city of Spin Boldak and back again, along the way becoming a village elder and a used-car dealer. He established a national youth organization, garnering positive attention from provincial authorities. At age twenty-eight he received the appointment as governor of the "unofficial" district of Dand. (As Kandahar Province's newest district, Dand had a constitutional status that remained in limbo for years.)

By then Sherzai had been transferred to Nangarhar Province in the north, and Nazak was operating on his own in Dand. He quickly moved to undermine the Taliban, and the Canadians began to spend money widely. Within three years Nazak had turned that money into a viable political system capable of resisting the Taliban's repeated incursions.

At the heart of Nazak's system lay a bargain he made with local maliks, or village headmen. He would send them projects, but only if they came to the district center to arrange the assistance. A steady flow of maliks began to stream into the district center, a visible sign of the success of Nazak's system.

In return for projects the elders also pledged security, and they would prove this security worked by opening the local school. To do this, the villagers would provide tips that allowed the security forces to weed out the Taliban. "Security depends on the maliks," was Nazak's oft-repeated maxim.

Under Nazak's bargain, if villagers provided no tips about the insurgents and the maliks did not visit the DDC, then projects would not flow to the village. If a village underperformed and the school failed to open, Nazak replaced the malik and the village tried again. Nazak reckoned his system created better security, improved the economy, and restarted the dialogue between the people and the government, without which the war could not be won.

As months passed farmers could see better security, and their perception of security became more positive, which in turn made them more likely to inform on the insurgents, which improved security even more. It was a virtuous cycle, but the system relied on a steady stream of quick-impact projects, such as a new well, that could be installed without a lengthy delay. Nazak needed people to feel he was responding to their needs, even if he was merely channeling foreign money while the foreign soldiers throughout the district actually handled most of the details.

The system worked, even though being a malik was risky. In 2009 the Taliban began a campaign across Kandahar to kill tribal elders and political leaders, including those in Dand. As late as 2010 visiting Canadian VIPs were shot at by insurgents who lurked outside the district center. In mid-2011 elders were still being beaten up or killed by Taliban infiltrators. One kidnapped malik gained his freedom only after a group of elders traveled to Panjwai District, where he was being held by the Taliban, and retrieved him.

It was risky for maliks to work with the government, but they gained personal prestige by bringing projects to their people. This played into the widespread Afghan desire to gain a public reputation. Tribal custom is based on pride and honor. The more honor an Afghan male possesses, the wider his reputation. Honor and reputation are bound together. In a small village in Dand a malik who brought money and projects to the people gained such a reputation. At the same time Nazak also exploited the tribal ties that people shared with the government.

I already knew a few dollars could make a huge difference in a village, despite the risk. The year before, on a patrol in a rural district north of Kandahar City where I worked with the Department of Defense, we had driven to the isolated village of Baghtu. Located near the main road to Uruzgan Province, the collection of two hundred mud houses built at the bottom of a deep valley drew few visitors from the passing traffic. Rocky hills covered in scrub rose on either side. The villagers in Baghtu wanted a stone wall to protect their crops and houses from the river that ran through the village and surged with snowmelt each spring.

"The village needs a wall to keep out the flood waters," one farmer said. "The recent flood destroyed a lot, and all the wheatfields are hurt. We have lost twenty-five acres of wheatfields this year due to the flood."

The protective wall would cost about $11,000, and it represented the first government gift to the village. But the risk was great. Several years before, the people in the Baghtu Valley had risen up against the Taliban and banned them from their village. But the Taliban returned in force to kill the ringleaders on their doorsteps. At that time the government had been no protection. Now the villagers just wanted help.

"If we take projects, the Taliban will be angry. They will come and beat us," the farmer told us. "But they will beat us anyway, and we want the projects. We want the work, and we will deal with it."[5]

In Dand, under the influence of projects, tribe, and pride, the maliks signed up en masse with Nazak. Information flowed in. Schools opened as projects flowed back into villages. Eventually most of the northern part of the district near the district center became safe. Then the southern half of the district grew safer. By late 2010 it too was mostly pacified.

In early 2011 the Canadians further regularized Nazak's system and persuaded him to divide the district into twelve different clusters of villages, each of which would receive one million Afghanis, worth about $20,000, to spend as one-time assistance. Each cluster of five to fifteen villages would hold a weekly *shura*, or consultation council, composed of local village maliks, and each cluster would send one cluster leader to the district center with requests.

Nazak disliked the idea of having cluster leaders, which he viewed as potential rivals for authority and who in practice unfairly favored their own villages when it came to apportioning the Canadian money.

"I don't want to work with the cluster leaders. I want to work with the maliks," insisted Nazak. "I don't like the cluster system."

But the ever-practical Nazak never turned down free money. He approved the plan and simply worked around the leaders as best he could.

With his system working and the district center humming, Nazak next attempted to bring the local mullahs on board. For nearly a year he assiduously courted them, but the Taliban closely monitored the mullahs. One mullah told Nazak that to visit the district center he needed the police to pretend to arrest him and bring him to the DDC, where they could discuss working together. He would then be taken back to the village by the police, showing some light abuse to keep his cover story intact. The pressure on the mullahs by the Taliban, plus the lack of funds to offer them, made this idea a challenging one for Nazak to implement.

Nazak's innovations were all the more remarkable when compared with neighboring Panjwai District, where the government made few inroads into the insurgency throughout 2011. Its political system floundered under steady insurgent pressure.

As Dand stabilized, Nazak began to look ahead to the next step in his career. Perhaps he would become deputy provincial governor or the mayor of Kandahar City or maybe even provincial governor, or one day he might even take Karzai's job. Why not? He had pacified Dand. But even in his triumph the years wore on without advancement, and his enthusiasm waned. The routine administration of villages seemed to become boring to Nazak.

Even as Nazak's system bore fruit in early 2011 it was threatened by outside forces. Though the system was built on projects, that spring the U.S. staff in Kandahar City began to discuss cutting Dand from projects as an experiment to see what would happen when the inevitable U.S. withdrawal began. Dand might become an early guinea pig to see how districts could handle the inevitable reduction of resources. In meetings with Nazak U.S. officials promised their full support, while in official channels they worked to cut aid and begin an experiment leading into the unknown. A few months later when Nazak heard about this, he complained this concept would destabilize the district and his own personal prospects. It was too soon to pull resources, he argued, because his system needed time to become fully entrenched. People needed to have a robust trust in their government when resources were drawn down in 2012 or 2013.

Nazak worried. He knew the Americans would leave and the projects needed to control the district would have to come from the Afghan government. But would the Americans stop the flow of projects before his own government, which until then had proved incapable of delivering almost anything, stepped up? And would the Americans pull the plug earlier than necessary in some sort of ill-advised experiment?

As Nazak looked ahead to the transition he suspected that the Americans would make pulling out a priority, and U.S. officials would find it difficult to understand Nazak's system. He suspected the Afghan government would fail to support the district for years to come, and therefore the eventual failure of his system was almost assured.

He said only half-joking, "When the Americans pull out, I am leaving too."

Three things would happen in the next year or two. First, the amount of money and troops the Americans committed to Dand would steadily decrease. Second, we needed to preserve the political system by finding a low-cost option that would let us continue affecting people's lives in a positive fashion while using only a fraction of the money we used now. Third, we would need to improve the economy so the people could see their lives improving as well.

And so we turned to thinking about the economy. A booming economy would ensure the viability of Nazak's system, while failure would allow the Taliban to return. Recalling Keith's turbulent experience with the people at KAF, I figured it wouldn't be easy to find a good economic plan that would pass muster back at headquarters.

# 6

## Priming the Economy

Floods in the Arghandab are reported to occur twice in the year, and result in damage to a greater or less extent to the canal-heads. There is a superintendent of canals, Akram Khan, and after a flood a new head is generally dug in the line which then strikes the eye as most suitable. The labour for this is supplied by the owners of the fields; no rent is charged by the State for the water, and no pay is given to the men for their labour. The canal continues in working order for about six months. —**Augustus Le Messurier**, *Kandahar in 1879*, 1880

Most of all, funnily enough, they want security. Who wouldn't? It's a very basic need for us all and is too often lost in an over-focus on governance. Secondly, irrigation, then roads and electricity all of which leads to the most important thing overall after security which is jobs. —**General Sir David Richards**, quoted in Sandy Gall, *The War against the Taliban*, 2013

During our training in Washington DC a favorite question had been, "So what does a field program officer in a district actually do all day?" We received no straight answer. Instead we were told, "Do not promise projects to the Afghans. Do not think you are able to fund projects yourself; there is no money for this. Do write reports. Do coordinate with the military unit that is on the ground with you."

No one explained why either the Afghans or the military would want to talk to a USAID district officer who had neither money nor any intention of using U.S. government funds. One recently returned USAID veteran had told us in vague terms that he spent his time "putting out fires."

In fact the district officer spent most of his time mentoring the district government to help it learn to manage projects that were funded by foreigners and would eventually be funded by Afghanistan's own national government. Unlike district officers in British India a century before who ran the district to which they were assigned with sovereign powers, the priority for a field officer in Kandahar was to engage and empower the local government, while simultaneously making visible changes in the district by managing projects. This simple but effective mandate was not always echoed at the embassy or at KAF, which often valued report writing over mentoring the Afghan staff, as well as rubber-stamping USAID programs over ensuring they actually generated usable and effective projects.

USAID spent millions of dollars every year in districts like Dand. In fact, however, USAID doesn't directly spend the money. Instead it hires large American companies or nonprofit organizations based in Arlington, Virginia, or Bethesda, Maryland, to run its multimillion-dollar programs. Once these companies receive the contract from USAID, they open in-country offices and hire local people and contracting companies to do the real work on the projects. These Afghan contractors all too often turn around and hire other subcontractors, and this subcontracting process might recur perhaps two or three times on a project before it is begun. The impact of the program dollars is diluted with each layer of the subcontracting cake. All of the nearly $15 billion spent by USAID between 2002 and 2012 passed through this USAID system.[1]

It is a convoluted and often wasteful process made necessary by the limited number of USAID staff working in the field. According to James Petersen, a former U.S. government inspector for Afghanistan, only about thirty cents of every dollar spent reaches actual projects in Afghanistan. And of that thirty cents, even more is swallowed up. Petersen stated, "Add in the cost of the USAID's bureaucratic superstructure—including $500,000 annually for each U.S. employee in Kabul, and the supporting staffs in Washington—and sometimes less than 10 cents of every dollar actually goes to aiding Afghans."[2]

Since the mid-1980s the number of USAID people posted around the world has steadily shrunk, and staff numbers dropped by half over twenty years.[3] In southern Afghanistan only a few dozen staff were in the districts at all. In 2012 there were 130 embassy staff members to cover four southern provinces and 3 million people. By mid-2013 that number had dropped to 40, with none in the districts.[4]

The USAID system, which is built around the international development companies that manage projects directly, has a historical precedent. Even in its heyday of the 1950s, USAID hired private contractors to build its projects. American engineering giant Morrison-Knudsen built the Kajaki Dam in Helmand Province in the early 1950s, bringing irrigation canals to farmers downstream. Now the USAID field officers spread across the country oversaw what they could of the projects they officially supervised, their access hindered by limitations in security, transportation, time, and the meager inclination of many USAID field officers to get in armored vehicles and visit villages where the projects were actually under way. Many, though not all, officers felt that the risks outweighed the benefits and avoided ever leaving the security of their bases surrounded by high walls and razor wire.

Within the USAID system the USAID field program officer is supposed to make sure the money is spent wisely and the district improves, with better roads, better canals for irrigation water, more wells for drinking water, or other projects that improve people's lives. When I arrived in Dand, USAID had about eight relevant programs there. Four of them were having a significant effect, one had a positive effect only part of the time, and three were moribund or almost completely ineffective. None of the latter three had been canceled, however.

Two of the best programs involved building fixed infrastructure, such as roads and canals, and training villagers. One program dug wells for drinking water.

Another program, the District Delivery Program, offered extra funding to district staff to compensate them for the harsh conditions they endured, though the money usually arrived late. It also paid for sofas and printers in the offices. Bizarrely it failed to fund the district staff's requests for fuel so they could visit the villages. This funding was denied by provincial officials, who exercised veto power over the disbursements and didn't see why the local Afghan staff should visit project sites to ensure the work was on track. In this matter the U.S. staff at KAF agreed with provincial officials, against our objections.

The District Delivery Program also represented a warm-up exercise in handling money—a training tool for the Afghans so they would be prepared when the national government began to release funds to the provinces. The program didn't go well and was canceled early, after only a fraction of the money allotted had been spent. It was an ominous foreshadowing of later problems we would encounter with the national budget.

USAID managed significant progress in some areas, such as improving access to health care, even as it fell short in a number of others. But it was not the only offender in designing programs that ran into trouble. I spent my first four months in Dand trying to determine what had been done by Americans and Canadians during the preceding two years, a nearly impossible task. Projects would be completed in villages only to wither and fade away. Mohammad Zahir and I tried to track down these projects when we visited villages with U.S. Army patrols. In one example a Canadian agency had sent a dozen hives of bees to Dand, and they all wound up in the backyard of one of the largest landowners in the district.

This diversion was a good thing, one of the elders explained, because ordinary people feared bees. "The local people do not accept them," he said.

Canadian-funded vocational training had been conducted in several villages, but these projects failed to create any new businesses. When we visited the villages, no one could tell us who had undergone the training or confirm that any training had taken place.

Another Canadian-funded project delivered between six thousand and seven thousand sheep to eleven villages. The animals had been given out in two lots: once to help poor farmers and a second time as compensation for working on communal improvements. The district agriculture director, Abdul Rashid, promised to get information about who received the sheep and what the result had been. That was the last we heard of the sheep.

Abdul Rashid explained apologetically, "The powerful village men try to take the sheep." Undoubtedly that was what had happened.[5]

Another time chickens had been distributed, along with a complete set of machinery to grind grain into feed. The machinery, which we never located, was apparently sitting within a mile of the district center gathering dust, and most of the chickens were dead or had been eaten. USAID also paid for 123 farmers to receive new orchards. For that project outlay we could at least get the details of which villages were supposed to benefit, though no one on the ground could ever point to any new orchards. Getting the full picture proved to be impossible.

Lackluster efforts that sank with barely a trace took tens of thousands of dollars with them. This waste drove District Governor Nazak to anger and borderline despair. He counted the waste as the cost of doing business with foreigners. He threatened to quit if the Americans continued to implement the projects they favored without making any of his wishes a priority. He wanted support for his staff, both in outside mentoring on a variety of skills and in money and assistance to help keep the district center running. Nazak lacked funds from his own government to cover the most basic costs of running the district. For instance, the U.S. Army had to pay for the fuel that ran the generator outside the DDC. He also wanted projects that would prompt people to cooperate with his government. Above all he wanted to improve the economy, enrich the people, and dispel any lingering temptation to work with the insurgency.

Nazak's priorities made sense. What he said was in line with what researchers had found in a survey for the Asia Foundation. When asked what they cared most about, ordinary Afghans said they most wanted security and an improved economy for their local areas (their replies differed for the problems of Afghanistan as whole). Of people surveyed, 32 percent said unemployment was the worst problem, topping even security, which 31 percent identified as the most critical matter.[6]

Research showed that one of the prime reasons young men decided to join the Taliban was to make money. It made sense that, if we improved the economy, we would remove the incentive for Dand youth to stir up trouble.[7]

Consequently the first priority was to create an economic plan. When I arrived I found no such workable vision to execute. Keith Pratt's plan had been smothered after he and the stabilization officials at KAF punted his ideas back and forth for six months without agreement.

Dand is agricultural and arid. Its scattered villages would wither and die without irrigation water, which people pump from canals or wells into the fields. Villages follow the German model, with dense settlement surrounded by green fields, the whole encircled by sandy dirt baked hard by the sun. The southern part of Dand was more arid than the north, in part because the Tarnak River cuts the district in half and prevents irrigation canals from extending from the north into the south. Water from the mountains north of Kandahar City moved along a series of canals in use for several centuries, but it benefited the northern area almost exclusively. Southern Dand remained drier, poorer, and less secure.

Keith developed a plan that proposed spending a million dollars to buy thousands of sheep to pasture in the north and to grow alfalfa in the south that would be irrigated by digging deep new wells. The alfalfa would be sold to the farmers raising the sheep, which would then be sold in Kandahar City. Everyone would make money. In his plan USAID would pay for the wells, the sheep, and new tractors to plow the alfalfa fields.

Keith's plan made sense only if all the moving parts could come together simultaneously. But I knew nothing about deep-water wells, and no one else I spoke with did either. I also did not know if the farmers in the south would grow enough alfalfa to feed thousands of new sheep in the north. My ambivalence became irrelevant because KAF said no to Keith. Back to square one.

A minority of rich landowners sold cash crops such as pomegranates or grapes in Kandahar City and made good profits. Most farmers worked as subsistence farmers or sharecroppers, renting the land by giving part of their crop to the landowners. Other small farmers tilled tiny allotments of their own. Poor farmers often supplemented their incomes by working as day laborers in the bazaars of Kandahar City or Kabul, or in very bad times they went to labor in the dismal coal mines over the border in Pakistan. Inequality was rife, and the sparse wheatfields of a subsistence farmer might lie next to the vineyards of a rich landowner, the grapes ripening before being exported to Central Asia, Pakistan, or India.

Our problem was how to spread benefits throughout Dand and set up a system so that, when we withdrew, the economy would continue to hum. Keith's plan had aimed to set up a sheep industry. Nazak had a few ideas, Antoine Huss had others, and the farmers still more. After spending $85.5 billion in Afghanistan for military and civilian assistance (while other countries had added another $29 billion), we still were playing these improvements at the district level by the seat of our pants. (Of course 60 percent of the U.S. money had gone to fund and improve the security forces, but what remained was still huge; USAID alone had spent $15 billion.[8]) The United States was spending millions of dollars to boost farm incomes with USAID programs such as AVIPA and CHAMP, which trained farmers and distributed subsidized seed. There were plans to bring several agricultural processing factories to Kandahar City, but these efforts were not properly joined up with an economic plan for the district. And many of the grander plans at the higher level ended up being canceled or delayed indefinitely.

Planning by the U.S. team fell short in a number of other areas, not just the attempts at improving the districts. The United States spent more than $11.5 billion to build bases for Afghan security forces, but a SIGAR report noted in 2012 that the United States risked constructing bases that were either inadequate or "do not meet ANSF's strategic and operational needs."[9] These issues made me question our war effort. I also wondered if the U.S. government could plan and execute a counterinsurgency campaign.

In Kandahar Province some USAID programs arrived in what seemed an almost haphazard fashion. Similar districts received a completely different mix of USAID programs, which was understandable because of the huge war effort and limited resources. District economic planning represented a haphazard effort of U.S. officials, Afghan officials, and individual aid programs that applied to different districts. The Afghan government developed an economic plan for Dand, but it languished, in part because it was mostly a wish list of projects. The overall strategy left much to be desired.

We on the U.S. district team began to look at the available resources and figure out what would work best. Some of our resources were more flexible than others, because some programs, such as one for microcredit for small businesses, could not be altered at all. Consequently they proved almost useless. But other programs, such as a large one to assist farmers, could change the kind of activities supported, and we could get more or less what we wanted from them. The military was exceptionally flexible in pushing money into activities that were Nazak's highest priority, because the local battalion commander, Brian Payne, could spend military money where he wanted, and he met with us and Nazak at least once or twice a week.

So within a few weeks, after getting input from Keith, Antoine, the district governor, district staff, and people in the villages, we developed a plan. It contained three parts—for short-term, medium-term, and long-term horizons. We hoped each stage would lead logically to the next.

District Governor Nazak said that he eventually wanted factories, electricity from the Kandahar City power grid, and more jobs. The district staff said they wanted to build more roads, refurbish irrigation canals, and give farmers free or subsidized seed and fertilizer. Irrigation canals in the past had been maintained by villagers without government assistance. But since the Soviet war, when many people fled to Pakistan, this practice had dwindled. Now the crops were at risk if the water did not flow. The villagers in northern Dand said they could get to the market fairly easily because ISAF had just built several roads, but they didn't know how to tap into the Kandahar City market for new types of crops and thus needed help.

We decided in the very short term to continue to expand the road network and try to bring outlying villages in the south into the orbit of the Kandahar City bazaars. By pushing the road south we would reduce the travel time to Kandahar City from four hours each way to about forty minutes. In turn it would help to cement the security situation there.

Our medium-term goal would be to develop villagers' market crops more intensively and help farmers sell more of their vegetables in Kandahar City. With more than 500,000 residents Kandahar City had a voracious appetite for fresh vegetables, meat from chickens and sheep, and other crops. Even poor farmers could increase production and boost their incomes. We would try to develop new products for sale in the city, such as commercially produced eggs, and also find ways to export the cash crops more efficiently.

In the medium and long term we hoped to develop craft businesses and tie the grapes and pomegranates into the new processing plants being planned at the provincial level. Nazak's ultimate goal of building new craft factories and selling tomato paste and other processed food would depend on the economy continuing to grow and ultimately on whether the Kandahar City power grid could be extended to Dand, an unlikely prospect in the next few years since the grid was already overstressed and improvements behind schedule.

So three weeks after arriving we had the outline of our first economic plan. The plan built on what Nazak wanted, repackaged his ideas, and added a few new elements, such as improving production and marketing of new crops. It would be cheap and leverage existing USAID programs, which would provide the money and labor. It also had plenty of unknowns, such as whether USAID's plans to build provincial processing plants would succeed, be delayed, or fail outright. But it seemed to have a good chance of working, as well as of boosting incomes.

We felt a great deal of pressure on us because the clock had already begun to tick. As the U.S. surge wound down and American forces left, U.S. civilian assistance would wind down too. Less money would be available to fund stabilization and development projects, which would benefit the villagers. Those were the projects that brought people onto the government's side and helped to create security where none existed before. Boosting the economy would, we hoped, allow us to remove the projects without people turning back toward the Taliban when the funding dried up. Getting the economy wrong would jeopardize all of the progress already achieved. We needed to get it right.

But it would depend on us not getting stymied at KAF. If officials at KAF heard we were concentrating some program efforts into activities they thought unproductive, they could easily block us. We worked closely with the international development companies that actually ran the USAID programs, which in turn paid for the projects we wanted. We needed Nazak to make the case to visitors that our plan would work. Antoine and I schooled Governor Nazak on how best to present the plan as a series of linked and progressive ideas. Nazak, a quick study, soon began to brief visiting VIPs on the short-, medium-, and long-term aspects of his plan to transform the economy and make Dand self-sufficient as outside aid steadily dropped over the next year. He assured his guests of his confidence that the district staff could manage the job of managing the new ideas, too.

Nazak told visitors the economic plan would enable the district to use less NATO money because farmers would be richer and would demand less from the government. Nazak, a clever and articulate advocate, soaked up ideas like a sponge. The visitors were typically delighted with this kind of talk. An Afghan with a multistage plan! At the district level this was as rare as a dodo bird. The Afghan district staff members were enthusiastic as well. They followed the governor's lead, ensuring that the farmers would continue to throw their lot in with the government.

Obstacles would soon emerge. In coming months we would face constant pressure to reduce resources in Dand. We would need to constantly refine our ideas for new business development. Improving the district staff's ability to manage and oversee projects would require months of concentrated effort.

But all that was blissfully in the future as we began to rapidly make changes that would prevent Dand from backsliding. We had less than a year to improve lives in the villages in order to solidify Nazak's system of political control. If the aid ran out before we finished, the entire district could be ripe for a Taliban takeover.

# 7

## Waiting to Work

The truth is, that in Afghanistan the only chance of exercising a considerable authority is when power falls into the hands of a very strong and wise man with money at his command. Without plenty of money, not an angel from heaven could rule that country.—**Sir George Campbell**, *The Afghan Frontier*, 1879

The constitution, which we are fighting, dying and spending getting on for £6 billion of taxpayers' money a year to support, is unstable, because it is highly centralised—I am glad to say that it was designed by a Frenchman and imposed by an American. But it is not sustainable, because it does not go with the grain of Afghan tradition. We need something much more decentralised.—**Sir Sherard Cowper-Coles**, in UK House of Commons, *Oral Evidence Taken before the Foreign Affairs Committee regarding the UK's Foreign Policy Approach to Afghanistan and Pakistan*, 2010

Almost every week a helicopter from KAF brought VIPs into Dand to kick the tires. They would fly in, walk from the helipad at the adjoining U.S. base, and spend an hour or two with DG Nazak in his office. Usually the visitors were the same and featured the Canadian general in command and a few civilians. Most weeks they covered similar ground and relied heavily on platitudes.

In early June the helicopter brought a quartet of fresh faces—a ranking delegation of NATO officials, including a NATO administrator and several parliamentary members from the smaller European countries.

They wanted to speak to Nazak and hear him explain the transformation of Dand over the previous five years from basket case to model district.

The visitors settled back in the deep couches arrayed around Nazak's office. The European officials were surprisingly young, well educated, and courteous. With only a shallow understanding of the Afghan situation, they listened attentively.

Nazak explained how security had changed, and how the people supported him now that he had made his bargain with them, that is, the exchange of projects for security. But now, he said, the way ahead was blocked. By now he'd guessed that KAF might prematurely cut support for Dand. He was also acutely aware that the appointed time for the withdrawal of the American troops, and the money that came with them, would arrive in less than a year. He worried about the future.

"What else can I do?" Nazak asked. "If you people leave halfway through this process, it will destroy this place. We need support for the economy. Without support we will lose this place."

The Europeans prevaricated. They promised that the Afghan government and Nazak in particular would continue to receive support from NATO.

"We want to support economically the programs you said make a difference for the district," one of the visitors told him.

Nazak knew the most important programs were from USAID and not the Europeans, and he took little notice of their assurances. He expected the Americans to continue to deliver USAID programs to the district and for the U.S. Army to provide money for small projects as long as it remained in-country. But he was talking about something else.

Nazak worried over two problems that seemed unsolvable. He needed the Americans to fund the new economic plan for several years. And his district staff was being starved of resources. He had carefully collected almost two dozen staff members to work in the DC, or district center. There were hundreds of teachers, nurses, and health-care workers scattered around the district, but many of them were unable to do much work.

His most valuable staff at the DC had the fewest resources. There was no money for them to visit villages, paint clinics, or build an additional classroom onto the most crowded schools. There was no money to run the generator at the district center or pay for computers or spare parts. The allowance for these things from the province was minuscule when it existed, and he did not expect to receive any additional money.

To attack these problems Nazak's strategy with high-level visitors was to tell everyone what he needed, hoping that there eventually might walk into his office the person who could and would do something to help. Like most Afghans, Nazak possessed a limited understanding of how important any particular VIP really was, and he had few resources for finding such information. So he used a scattershot approach typical of Afghans looking for help. Antoine Huss and I would review the list of visitors and surmise how important they might be. Often the visitor of the day could not help Nazak. But Nazak never stopped trying.

"I don't see sustainment for the Afghans," Nazak pressed his European visitors. "There is no effort to help the Afghan economy. We here don't have the tools to do this ourselves. We have the people, but not the stuff."

The NATO visitors looked bemused. They didn't grasp that Nazak desperately wanted two things: money to fund the economic plan and money for his officials to do their jobs. To Nazak this would be the focus of the next year. Catastrophe loomed if we got this wrong.

"If you leave there will be massive destruction as we fight each other," he insisted, looking from one visitor to the next. "Politicians say they will fight. There is no system to give us taxes. We need this help." Nazak knew that districts were forbidden by law to collect their own taxes, so they relied entirely on the province and outsiders for funding, though this key point was often lost on his VIP guests.

The NATO visitors looked embarrassed and changed the subject. They asked about how many Taliban had given themselves up, a moot point because fighting had largely ceased by this time in Dand. There were no Taliban there to surrender. But the new topic was easier to discuss than addressing Nazak's problems. The visitors lacked an understanding of the situation and the power to influence it. Nazak told them the Taliban operated in Panjwai instead, where the fighting raged. The VIPs departed fifteen minutes later, leaving behind a frustrated district governor. This meeting, as with countless others, consumed his time but proved fruitless.

Nazak was not shy about his problems. He repeatedly expounded on them to Lt. Colonel Brian Payne. Our whole team worked closely together, from Nazak and the district staff to Payne and his staff to our USAID element. We met frequently in Nazak's office.

One day in June Colonel Payne came to visit Nazak, who laid out his points concisely. Payne was Nazak's greatest ally among the Americans, and he trusted the officer.

"We have our plan for long-term, short-term, and medium-term projects," he told Payne. "But ISAF does its own thing. I've tried to resign eleven times because of it. I will resign if I get no support. I will not ruin my name by having the district go back to the way it was," he added.

The situation seemed tenuous at best to Nazak. Not only was his district secure, but he had also eradicated poppies, which remained a scourge in Panjwai and districts farther west. But the elements he relied upon from KAF, including U.S. support and the development of food-processing factories in Kandahar City, were stymied by slow progress, an erratic electricity supply, and uncertainty about the intentions of the Americans. Nazak's consolation was that Payne seemed to appreciate the big picture.

In fact Nazak's problems stemmed from a deeper issue. They lay at the roots of policy making and decisions made at the highest levels months earlier. More than that, they emanated from a mindset among U.S. officials, one in which they had failed to foresee that someone as proactive as Nazak could come to power in a district at all. Or that he could bring together his kind of staff.

The official work day for the district staff began at 8:00. Staff usually filtered in sometime around 9:00, walking across the threadbare red carpets to slide behind their desks, exchanging welcomes as they progressed along the hallways. Everyone, even latecomers, received hearty greetings. The DC was a convivial place in the mornings.

The routine seldom varied. Antoine disappeared into DG Nazak's office. I made the rounds of the other district officers.

I mentored everyone that Antoine didn't, which in practice meant everyone aside from the DG. For the first few months I was the only USAID person present until Cip (pronounced Kip) Jungberg arrived later that summer. Four staff members represented the four major ministries in Kandahar City: health, education, agriculture, and rural development, which handled village projects. Other, less crucial employees dealt with correspondence, village affairs, legal disputes, and the routine operations of the DDC.

It soon became clear that the line directors did not do very much. The education director stayed the busiest, with hundreds of teachers to keep track of, but all of the directors were at least partially idle. Yet they all had jobs to do that should have taken them routinely into the villages. For instance, the education director ran twenty-eight schools across Dand but usually failed to visit classrooms.

While he and his staff worked to ensure textbooks and salaries flowed smoothly from the province, his participation inside the schools was minimal. His absence from the schools resulted in a lack of follow-up to address the needs of teachers and students. The headmaster at one school complained of a lack of books, and his requests for more were ignored. The education director assured us there were plenty of textbooks in the district, but I suspected he had not seen the problem for himself.

Similarly the health director seldom inspected the five clinics under his purview.

The official responsible for reconstruction and rural development (or RRD; his title was "social mobilizer," but he was accorded director status in practice) was to ensure that work on projects funded by ISAF proceeded smoothly. Visiting work sites was a vital part of his job, but he and his office mate seldom bothered.

Meanwhile the staff under the agriculture director should have been training farmers and assessing problems in the villages. Instead they spent most of their time in their office, watching Iranian soap operas and news shows on satellite TV.

In practice all the line directors intermittently visited villages. Some schools had not seen the education director in months or years. Instead the staff sat at their desks and filed reports to their provincial offices. It was startling. I wondered if they all suffered from a poor work ethic.

The lack of dedication on the part of the health director, Dr. Mousa, made sense. Although a few months into his appointment, he hadn't yet been paid. With a full-time job as a doctor at a hospital in Kandahar City, Dr. Mousa showed up for work once a week. He doubted he would be paid anytime soon. For the others, however, there was little obvious explanation.

At first I figured that they were so busy handling ISAF assistance projects that they simply had no time to leave their desks. After all, the Canadians were throwing money at the villages in a highly effective but somewhat indiscriminate manner. Canadian civil-military soldiers worked in a half dozen locations, all of them pushing quick-impact projects into villages. They were also finishing two major asphalt roads. That was a lot for the RRD officer to keep track of.

Plus there were USAID projects. Over several months' time they'd graveled a handful of roads and distributed seed and fertilizer to thousands of farmers. This, too, would absorb the efforts of the district staff, who would need to find the farmers and help with the distributions.

Still it was odd. Eventually after weeks of cups of tea we asked them if they wanted to be busier. They answered with relief that yes, they wanted to do much more. They couldn't, though. They had the same problem Nazak had scolded the NATO people about.

In general the district staff wanted to visit the villages. The development director chafed at the bit, but going required money for fuel. When they visited villages, they paid out of pocket for the gas and drove their own vehicles.

One member of the staff, the *huquq*, constituted the district's entire legal department and settled disputes across the district. One day in an effort to explain the problem he talked about his motorcycle.

The huquq handled land claims and civil disputes in the villages. It is a demanding job because Afghans can be independent, stubborn, and fractious. This volatile mix of temperaments led to a steady stream of problems in villages. Land and women have provided a never-ending source of tension in Afghan society for centuries. The recent troubles had done little to temper those issues. Many complaints also involved American armored vehicles on patrol damaging crops and houses. To solve these issues the villagers needed to find a respected elder to decide the merits of the case. Depending on the seriousness of the case, they might turn to their local village elder or go to see Nazak or the huquq, traveling to the latter's small office wedged in an old building at the side of the district center.

The huquq would record the details of a case and then set off on his motorcycle to visit the village, where he would seek out witnesses and inspect the damage. Sometimes a single case would require two or three trips to the village. But because the Afghan government paid the huquq no money to put gasoline in his motorcycle, his job placed an enormous burden on him.

Gasoline cost $4.60 per gallon in Afghanistan. An average government worker made perhaps $350 per month. Since all the officials lived in Kandahar City, their commute to work every day on a motorcycle cost a dollar or two. Visiting villages on top of this would cost the huquq even more. Visiting ten villages a month, several times each, probably ran up a gas bill of $100 a month, including commuting. The remainder of his paycheck would have to cover the costs of food, clothing, rent, and health care for his family. An educated man, the huquq lived a tenuous existence; he could not even afford to replace his shoes, which were old and split down the side.

His trips to the villages cost him money he could not spare. His wife had fallen ill, and he said he could not afford to pay for her medical treatment.

When I asked other staff members about this, they all confirmed they suffered similar problems. No government employee was receiving much, if any, gas money to inspect the villages. They did what they could, visiting occasionally and spending far more time behind their desks than they wanted. They were, in effect, chained to the district center.

Looking more closely made it obvious there was no money for almost anything at the district center. The government provided only a modest operational allowance. Nazak could spread that money around or keep it for his own needs. There was no money for generator fuel, or travel, or new computers, or roof repairs. When things fell apart, the staff were forced to approach the foreign soldiers, but the soldiers refused to pay for gasoline for motorcycles.

The shortfall of government money did not stop with a lack of gasoline money for motorcycles. It extended to all aspects of the staff members' jobs. Nazak paid for the staff's lunch of flat bread and fried eggplant every day, but there wasn't enough money to buy tea for guests.

As difficult as the shortfall made their lives personally, it also hobbled their initiative. If the staff wanted to consult villagers or teach them new farm techniques, they seldom had money to do so. Paradoxically there was money to build new schools, which came from a central fund, but little money to maintain them because the central fund for maintenance was starved of cash.

Under the Afghan system, in theory, the provincial ministries would provide funds for development projects and for operational expenses such as fuel or paint for a clinic. In reality, however, the provincial ministries seldom had money for such activities. The Afghan budget was poorly funded and poorly executed. Budget funds seldom trickled down to the province, let alone from the province to the district in the form of projects. DG Nazak said it was futile to rely on the province to get things done.

Many development projects were supposed to flow through Afghan programs such as the National Solidarity Program, set up specifically to help villages with their needs. But we saw little evidence of this work being done in the villages of Dand.

This problem was made starkly clear months later when the deputy education director of the province came to Dand and wrote out a chit asking ISAF to help maintain the schools. He sat in Nazak's office, explaining the lack of money to maintain schools in Dand. Then he wrote, "As you respectfully know, the government cannot reach out to all the problems as we do not have enough in our budget." He told Nazak he had $35,000 to fix all the schools in the fourteen districts of Kandahar Province. He had decided to concentrate the money on schools in Kandahar City, leaving the districts to their own devices. The unwieldy government system required district staff to send requests for even minor repairs to offices in Kandahar City, which then routed them to Kabul, where a year later the requests would be turned down. An ineffective system for providing projects in the villages, it fell apart completely in terms of providing funds for small incidentals such as gas for motorcycles.

And so the district education director usually didn't take his car to the villages. The agriculture director didn't send his staff out to supervise the training for farmers conducted by USAID contractors. The health director, poor as a church mouse, didn't regularly inspect his clinics. The rural development staff periodically ventured out, but not often. And they all used their own gas money.

This persistent lack of adequate support snowballed into a palpable sense of deprivation at the district center. With no money to paint the halls or feed the generator, a feeling of beleaguered austerity prevailed. The Americans were generally the last resort for addressing the most important problems.

Though there was the USAID-supported District Delivery Program, or DDP, which was meant to help with expenses such as fuel and furniture, it worked poorly. It was a short-term experiment designed largely to see if the national levels of government could handle money. DDP funds arrived chronically late and seldom bought what the district needed at that moment. Each section had its own DDP budget, but it was hit or miss as to what would be approved.

DDP also topped up the staff's salaries, effectively doubling many of the salaries from $225 a month to $450. This boost was a great success, creating huge incentives for staff to do a good job.

When USAID suspended DDP six months after I arrived, there was genuine consternation among the Afghan staff. They considered useful the phone cards and extra printers supplied by DDP, even if the supply remained erratic and unreliable. The salary top-ups, which had generally arrived at least four months late, had been an enormous boon. They sorely missed the extra money.

DDP was canceled, paradoxically, for not spending money quickly enough and for poor oversight. Having gone through less than $2 million out of a $40 million budget, high-ranking USAID officials got nervous. Cumbersome and slow but ultimately popular among the Afghan staff, DDP represented a wasted opportunity.

And DDP did not solve the central problem of the district center not having enough money to pay for basic operating functions such as its staff visiting the villages.

It transpired that official U.S. policy called for district staff to receive no direct support to do these things. No one at KAF or the embassy in Kabul ever took seriously the need for the district staff to leave their offices to inspect the situation in the villages or the need for resources for them to do their jobs.

It took me far too long to figure out the basic problem. I had plenty of clues. During our week at the embassy in Kabul we had a session about this exact point. A middle-aged bureaucrat walked us through two planning documents he had penned, in late 2010 and early 2011, five months before we arrived. These unclassified planning documents laid out U.S. priorities when dealing with the Afghan government.

The documents stated that the embassy should concentrate its resources at three levels: the national level, the provincial level, and the large cities. Cities like Kabul, Kandahar City, Herat, and Mazar-i Sharif should be able to spend their own money. But not districts.[1] Districts would not be a priority because there were too few resources to help them, and the Afghans did not have the capacity to manage improvements there.

A second embassy planning document asserted that if we tried to help districts spend money, we would fail. Funds for individual districts could not be provided because it would be too "difficult." The document noted, "At the district level it would be difficult to implement such a fund while the province's capacity to manage public finances is not sufficient. A District Fund (other than the current District Delivery Program) would at this time outstrip sustainable Afghan capacity."[2]

The document went on to say that the American district advisors in district support teams (DSTs) such as ours should merely encourage district and provincial officials to work together to provide resources for the district, given the districts' limited ability to govern. It said, "A more viable approach in the year ahead would be for U.S. civilians in DSTs to concentrate their efforts on supporting stabilization activities, implementing DDP, and helping district officials push their priorities up to provinces and center, while U.S. officials at PRTs encourage officials to allocate resources in a way responsive to district priorities and needs."[3] PRTs were our counterparts at the provincial level.

This bureaucratic tussle from late 2010 ensured that district staff would be inadequately resourced to do their jobs. There would be no effective way for them to get money. Districts would instead rely upon the Afghan provincial ministries to send chits for gasoline or to arrange for contractors to fix the school roofs. It was a cumbersome process, one that ensured nothing would ever reach the districts, because the Afghan government had little money of its own to spend and no mechanism for spending what they did have. The staff at KAF and the PRT advised us in Dand that only in 2012 would the Afghan government be expected to handle even half of all the development money in Afghanistan. Until then it handled a small fraction of the funds and did so badly. (Even this estimate would later prove to be wildly optimistic.)

And it all constituted official U.S. policy.

We flagged this issue to the higher echelon at KAF, but we were informed that the system was set and nothing could be done to alter it. Given the serious nature of the problem, we felt even more discouraged, especially because, in other cases, workarounds had been found and implemented.

When the Afghan government had failed to act in previous years on other important issues, international donors found ways to circumvent the government process. For pet projects, such as the national airline, donors funded the task directly or they outsourced the problem entirely to private organizations. DDP was, in its own way, an attempt to circumvent this problem.

Under the embassy's scheme nothing incentivized the Afghan government to meet the needs of the districts. The system even created disincentives, hence the frustration and despair at the district center in Dand.

Without money flowing through its system the district government could not meet many of the needs of the people. It would need to rely upon USAID programs, or projects from the military, none of which was handled directly by the provincial government. The district government could weigh in on what should be done. In districts such as Dand foreigners did their utmost to comply with the district staff's wishes. But the district government could not do what it needed to do, which was to help its own staff help the people directly.

This gap in intention and credibility was old news. The pernicious effects of this system were generally recognized, even in official channels. One British report from 2008 noted, "The resulting inability of the government to provide or direct (through the private sector and civil society) services to its citizenry has led to a legitimacy gap. The State is, thus, believed to be ineffectual or, considering the corrupt and criminal behaviour of many ANP officers and public officials, a greater source of predation rather than protection."[4]

Even the basics of counterinsurgency (COIN) theory put the greatest emphasis on pushing the initiative down to the lowest levels possible, even in poorly developed countries like Afghanistan. A primer of COIN practice from 2007 noted, "Establishing workable financial controls without a banking system and in the absence of communications is a tall order. However, simple but robust financial controls can limit corruption. *First, every school, clinic, police station, or other operating unit needs a budget.*"[5]

The embassy plan to fix every level of government except the district, which most affected the people, reduced the district staff to being the least empowered officials in Afghanistan, although they wielded the most influence with the people.

When our training class rotated through the embassy, we received the planning documents. We raised some of the above points with the author of the plan. Why, we asked, had the United States developed a system that was bound to give second- or third-rate service to rural Afghans? And why ignore the district staff, who have the most direct contact with the people?

The embassy bureaucrat responded that there was no problem with creating a system that did not work very well. He said the Afghan system was designed to be third rate and that the villagers wouldn't know any better because they had never seen a decent government. Anyway there were not enough qualified Afghans able to work in the districts, and the task would have been impossible for that reason alone.

In Dand I found the consequences of these ideas were most felt by the Afghan district staff, who needed the most help in winning the war. We had qualified and competent Afghan officials who wanted to do their jobs to a high standard, but they were starved of the resources to do so.

This was equally frustrating for ordinary Afghans, who expected their district government to improve their villages and maintain a very small number of functioning clinics and schools. People expected the district governor to respond to their needs and demanded more than a third-rate performance. Nazak's bargain with the people depended on it.

The monies needed at the district center were modest. A generous gas allowance for the huquq might cost $100 a month. Funds for district staff to train farmers in the village might cost $1,000 a month.

When Nazak harangued the NATO visitors about his problems, he was talking small potatoes. We would work to fund his economic plan by folding the ideas into existing USAID programs, which might or might not work because the programs were designed to do a limited number of things and his ideas might not fit those plans. We also sought ways to work around Nazak's other problem—that his staff could not visit the villages on a regular basis without a budget.

Every morning when we went to work at the district center we felt the pressure. Unless we helped to solve Nazak's problems, most of the gains that Nazak and his foreign supporters had so painfully made over the previous few years would likely prove fleeting.

# 8

## Kick-Starting the Staff

Under the old regime the city revenue amounted to about 6 ½ lacs of rupees, and this was sent direct to Cabul, not a pice of it being spent in municipal improvements or otherwise at Kandahar.
—**Augustus Le Messurier**, *Kandahar in 1879*, 1880

Every Friday several four-wheel-drive armored trucks called MATVs left our gate at COP Edgerton and drove ten kilometers south to the main battalion base near the Tarnak River in the center of the district. At the base the few of us who worked every day with the district government climbed out of the vehicles with their reinforced doors and went inside for the weekly staff meeting.

The battalion base was a maze of tents and workshops, with razor wire and mud walls surrounding the camp. Three large wooden buildings with sloped roofs held the offices of the battalion staff, including the operations room, where soldiers kept tabs on every military patrol out in the area. Made of prefabricated sections standing fifteen feet high and forty feet across, the sun-bleached pine of the buildings reflected bright amber light from the late afternoon sunsets, like three Swiss chalets that some madman had planted in the middle of the desert.

It represented the nerve center of the 850 troops of the battalion, which had companies spread across the district. Every Friday the staff officers and company commanders assembled in the conference room, with a long table facing two screens and wooden benches arranged in stadium-style seating against walls. The company commanders, all captains in their late twenties, sat at the foot of the table while the senior battalion officers sat at the head. Straphangers from units attached to the battalion sat on the benches. Everyone faced the two video screens. The meetings could take hours as up to forty PowerPoint slides flashed on the screen, one after another, each slide filled with words, arrows, and staccato phrases hard to understand without further explanations.

Lt. Colonel Payne would inspect the list of activities he expected the companies to do, read the PowerPoint descriptions of their activities, and listen to the explanations. Sometimes company commanders explained their slides. Other slides came from Captain Matt Kotlarski, who explained how the battalion was helping DG Nazak. Other slides from supply people, the intelligence officer, and other staff officers flashed on the screen. Everyone presented in turn.

Each meeting began with Payne explaining the grand scheme, which often involved the need to help the Afghans take over from the United States. Antoine Huss, and later Cip Jungberg and I, commented on how we could improve operations or added cautionary notes. Meetings were long and tedious but also useful and necessary. This weekly gathering was where the nuts and bolts of our help for the Afghans could succeed or fail. The weekly pilgrimage to Tarnak was also a chance to get away from the district center for a day, so we made the trip every week in reasonably good humor.

The meetings were a mix of plans to kill Taliban who continued to pass through the outskirts of the district, to shift the battalion from Dand and into Panjwai, and to support the government. As weeks turned into months and the line companies began to leave Dand for Panjwai, the emphasis turned more and more to the security problems in Panjwai. The meetings proved important, because we could explain in detail to Payne why he needed to spend money on ideas that would help the district government.

Payne, a blustery and aggressive man, responded well to ideas that promised results. Unfortunately the results we promised would be hard to measure, which could potentially cause serious problems because the military and their civilian counterparts in Afghanistan were obsessed with metrics. How well are we doing? Are we winning the war? Is the situation better this week than last week, last month, or last year? How to measure progress has never been satisfactorily answered. In counterinsurgency almost no simple metrics used in a vacuum, such as the number of attacks, are suitable.

Payne had to report progress to his higher headquarters, and the only real progress on the civil side we would show would take months to appear. If events went awry and the Taliban seeped in and undermined the government, it would happen after Payne's companies had already left, and thus it would be too late to remedy the situation. In supporting USAID and the battalion's governance people, such as Matt Kotlarski at the district center, Payne took a leap of faith in a result he could not hope to measure beforehand. He had no real choice in the matter, because our ideas were the only game in town.

In the meantime we measured how well our civil initiatives moved forward as best we could. There was no alternative, because how else could we evaluate progress? The number of bombs and attacks? That worked poorly. If there were no attacks, that might mean the insurgents controlled an area but that the security forces were not strong enough to fight them, and so paradoxically a lack of attacks could be a *bad* sign. The amount of money spent on projects? Possibly. But money did not always bring results. In many districts the U.S. government spent millions of dollars and achieved little in improved security or in attracting more residents firmly to the government's side. Complicating matters was that the U.S. strategy called for the most money to go to the least secure areas; 80 percent of the aid flowed to the restive east and south. The amount of money spent could misleadingly suggest that more aid led to more violence.

One true measure of progress in Afghanistan is the relationship between the government and the people. The more the villagers support the government, the better the war is going. And this is relatively simple to measure. The best metric is how many people visit the district center every week. The presence of many elders indicated the government was doing well, because the people weren't afraid to work with government staff.

It was significant that the hallways of the Dand District Center were busy almost every day. Some elders sought identity cards. Others talked to the agriculture director about USAID programs, while others met with the rural reconstruction officer. A small crowd always wanted to talk to DG Nazak, and they lounged on plush couches next to the peeling paint in the hallway outside his office as they waited to see him.

Our challenge was to keep them coming and to figure out ways to keep them coming even as the aid dollars dwindled in number. At the same time, we needed to get the line directors back into the game and make sure they were able to help people, not just channel USAID programs, which often did not address what the people most wanted.

The district's Afghan line directors saw many people, but when I arrived their work mostly involved handling paperwork that turned ISAF money from USAID and Canadian Army civil affairs soldiers into projects in the villages. Pushing paper often left the staff overworked but underfulfilled. It drove the heavy traffic of elders into the district center. The staff were reduced to observing more than managing, but they believed they could do better. More than shuffle paper, they wanted to act on their own ideas.

The problem stemmed from the way projects were run. The Afghan staff had limited input on the course of USAID programs. And they oversaw projects that the Canadians and the villagers had worked out. But they had their own ideas to contribute. Sometimes the flow of projects completely bypassed the district staff, with the villagers talking directly with Canadian soldiers. Improvements to schools and clinics were seldom high on the agenda for village elders in search of a new well. This problem needed to be solved quickly, because when the Canadians left in midsummer of 2011, they would take their pot of village assistance money with them.

This problem was brought home sharply one day when the district health officer, Dr. Mousa, became unhappy and loudly expressed his feelings. He spoke with me and Captain Kotlarski, who had recently moved to the district center to fill the gap left by the departing Canadians.

Dr. Mousa, a thin, intense man of about forty-five, spoke in a fluid wave of Pashtu. He began with a frustrated wave of the hand. "I cannot get the projects I need to improve the clinics approved," he complained. "They are never done!"

For five minutes he described how his five clinics needed more storage space, more electricity, and a coat of paint. Because he received no funds from the provincial health department, he could not make the most rudimentary repairs. Neither the Americans nor the Canadians appeared willing to fix the problems.

Dr. Mousa was passionate and committed. After all, he worked for no pay. He just wanted something done. Eventually I broke in. Already familiar with Dr. Mousa's issues, Matt Kotlarski and I had prearranged a solution.

"Dr. Mousa," I said when he paused. "We have discussed this, and we insist that you spend $10,000 in the next two weeks. We will not take no for an answer."

He barely listened, instead resuming his complaints. It took him about fifteen seconds before he stopped. I repeated our offer. I explained that we all wanted improvements. He would need to prioritize, provide us with a list, and we would get started immediately using military funds.

Understanding and shock filled his face. Did we mean it? Yes, we did. We would spend U.S. and Canadian military money to help him. And with that we took our first step to get the district staff to begin addressing their own priorities.

Dr. Mousa would need to take his list to the ministry and have his proposals approved. He would need to check on the projects as they were built. He would coordinate the work with the clinic directors. Dr. Mousa, in short, would need to start doing his job of managing the district's health-care system. For good measure we suggested ways he could improve his reporting to the province. In time he would be able to secure official Afghan government money to pay for needed projects, even if there was not yet any money available from the province. By the time we explained all the things we wanted him to do, he was beaming.

Dr. Mousa was not alone. Every line director faced the problem of receiving no money from the Afghan government to do anything—none to visit the clinics and none for making repairs. This lack of money had several effects, all of them bad. Some district line directors stopped working and simply waited for ISAF to hand out projects. The agriculture department in Dand simply handled requests from farmers, hoping to tap into USAID programs. Just as bad, the normal planning and coordination that should exist between the district and provincial staffs atrophied from the lack of anything substantial to discuss. The district staff informed provincial officials what was going on but rarely consulted the province about anything because no one had insisted they do so before.

Worst of all, the lack of money stifled initiative. Line directors had many good ideas about what would help people. Those ideas wouldn't cost much to implement, but there was no way to do so. Their ideas were routinely ignored by the province. And ISAF usually went to the elders and villagers, while making little use of the district staff.

Unfortunately this practice reduced the staff to managing the run-of-the-mill projects ISAF had been doing for years, such as digging wells, refurbishing mosques, or building walls. While useful, the line directors lacked the power to initiate good ideas. The district lost its finest resource: the expertise of its own staff. While there were weekly meetings between the staff and village elders to work out priorities for projects, these short-changed any initiative by the staff. They often tried to manage the desires of elders, who pressed to obtain scarce resources for their own villages with little regard for the district as a whole.

We were determined to change this dysfunctional dynamic. Henceforth, if the staff had innovative ideas, we would do our best to find the money to back them.

The easy answer would have been if the Afghans had called up the ministries and asked the Afghan government to pay for whatever the district needed. Not possible. The Afghan government had little money for projects. They rarely spent a fraction of what money they did possess, because top officials performed poorly, the system was flawed, and the financial workings were too complex. The provincial officials resisted help that was offered by their American mentors, who only visited once a week.

The numbers were astounding. Aid in 2010–11 amounted to more than $15 billion, roughly the GDP of the entire Afghan economy.[1] The bulk of those funds paid for the Afghan security forces, though considerable sums were also spent on the civilian side. But most of that spending was not handled by the Afghan government. Outside players such as USAID and the U.S. military spent the bulk of the money, and while the Afghan ministries in Kabul were consulted, they often did not actually dispense the money. As the World Bank described it, "In 2010, of the roughly US$16.9 billion in total public spending, only US$3.3 billion were channeled through the 'core' budget and was under the control of the government's PFM [financial] systems."[2] So for every dollar spent by an Afghan ministry, five more were spent by its international partners.

This imbalance was due to be evened out by 2012, when half of the money allotted for development projects would be spent by the ministries. We planned for this to happen. It promised to give district staff some positive answers to their requests. Little did we know the whole idea would prove to be unworkable and the timetable hopelessly optimistic. The extent of the problem was hard to imagine. In the three years leading up to 2011 the Afghan ministries managed to spend 40 percent of the money they were given for development projects: they spent $950 million, leaving more than $1 billion sitting idle in bank accounts.[3]

The Afghans did manage to spend the operations and maintenance money that the ministries received. The bulk of this money paid the salaries of government workers, such as teachers and the police force.[4] This money also paid for the maintenance of schools, clinics, and district centers. But relatively little money was actually devoted to this funding pool—a paltry $335 million in 2011, according to the World Bank.[5]

The money that was being spent also didn't flow easily from Kabul to the provinces. The World Bank reported, "There are problems with efficiently allocating funds from the center to provinces/districts."[6] This inefficient disbursement explained why Nazak never had money to pay for the fuel for the generator at the district center and why the staff lacked fuel for their motorcycles. There just wasn't enough money making it through the system to all who needed it.

This bottleneck in the distribution of funds would not have mattered if the district staff was performing badly, because they would not have needed the money. But for the most part our district staff were raring to go.

We focused our daily mentoring of the line directors for health, education, rural reconstruction, and agriculture on helping them decide what project would most improve the district and then try to fund it. Their lists of previously unfunded projects were long; they wanted to repair roofs, add classrooms to schools, and repaint clinics. In previous months villagers had asked for rugs for mosques because that was what the village could absorb. (For instance, projects funded by the Canadians were required to benefit the entire village, which led to an unusual number of projects installing new solar lights in mosques or building a new village shura room, because that fit the criteria). Now the district staff asked for a new storeroom or solar panels at a clinic.

We slowly shifted from empowering village elders to empowering the district staff, because the number of projects that could be addressed would shrink as the Canadians and their dollars departed. This would be how the system would work in the coming years, as the Afghans used more of their own government money.

Some interesting ideas arose within just a few weeks. The rural reconstruction and development director, Mohammad Naseem, decided that we should repair the wells in the villages. In many villages old drinking water wells stood dusty from disuse. Often a well had one or two minor things wrong with it but otherwise functioned adequately. For want of a metal part or a new join where the plastic pipe had separated, the well was useless. Residents said hundreds of these wells needed to be fixed, and we figured we could do it for about $100 each.

Mohammad Naseem decided to hire a two-man team to go to villages and fix the wells. The team would repair two wells each workday, forty-eight wells per month. This would cost about $6,000 per month. Because several families used each well, the project would help hundreds of families very quickly, which would turn the villagers toward the government and improve security. Lt. Colonel Payne dedicated military funds to cover the costs of the well repairs.

So Mohammad Naseem quickly hired two men, who piled $2,000 worth of spare parts into a beat-up van and started to visit the villages. Naseem took requests from village elders and placed a list of villages on the wall of the district center by the staircase.

Within weeks the well repair project proved to be a howling success. Mohammad Naseem did everything. He planned, prioritized, budgeted, and wrote the monthly reports. Matt Kotlarski read the reports, checked their accuracy, and then paid for the next month's repairs.

Well repair represented a low-cost service that answered the villagers' needs. Because it was low cost, Afghanistan could probably benefit from similar homegrown ideas in years to come.

Some U.S. officials at KAF would criticize the program in the months ahead, unsure how it would continue in the future. But DG Nazak and

Mohammad Naseem assured us the ministry would be happy to fund the repair team when the official budget money finally came through.

Meanwhile the education director, Abdul Ahad, came to us and complained that little progress was being made on his pet project, a school offering vocational education. With Kandahar City a few short kilometers away, a huge demand existed for skilled workers such as plumbers and mechanics. The U.S. Army had been considering a proposal for a vo-ed school for months, and the budget had ballooned north of $1 million.

After Abdul Ahad complained to Lt. Colonel Payne that the officer in charge of the vo-ed school had made little headway, Matt Kotlarski and I took a look at the plan and trimmed it down by about 95 percent. Assured that the project might work, Payne approved a modest budget of $52,000, which paid for a new teaching shed, some equipment, and tools for the initial enrollment of 120 students.

Abdul Ahad had not been able to get approval for a new school building to be built and equipped. By refurbishing an old madrassa at the edge of a village in southern Dand, we saved hundreds of thousands of dollars and got a vo-ed school up and running within four months. Education ministry officials in Kandahar promised Abdul Ahad they would pay for teachers and a nighttime security guard. The U.S. Army paid for the improvements, because what we needed to do could not be fit into any USAID programs, the latter being devoted mainly to aid for agricultural and infrastructure such as roads. The school opened in the fall.

In trying to empower district staff we were not always successful. The agriculture department in Dand had little interest in increasing its workload. The office had five men on staff, but they continued to watch television for much of the workday and wait for ISAF handouts, no matter how much we poked and prodded them.

The agricultural director, Abdul Rashid, had worked in Dand for nine years, but he spent several days a week at his large farm in Helmand, fifty miles to the west. He was also recently married. In the past he had worked in the powerful secret police under the Communist regime, which led to a sense of entitlement on his part. He ruled absolutely. One of his men begged to be given something to do, even raising the problem in front of Nazak. Enraged, Rashid soon eased him out.

We suffered other reverses. The village affairs officer, in charge of keeping a list of elders who ran each village, was a tall and very thin man with a sparse beard. He had a problem showing up for work, missing days at a time. Eventually word filtered through from the maliks that he was soliciting kickbacks on construction projects, which was doubly outrageous because he had nothing to do with managing the projects and was relying on the gullibility of the villagers, who assumed he had influence. Nazak fired him. A month later, he popped up again on the staff in neighboring Panjwai District.

Other staff were found with their hands in the kitty. In July word came that agricultural director, Abdul Rashid, had been beaten up. Two district officials, the executive manager and the administration manager, both young men, had been demanding kickbacks from Abdul Rashid. A USAID contractor company called IRD was distributing subsidized wheat to hundreds of farmers, each of whom received bags of seed wheat and fertilizer. The two officials pressed Abdul Rashid, who oversaw the distribution, to set aside seed wheat and fertilizer for them. A single bag of wheat fetched forty dollars in Kandahar City.

Nazak told us the story the next day in his office. Abdul Rashid had refused to cooperate with the men, even after being beaten and threatened, and he had instead sought help from Nazak. Nazak called in the police and the Afghan intelligence officer for the district.

Confronted by the DG, the two officials made up a story that flipped the blame. "I'll fire either Abdul Rashid, or the executive manager, or the administration manager," vowed Nazak. He also ordered security forces to keep a closer eye on the seed distribution.

This was not the first time the executive manager had run afoul of Nazak. Six months earlier Nazak had gone to Dubai and left the executive manager in charge of the district. The executive manager and another official had pressured Abdul Rashid to pay them 100 Afghanis, worth about two dollars, each time he handed out subsidized seed wheat to a farmer. Presumably Abdul Rashid would in turn have dunned two dollars from each farmer so as not to be out of pocket, if he had agreed to the scheme. Eventually Nazak returned from Dubai and Abdul Rashid informed on the officials.

"Abdul Rashid was ready to quit," Nazak said. "I sent a letter to the prosecutor. They needed to interrogate these guys."[7]

As this situation unfolded we received anecdotal reports that seed and fertilizer had been stolen by the chief of police and other district officials. Distributions offered an opportunity for corruption that brought out the worst in people. We took extra precautions, such as guards, razor wire around the piles of wheat and fertilizer, and careful paperwork, but it proved almost impossible to deal with the vultures. Every time a new farm commodity distribution was announced we improved the measures to thwart corruption, but the cycle of attempted thievery and new precautions remained unbroken.

Over time our scorecard with the district staff was pretty good. The line directors planned, prioritized, and managed projects. The requests were countersigned by the provincial directorates, which solidified the relationship between the district staff and their provincial counterparts.

Even as the Canadians left and Dand's aid budget steadily declined over the summer and fall, villagers saw that the government was working for them. Because the staff developed ideas that cost little to implement, such as well repairs, there was a good chance they would eventually be funded by the Afghan government. Over time our informal motto became, "Spend a small amount of money that gives big results in the village. Always respond to people's needs."

The fly in the ointment would be twofold. First, when would the Afghan government have its own money to spend and could they spend it? And second, how much opposition would our ideas run into from KAF?

Soon after July 2011, when our aid budget began to shrink, the number of U.S. soldiers also began to shrink. We had one chance to set up the district for the future. We hoped that when we stepped away, the Afghan government would step up. From the district all the way up to Kabul the system would have to work properly or the peace we had won would be in trouble.

# 9

## Outpost Life

> To be allowed to sit in the Amir's presence is a sign of great favour and an honour accorded to few, and chiefs and high officials when asked to sit down, would do so on the floor, sitting with their backs against the wall, and if many were present they would sit in a line along the wall on either side of the Amir, those highest in rank or favour being nearest to him.—**Frank A. Martin**, *Under the Absolute Amir*, 1907

As summer turned into fall, one day dissolved seamlessly into the next. We would arrive at the district center, speak with the line directors, and brainstorm on their ideas and how to carry them out. We talked to whomever was in their offices—the directors of health, agriculture, education, or rural development. Matt Kotlarski, Mohammad Zahir, and I, accompanied by Sergeant Brian Hull, who wrote reports for the army, walked from office to office. We talked over ideas for projects the line directors considered viable and figured out how to fund them.

Assisting Matt were several civil affairs soldiers. They helped the staff learn about computers, in particular how to use spreadsheets and compose reports. The line directors' computer skills were good, but their assistants' ability ranged from good to basic to nonexistent. One of the agricultural assistants taught at Kandahar University and used his computer for a wide range of tasks. The education staff were generally well up to speed, while the assistant for Mohammad Naseem in the rural development office worked mostly with pen and paper. The village affairs officer never turned on his computer. The Afghan governance advisor assigned to the district had considerable expertise in computer use (he was in his twenties and working on a bachelor's degree at Kandahar

University, where Mohammad Naseem also studied). Governor Nazak was completely fluent with his laptop, posting most days on his personal Facebook account, while he employed several aides who had had little experience with computers. We spent considerable time trying to teach the basics of computers and cameras. Those skills became increasingly important as we began to demand reports with photographs to prove the projects we'd commissioned were being done.

In Afghanistan it is impolite to refuse tea from a host, so in the course of the daily rounds we might get four or five cups of piping hot tea, one after another. We sipped from dirty glass mugs with bits of the tea leaf floating on top. Some days the cups were reused endlessly as more guests arrived, with the remnants of the lukewarm tea tossed out and the cup refilled immediately. You looked for a clean part of the rim before sipping. Refusing was out of the question, because that would be an insult.

Lunch presented the same dilemma. Most days lunch would arrive in whichever office we were in. Sitting around communal bowls of eggplant swimming in vegetable oil accompanied by freshly baked loaves of flat bread, each person ripped their bread and dug out a chunk of oily eggplant. Decorum required leaving a little distance between your bit of eggplant and that of the person next to you. Life in Afghanistan was not for the squeamish. Some people avoided tea and lunch altogether, heading back to the base as soon as lunch appeared. Most soon adjusted.

In Afghanistan it is also impolite to discuss business at lunch, so we generally talked about life outside Dand. Karim Kamin, the governance advisor assigned to the district by the Independent Directorate of Local Governance (IDLG), faced two more years in his university studies. The rural development director was a former businessman who had traveled to Greece and India and was studying many subjects at Kandahar University. DG Nazak had his own colorful history.

In midsummer Cip Jungberg, the second USAID officer for the district, arrived. As Antoine Huss left, the district needed two officers to work there, plus Mohammad Zahir, our local cultural advisor-cum-interpreter. Cip, who was from North Dakota, had worked on a provincial reconstruction team in Iraq, knew plenty about working in war zones, and had good ideas about developing new businesses. With a wiry beard, a wry sense of humor, and midwestern common sense, Cip was an immediate hit with the Afghans, who were impressed by his empathy and willingness to try anything at least once to get results and back them up. Cip was not a fan of the eggplant and oil.

The district center in Dand stayed busy during the work day. Maliks and elders came to talk to district staff about the projects they'd requested. We often waited our turn until a particular director's office was clear of elders so we could sit down and consult with him on our next moves. Villagers also came to have their disputes settled by the district governor or the huquq (the government legal representative). To speak with DG Nazak we sometimes waited an hour, though usually he had us sit in the office as he dealt with his stream of visitors. The closer to your turn you got, the closer you moved to Nazak, shuffling from one sofa to another as the visitors came and left. If we were at the top of the square and speaking with Nazak, we were often dislodged by important visitors, starting again at the other end of the room. This was convenient because when we had VIP visits from the military, Nazak could easily cast a subtle glance down the room at our district team to get visual confirmation on specific points, and visitors seldom would notice our nods or headshakes in return. When Antoine was in the room, before he left in early summer, he seldom left Nazak's side and always occupied the plush chair next to the district governor's in almost every meeting.

At the entrance and in the hallways the police bodyguards carefully eyed the visitors, checking papers and bringing tea for Nazak and his guests.

In the midst of this bustle we would hear the whirl of helicopter blades as a green or tan helicopter swooped onto the base next door. A few minutes later most of the activity at the district center would pause as a general officer, a foreign dignitary, or a U.S. civilian arrived to kick the tires. Most often it was Canada's Brig. General Dean Milner, come to inspect "his" district. Dand was one of three districts in Kandahar Province assigned to Canada, and he visited about once a week, often bringing high-ranking guests with him.

His forces covered Dand, its neighbor to the west, Panjwai District, and its neighbor to the east, Daman. Dand and Panjwai resembled twins in a dysfunctional family: Panjwai, the violent ne'er-do-well, and Dand, the shining boy wonder.

Canada had varying experiences in Kandahar. On one hand it had showered its districts with largesse, and Dand had been among the biggest recipients of this bounty. Canadian money improved security in Dand by allowing the villagers to see the benefits of working with the government in the form of freshly dug canals, new roads, and better mosques.

On the other hand, for years the Canadian Army was overtaxed in Kandahar Province. The Canadians had too few troops to control all the ground. In the early years of its deployment, its units would rush from one spot to another, trying to put out fires. As soon as one fire was out, the troops would be moved to another sector and insurgents would simply filter back in again. So the population saw much violent action but little permanent security, which proved intensely frustrating for soldiers and farmers alike.

The Canadians benefited from two things. First, in their early years in Kandahar they saw few IEDs. Running in eight-wheeled light armored vehicles (LAVs) armed with 20mm cannon, the Canadians could defeat any opposition they encountered. When IEDs began to appear in volume in 2008, the LAVs began taking casualties. This problem would later plague the Americans, who supplemented the Canadians and who used an American version of LAVs, the Strykers. These would eventually be redesigned because they offered too little resistance to IED strikes.

The Canadians benefited as more Americans arrived, which allowed them to reduce their territory and exert a much greater effect on the area they retained.

Now Dand was part of the rump of Canadian-controlled territory. Like clockwork every week the Canadian general visited District Governor Nazak. By the time the helicopters dropped their passengers and departed, the general would be sipping his first cup of green tea.

Nazak had steadily improved the district center to impress guests. The walls of the large meeting room were covered in shiny plastic patterned to resemble wood. Glass coffee tables stood on red embroidered carpets. Nazak called this conference area his "corruption room."

He boasted that although a contractor offered him a kickback, he declined, saying, "I won't take the money. But now you can use that money to refurbish the shura room here so all the people can benefit." Dand was known for having the nicest district offices in Kandahar Province.

Nazak often explained with a sly smile, "Having nice offices is good, because people can see I am not just walking off with the government's money."

Nazak and the general sat at the end of the room with the rest of the visitors seated on the sofas lining the walls. Ordered by rank, the meeting resembled some bygone imperial court. Cip and I usually parked ourselves far down the line, among the lowly lieutenants.

Nazak took full charge when he hosted visits.

Brigadier Milner's visits helped to build a personal relationship with Nazak, but their discussions seldom centered on anything specific or even very useful for the district. The men talked in generalities—how Nazak was dealing with his maliks, how things in Dand were better than elsewhere, the Canadians' plans. They typically exchanged the latest gossip about Kandahar Province's governor Tooryalai Wesa, a divisive figure and former college professor in Canada who did little to tamp down the rampant corruption in the province.

After an hour or so the visit would conclude. Sometimes there would be lunch, with rice, flatbread, and meat. Then the general would be whisked away and we would return to business in the DDC.

As weeks passed the absence of substance in these VIP visits became more and more astonishing. At that time the district center lacked electricity from the power grid (generators ran on expensive diesel fuel paid for by the Americans), and the U.S. cohort was looking to take over the area. It was one of many problems left unsolved. But by then, in the waning weeks of the Canadian presence in Kandahar, what was there left to say? Other VIP visits seldom got past the same vague generalizations about the district. Eventually we stopped hoping substance would come out of these meetings. They were part of Afghan culture—strictly for show, not for solving problems.

This waste of time did not bother Nazak. His expectations were low. He mostly wanted to look good in front of ISAF, and avoiding any discussions of substance was a good way to accomplish that. He figured if he looked good to ISAF, they would help him get promoted. He wanted to become Kandahar City mayor, or deputy provincial governor, or even governor. Convinced that ISAF wielded major influence on President Karzai's appointments, he aimed to project the image of a savvy governor firmly in control of his district.

The weekly bustle at the DDC was followed by an abrupt quiet on Thursday afternoons. Friday is the Sabbath in the Islamic nation, and by the afternoon before the Sabbath the DDC would be deserted. Then Cip and I would go back to our accommodations on the military base next door and write the weekly report to KAF. Every Friday we would make a trip to the battalion's main base for the weekly planning meeting. On Saturday the cycle started again. We didn't get a day off.

On most business days the DDC would clear out after lunch, which was served at about 12:30. The district staff worked on average three or four hours a day. But they did actually work. They talked to maliks and wrote reports for their own headquarters in Kandahar City. After lunch most of the district staff headed home. No one lived at the district center, because Kandahar City was only ten minutes away by motorcycle. Dand was a commuter district with a twist: people kept an eye out for insurgents on the trips to and from the city.

After everyone left the DDC the Americans' second workday shift began. Cip and I would wade through emails and write reports; some days we worked as late as 10:00 p.m. Some emails were about the USAID programs we were overseeing, while others were requesting information needed to help the staff with their jobs or simply expressing new ideas to staff at KAF or in Kandahar City. Was Dand slated to receive any new schools? Could USAID boost farm exports to India? Reports covered USAID-funded projects such as roads, seed distributions, or new wells.

Many of the USAID programs essentially ran themselves. Others did not because some partners were unreliable, doing shoddy work and failing to make progress reports. The bad ones would require us to write reports to KAF and correspond with the embassy people to exert pressure on the companies to work harder.

One of our USAID contractors was digging eighty drinking water wells in several villages. Several wells failed the water quality test. They were retested, but the company dragged its feet on the retesting and didn't update us on progress or even pass along basic details such as the depth of the wells. The coordination between us, KAF, the embassy, the contractor, and the district government dragged on for weeks. There was no real way to take shortcuts.

Usually we finished up the work at about nine o'clock, and then it was time to put on the music—usually from YouTube videos—and write a few emails or call home or have a chat.

Cip lived in Antoine's old trailer neighboring mine, and sometimes we would walk fifty yards to the dining tent, in which eight wooden benches faced a TV that, if it was working, could be used to watch movies. But most people stayed in their tents at night and played video games or went to the morale tent, where they could phone home or send email on a handful of communal computers. There was also a laundry tent, where the washing machines broke down frequently, a shower tent with a few moldy stalls and water that was usually hot, and a small gym inside another tent. That was the extent of the facilities; we had all the essentials and couldn't ask for much more. Who needed the boardwalk fast food of KAF when you had autonomy instead? It was liberating. The stars at night were amazing, bright dots easily visible through the clear desert air.

Most Westerners in Afghanistan tended to have one of two experiences: either they had cushy assignments on bases such as KAF, complete with dining halls and coffee shops, or they lived on tiny forward outposts where soldiers had to cut each other's hair. Our life in Dand lay about halfway between the extremes, because our small base actually had washing machines—something the smallest outposts lacked. Most people enjoyed movies and games on their computers, and the base never suffered an attack.

On the other hand, the toilets were portables, the water in the showers occasionally turned cold or stopped altogether, and patrols were sometimes attacked. In one year in Dand one U.S. soldier and about a half dozen Afghan police and soldiers died on patrol. More were wounded. In Dand things were generally okay, with a small frisson of bad. It was dangerous and inconvenient enough to be interesting, but the danger for most of us who spent the majority of our time on base was remote. I would try to get out once or twice a week, accompanied by Mohammad, to inspect projects or the sites of proposed projects or to visit villages and get a sense of how the people lived and what they thought about the government, the United States, their jobs, and life in general.

One of my earliest trips involved the village of Bellanday on the western edge of the district, near Panjwai. An infantry company had located its base next to the village school. We walked to the school, passing through a gap in the fence. The school was clean and modern, with classrooms arranged along three sides of an open square. Inside a small common room with dusty floors and a few wooden tables we found the teachers, who were friendly and offered us apricots.

They said the school was safe and secure, though three years before the Taliban had come and killed two teachers and a school worker. They experienced a few problems. They hadn't been paid for a month, which happened all the time because the provincial ministries were notoriously slow in processing the budgeted funds. The school stood empty, because the children were on summer vacation and would not return until the fall.

Eight teachers taught three hundred schoolchildren up to grade eight. They needed books, although they'd received some supplies from the province and 150 notebooks from the Canadian civil affairs soldiers located at the base nearby. The books were important because each student took seven courses: Pashtu, drawing, science, math, life skills, religion, and, for the older children, English. It was a well-run, efficient school. When we followed up with the district education staff, they said the book shortage was being solved and it was not a problem (several other schools complained of the same problem and we received the same stock answer).

The teachers lived in Bellanday village, where the Canadians had built a system of concrete-lined ditches to carry water from one end of the village to another, channeled by metal sluice gates set at intervals. We walked past the project, and the quality was top-notch. But the teachers told us the project was supposed to include sixty sheep. Meant for the local people, the sheep had been diverted to the contractor and to people at the district center, and the livestock had probably been divided up among the contractor, the local elders, and various district officials.

"If the people at the district center were not involved, the contractor could not have taken the sheep," one teacher explained, offering an early lesson in the corruption that reached into almost everything in Afghanistan.

The opposite side of the village lay right against the border with Panjwai, and teachers said that side of the settlement was less secure. While we were at the base the soldiers told us the next village, situated across the border, was a hotbed of insurgent activity. Because it lay in Panjwai, clearing it would require additional troops. It was a problem they would solve once they shifted to Panjwai for good. Our trip lasted a day.

In July the Canadian Army cleared out the last thirty men at COP Edgerton, and the base grew very quiet. The battalion staff lived primarily at the main U.S. base ten kilometers to the south of the district center. The Americans at our little base either worked with the Afghan government, ran the base, patrolled the nearby villages, or mentored the Afghan police. Everyone had a purpose and time passed quickly.

There were horror stories on the large bases—booze, prostitution, sexual assaults, and despair. At our little base we lacked such problems. Life for us remained low-key, and we knew we'd lucked out.

We had occasional diversions. The soldiers in our headquarters element became enamored with a local cat that was striped and cute. He promptly acquired the name Carl and a feeding schedule. From there he became an Internet star for the soldiers' families back home at Fort Wainwright, Alaska. As the unit's tour wound down, an Internet appeal went out. Carl needed about $2,500 to be shipped home. The families back home took about a week to raise the money. Even before the soldiers arrived home, the cat had already arrived and was waiting for them. The whole thing was amusing and bemusing; the average Afghan lived on about $450 a year, and kids in the villages often went shoeless in winter. Other units didn't take as kindly to pets. One day at dusk we heard a sharp crack as a senior enlisted soldier of another unit shot a base cat through the head with his 9mm pistol.

As USAID civilians, Cip and I each lived in a shipping container that was half house and half office. We had our own computers and phones to call home anytime we liked. We could complain, and sometimes we did. Our setup was so good, it was slightly embarrassing to tell anyone the details. A satellite dish sat atop my container, providing twenty-four-hour Internet and free phone calls via the embassy in Kabul direct to America.

Cip and I were spoiled, and we knew it.

# 10

## Security Holds

You will naturally ask what remedy I propose for this state of things, and I will briefly state the principle on which I would proceed. First of all, I would endeavour to meet the danger as far as possible from our own frontier, without placing any hostile power between us and our Indian base. Some of those measures I have already described. They involve the establishment of a perfect Intelligence department of European officers in Affghanistan, and, if possible, a preponderating influence there; but I would not attempt the subjugation of the country nor its military occupation, because I believe that we can effectually keep out all rivals by supporting a national government.—**Sir Bartle Frere**, *Afghanistan and South Africa*, 1881

When I announced this surge at West Point, we set clear objectives: to refocus on al Qaeda, to reverse the Taliban's momentum, and train Afghan security forces to defend their own country. I also made it clear that our commitment would not be open-ended and that we would begin to draw down our forces this July.—**President Barack Obama**, Speech on Afghanistan, June 22, 2011

By the spring of 2011 the crack of rifle fire in Dand had been replaced by the steady chug of tractors tilling the fields. Insurgents were reduced to intimidating maliks, assassinating isolated victims, and setting bombs at the fringes of the district.

Then, on June 2, we learned the Taliban had killed Haji Kakar Mohammad, who was a cluster leader in the northeast of Dand, a Barakzai tribal elder, and one of the most influential men in the district.

It was not surprising the Taliban had taken out someone of his stature. Over the course of many years the Taliban had conducted a series of assassinations targeting anyone connected with the government. A few months earlier the Taliban in Dand had captured a man named Asadullah, the cluster leader for Deh Bagh village, and killed him. Speculation mounted as to whether he had been killed by the Taliban or by drug dealers operating out of Panjwai, but several members of his family insisted it was the Taliban who had done the deed.

Assassination was a favored Taliban tactic, and life in the province had grown increasingly violent. One study suggested insurgents had killed 515 elders and officials connected to the government in Kandahar between 2001 and mid-2010.[1] No one was safe—not aid workers, clerics, government officials, or progovernment tribal elders. Later that summer the Taliban killed a female aid worker in Dand after they captured her in the eastern part of the district. She died in a village midway between the strongholds of the Karzai and the Sherzai clans.

The higher the profile, the bigger the target. In quick succession the Taliban killed the mayor of Kandahar City, the provincial police chief, and one of the most prominent women in the province, Sitara Achekzai. A member of the provincial assembly, Achekzai was the only woman police officer in Kandahar. And in mid-July 2011 Ahmed Wali Karzai, Hamid Karzai's brother, was killed. The chief of his bodyguard detail, a man who had worked for Ahmed Wali Karzai for years, took out his pistol and shot Karzai in the head at his home in western Kandahar City. The shooter, quickly gunned down by other bodyguards, never revealed his motive; the Taliban claimed the man as one of their own.

The reach of the Taliban's assassination campaign seemed to extend everywhere, putting the city on edge. They'd tried to kill Nazak twelve times, usually when he traveled by car between Dand and his home in Kandahar City. Once a suicide bomber infiltrated the second floor of the district center before he detonated his explosives outside Nazak's office, blowing out the windows and scorching the interior. That event happened the year before I arrived. There were few reminders of the explosion except the extra careful screening that Nazak's bodyguards gave all visitors.

The persistent threat of assassination became a source of tension when Nazak's armored car reached the end of its useful life and he asked for a replacement. The political staff of the U.S.-run Kandahar Provincial Reconstruction Team and the officials at KAF balked at the $120,000 cost, though the military generally paid for these political perks. They suggested that Nazak buy his own armored car, even though several district governors in Kandahar had just received brand new armored Toyotas at no cost. The officials argued that, because Nazak had an independent income from his business interests, he should pay for his own vehicle. Of course the Afghan government had no money to pay for such a vehicle, and the option was not even raised.

Nazak replied that he had an income but was not rich, and $120,000 was a lot of money. Eventually a solution was found by Captain Matt Kotlarski, who paid $80,000 of the cost from military funds while Nazak covered the rest. Inevitably Nazak arranged the sale and got a better deal on the car than the military could have, saving himself some money. In return for Nazak kicking in his own money the military allowed him to take the car with him to his next government job in 2012. Despite Kotlarski's compromise solution, it rankled Nazak that the American civilians had tried to force him to foot the bill for his armored car when other district governors received funding for their vehicles. This kind of small and irritating incident was typical and acted as a constant burr under the saddle of the U.S. relationship with Nazak.

The assassinations accompanied a trickle of other security incidents in Dand in mid-2011. A U.S. patrol operating in the southwest corner of the district near the border with Panjwai heard about a suspected IED. As it arrived in the area, one of the eight-wheeled armored Strykers hit the IED, which exploded near the driver and killed him—one of a series of incidents over the previous two years that demonstrated the Strykers' vulnerability to IEDs when hit in the wrong part of the vehicle. Eventually the army redesigned the bottom of the vehicle and mothballed the old-style hulls.

Earlier that spring a patrol with Canadian, U.S., and Afghan soldiers had struck another IED in the northwest fringe of the district, killing a popular sergeant major of the Afghan National Army (ANA) and destroying the Ford Ranger he rode in. Because the ANA had few armored Humvees and usually traveled in unarmored Ford pickup trucks, an IED strike was usually devastating and often killed several of the occupants riding in the cab or in back. Mangled Fords of the Afghan army and police littered many of the American and Afghan bases, unwelcome reminders of the poor equipment the Afghans were forced to use. Humvees were armored but harder to maintain, and the ANA and ANP at the district level were chronically short of parts for the few Humvees they possessed. After years of delay the United States planned to deliver more than seven thousand Humvees to the Afghans in 2011.[2]

On July 4 the Taliban placed two IEDs in eastern Dand near some road-work contractors. One of the bombs detonated while the other malfunctioned. The police investigation revealed that the Taliban planned to detonate the second IED after the first one had exploded and drawn people to the area. Luckily the plan went awry and the contractors continued to rebuild the road.

Nazak was unhappy that the IED had gone off at all. He blamed the villagers for not being more alert and cooperative. "For better security, people must work more closely with the government," he told his staff and several maliks who visited his office.

So the insurgency in Dand continued at a slow boil, with a small but steady trickle of incidents, with maliks kidnapped and occasionally murdered. Meanwhile farther west in Panjwai District the fighting reached full throttle. Matthew Roberts, a USAID field officer in our training class in Washington, reported difficulty in getting into the villages because the security situation had become too tenuous. Also the local battalion expressed reluctance to take him into the villages, because it had few vehicles based at the district center in Panjwai, where he lived, and it did not want to make special trips along a hazardous road to pick him up. Matthew had purchased Kevlar underwear prior to coming to Afghanistan, for which he had received weeks of ribbing. It looked like he would not be using his innovative undergarments any time soon.

By contrast it was easy for those of us with USAID in Dand to get out on patrols. Mohammad Zahir and I tried to get out once a week, tagging along with the scouts based near the district center or going to visit the companies based around the district and hitching rides on their patrols. Lt. Colonel Payne recognized that if we could not see what was going on, we would be of little use. We needed information directly from the villagers, on whether the government worked, if it could be trusted, and what they really needed. As Antoine Huss moved out and was succeeded in August by Cip Jungberg, we were able to complete the picture we had received from the district staff by talking directly with the elders in their own villages. Without a weekly hands-on encounter, we would not have a good feel for the current situation.

These side trips could take a few hours or several days. We might be picked up at the district center, visit several villages, and be dropped off at the end of the day. Or we might spend the night at a combat outpost manned by an American company and go on two patrols, one on the first day and one on the second. The local people gave their candid views of the security situation, even in the more insecure areas.

During an early trip Mohammad and I headed to COP Ainsworth in southwest Dand, an area still unstable because it bordered Panjwai. To the south of the COP lies a large desert called the Reg. A mass of rolling dunes covering hard rock, this desert spread for miles, running from Helmand in the west to Pakistan in the east and the south. Kuchi nomad settlements dotted the desert, hugging the river that bordered it to the north and cut it off from Dand.

Insurgents coming from Pakistan often wound their way through the desert, heading to Panjwai, a few miles west of Ainsworth. The trouble they caused in Panjwai had spilled over the border into Dand. Our destination, a village named Nahre Shefe (pronounced NAH-ree SHEE-fa), lay almost exactly at the nexus of the two bars of an upside-down T formed by the desert to the south, Panjwai to the west, and Dand to the east.

Nazak had failed to persuade the village elders to send a representative to the district center. They refused, complaining of the danger because the Taliban had easy access to their houses. In retaliation Nazak decreed the village would get no projects until they sent someone. The soldiers also reported no success in persuading the villagers to go. Life was especially difficult for the villagers, who had only one drinking water well for all the houses within a kilometer. They desperately needed another. Mohammad and I wanted to hear the stories for ourselves.

We had spent the previous night in dusty green tents surrounded by the high HESCO walls of the base. The COP, comfortable if cramped, boasted a gym, a small chow hall, and a shower tent. Plywood walls separated the officers' "rooms" inside the accommodation tents. Afghan soldiers, still in Dand at the time, shared the base with the Americans.

We set out early one morning, bouncing in the back of a Stryker with two other soldiers. Mohammad sat inside the back and dozed, and I stood with my head out a rear hatch. The view inside the hull consisted of the legs of the two men standing on the rear seats with their heads out the hatches and a small monitor attached to a forward bulkhead fed by a video camera on the nose of the Stryker. Swirls of dust rolled into our faces and down through the hatches, coating everything with grit that resembled beige ash from a fire.

Mohammad wore his usual outfit of well-used U.S. Army cargo pants in the old desert pattern, topped with a tan-painted helmet issued by the embassy. We both wore embassy-issued tan flak jackets that were bulky, heavy, and uncomfortable. A veteran of hundreds of patrols, Mohammad had spent years working with U.S. Special Forces, so these jaunts into the countryside were deeply anticlimactic for him. Growing up in Kabul when the Taliban controlled it, Mohammad had been living this conflict since primary school, and it had become routine. But we both welcomed these patrols as interesting diversions that allowed us a break from the stifling confines of the district center. As for IEDs, you either let the threat bother you or you didn't. Since the locals used this road frequently, it seemed more appropriate to doze than to worry.

The Strykers approached Nahre Shefe via a dirt track running across the scrubby desert. The Americans and Afghans kept a sharp lookout for IEDs. Eventually we passed some sparse green wheatfields with still visible traces of old irrigation channels carved in the hard-baked dirt. We followed a narrow road into the village, winding past several scattered compounds. Once we pulled off the road the vehicles spread out. The rear ramp dropped. Several soldiers dismounted. Others remained crouched behind their guns. An Afghan army pickup truck faced the desert.

Walking past several mud houses, we found the drinking water well and asked around. The village elder was in, and we were led by the ANA troops into his large mud house. We shook his hand and settled down onto thin wool rugs inside the thick mud walls. A young boy brought us hot tea, and we began to chat.

The elder was in his late sixties and rail thin, like most rural Afghans. With high cheekbones, his face bore lines that framed shrewd eyes. His mouth turned upward into something just short of a smile. He spoke freely and easily even though our visit would almost certainly cause the Taliban to pay him a visit in the next few days.

The elder said five or six tribes lived in the village, and he confirmed the existence of only one usable well. "This well was done before the Taliban came, and was done by an NGO," he said.

There was not enough water because the other five wells in town were too salty to use, and the people were having to haul water to their houses from the next village over, about three miles to the east. This cost a lot of money, he said, and the people were suffering.

But the elder again refused to go to the district center. He explained that the tribes could not agree on a single representative, so sending one was impossible. This was a convenient evasion of the central issue—working with the government—which he was clearly reluctant to do. Instead he said he wanted to work through the local tribal elder, who lived in the town nearest to COP Ainsworth, where security was better. Working through the elder would be less visible and allow him to deny any cooperation with the government when the Taliban inquired. He said that villagers had gone three or four times to ask this elder for a new well, but nothing had been done.

We pointed out that the people in Nahre Shefe were missing out by refusing to work with the government. Other villages sometimes received sacks of subsidized seed wheat, and the only way to secure a new well would be to work with Governor Nazak. In the end the elder declared he would make a concession, and, if someone came to see him, he would send someone to the cluster shura associated with the government, which met every week near COP Ainsworth. Of course he never followed through on his promise, nor did we really expect him to. As for going to the district center, that would remain a nonstarter as long as the Taliban passed by so frequently. Stalemate.

As we chatted he also told us the sorts of details we needed to plan projects for the area: what the village grew (wheat), where they traded ("We sell in Kandahar City, and it takes two or three hours to get to

Kandahar City by tractor"), and how safe they felt ("We are close to Panjwai and we have some fear. But the Taliban cannot stay here inside the village"). After an hour we shook hands, thanking the man for his tea and for telling us what he wanted. The soldiers piled back into the Strykers, I popped my head through the hatch, adjusted the headset, the ramp came up, and we lurched down the dirt track again, kicking up a great plume of dust. We stopped at two more villages and repeated the entire process, speaking to the elders and hearing their thoughts about the government. Located in safer areas a few kilometers farther away from Panjwai and the desert, these villages sent elders to see Nazak. In return they received projects. One village even opened a school. Nahre Shefe proved the exception rather than the rule.

The soldiers were happy to confirm this information. By seeing it for ourselves we heard the nuances and assured ourselves that when we discussed strategies with Nazak, he was giving us the straight information. We could talk to him as equals and better understand the people he governed.

The fact that people even in the more unstable areas were willing to talk was a testament to the ground covered by Nazak and the soldiers from the Afghan, U.S., and Canadian military forces. It was a remarkable turnaround in a short space of time. In other parts of Kandahar Province district governors struggled to do what Dand had accomplished by building or reopening schools and health clinics and persuading maliks to work with the government. Dand was quiet and that was good. It suggested few insurgents were operating freely.

In early June the security situation was poised to change. The Canadians would be pulling out in July and returning home, although some of their forces would shift to Kabul to help to train the Afghan army. But the kinds of intensive patrolling and fighting in the villages they had done so much of over the previous six years would end.

The ANA left Dand that summer, too. The U.S. military started pulling out its companies and reassigning them to Panjwai a few weeks later; their pullout was spread over several months.

To settle all the questions surrounding these wrenching changes, Nazak hosted a security shura attended by the ANA general in charge of the province, the Canadian general, and Lt. Colonel Payne. Nazak worried that he would be shortchanged as the forces shifted out, but he was a gracious host as the officers trooped into the district center on June 4. A dozen village elders waited to greet them, as the military and Nazak tried to get everyone on board with the changes coming soon.

The Canadian general, Brigadier Milner, noted that security efforts in Dand had been successful. "Last September there were insurgents here in Dand. But you don't let the insurgents back in. That is the most important thing," he stressed.

Several maliks complained, though, that someone had set up a checkpoint the previous week, and no one knew if it had been ANA or the Taliban. The elders said they could keep the Taliban out of the villages, because they would not let in strangers, but they also stated that this problem with checkpoints on the roads was almost impossible to solve by themselves.

Nazak piped up and said the only solution was for the ANA to step up the number of patrols. Checkpoints were useless because they were too static.

"Patrols are better because they reach more places," insisted Nazak.

Several maliks agreed. They said the ANA needed to patrol more, especially on the border with Panjwai. Insurgents had set up temporary roadblocks on the border with Panjwai, and the people were afraid. The insurgents viewed anyone who helped the government as the enemy.

"The Taliban says that by cooperating with the government we are invaders and infidels," one of the maliks complained loudly. The elders declared they could guard the new schools and the villages, but they were wary of getting caught by the Taliban roadblocks when moving around the district.

Nazak urged the maliks to work with the government, pointing out that in return for security the maliks would get projects. This prospect made the maliks happy, and they agreed to provide security.

The upshot of the meeting was that the security forces would think about patrolling more. But the drawdown was inevitable. This kind of balancing act, between the demands of the elders and the steadily diminishing resources of the security forces, meant that the future of Dand would hang in the balance.

But as much as Nazak could control the maliks, a number of factors exceeded his powers of persuasion and threatened to destabilize the district as the troops started to pull out.

He could not fight geography. To the west sat Panjwai District, unstable and violent. Panjwai weakened Dand, because insurgents staged weapons there for use in Dand and Kandahar City. Forty miles to the east lay the border with Pakistan. Since the 1980s fighters from Pakistan had infiltrated in from the east and south, passing through or along the fringes of Dand. The border was irredeemably porous, and drug and weapons smugglers used the desert south of Dand to move their wares. Dand represented a pit stop on the underground highway from Quetta to Kandahar City, as it had been for years.

Meanwhile the Taliban and drug smugglers sent a huge amount of traffic through the district to the east abutting the Pakistani border, an area called Spin Boldak, which was poorly patrolled. Few border police or customs officers made much fuss beyond collecting customs revenue. The problem expanded when in 2011 the head of the border police at Spin Boldak, Brig. General Abdul Razziq, was appointed chief of police for Kandahar Province as a whole. Little would change on the border, where making an end run around the official border crossing could take as little as two hours. More brazen individuals drove right through the customs post, offering bribes on each side of the border.

If the porous border threatened Dand, so too did centuries-old tribal problems. More than 40 percent of the population of Afghanistan is Pashtun. Areas where Pashtuns reside span the border between Afghanistan and Pakistan. The border zone on both sides, known as Pashtunistan, extends from Kandahar along the spiny border leading north. Consequently crossing the border is perceived as an age-old right rather than a pressing national security issue.

The Pashtunistan concept has irritated relations between the governments on both sides of the border for decades, because reuniting Pashtunistan at the expense of Pakistan was official Afghan government policy. Afghans continue to lament the loss of their tribal members to Pakistan, and it is national lore that the Durand Treaty, which established the border line in 1896, is an injustice.

Ideology also drives the war. The Pakistani government is comfortable with insurgents' radical Islam. For thirty years it has supported Islamists such as the Taliban and Gulbuddin Hekmatyar, because it approves of their view of the world. In the 1970s President Zia ul Haq, a devout Muslim, pursued policies to support and spread a strict version of Islam. Then in the 1980s Pakistan supported the most hard-line and Islamist of the mujahidin commanders, who received the lion's share of the assistance channeled to fight the Soviets. Pakistan continued to support these same commanders in the 1990s, when it helped to develop the Taliban, and it supports them even now, according to many reliable sources.

Taliban commanders have reported the movement derives direct support from Pakistan's ISI, or Inter-Service Intelligence Directorate, the intelligence service. One study noted, "According to Taliban commanders the ISI orchestrates, sustains and strongly influences the movement. They say it gives sanctuary to both Taliban and Haqqani groups, and provides huge support in terms of training, funding, munitions, and supplies. In their words, this is 'as clear as the sun in the sky.'"[3] The same study noted, "As a south-eastern commander put it: 'We receive a lot of training, weapons, ammunition and expenses from the Pakistan government. . . . Everyone knows Pakistan gives money, it goes centrally, then flows down.'"[4]

Pakistani support is both a strength and a weakness for the Taliban. The average Afghan tends to believe the war is a Pakistani creation. Nazak fully exploited this belief as he tried to persuade elders to work with the government.

But Nazak had good reason to be worried. The ANA and ANP were still ramping up to a full strength of 352,000 men. Even this was barely adequate to the task, according to the ISAF commander, General Stanley McChrystal, whose internal studies showed 400,000 Afghan security forces would be needed in a country the size of Afghanistan.[5] Since the surge was due to conclude within a year, the size of the Afghan forces was a key concern that would increase as security forces started to withdraw from Dand itself.

By midsummer 2011 the ANA had pulled out of Dand. Soon after, the American soldiers began to reduce their forces in the district. Security stayed about the same. Spending on projects remained strong, if slightly lower with the loss of the Canadians. The government continued to work with the maliks and people.

By early 2012 almost all the Americans were gone. Still the government remained strong and maliks kept coming to the district center, working with DG Nazak. He had produced a fragile but functioning government.

The deadline for the end of the surge was mid-2012, and most districts in Kandahar were unlikely to improve after that. Continuing security depended on good performance by the district governments. The Taliban had no reason to ease off just because U.S. forces were leaving; it had every incentive to go all in.

Looking ahead, so it proved. In late spring 2012, the start of the fighting season, the number of attacks was 11 percent higher nationwide than at that time the previous year.[6] The pressure continued to rise thereafter. We hoped that our experiment in nation-building in Dand would survive, despite signs that the United States' focus had shifted to simply getting out, with scant regard for conditions on the ground.

# 11

## Women's Work

The largest houses also have a garden attached to them, which is surrounded by a high wall to ensure privacy when the women walk in it, for no woman must allow her face to be seen by any man excepting her nearest relations. The door leading to the women's quarters in all houses has a kopchee or door-keeper, and no one is allowed to enter any house until its master has given permission, and no woman is allowed to leave the house unless the kopchee has been told by the master to permit it.
—**Frank A. Martin**, *Under the Absolute Amir*, 1907

A small group of Afghan police guards, invariably with long hair and sullen eyes and scruffily clothed in dirty blue coveralls, stood watch at the entrance to the district center. What they lacked in presentation they made up for in effectiveness. No one made it past the guards without being searched thoroughly. Visitors were searched at the front gate to the compound, the front entrance to the district center building, and at the door to Nazak's office. Every morning elders would arrive, bearded and proud, to speak with Governor Nazak about the state of their villages and to inquire about projects.

Into this stream of haughty, turbaned men a few shadowy figures would try to insinuate themselves. Covered completely in black burqahs, taking slow and often hesitant steps while keeping close to the walls, the women cut quite different figures from the purposeful striding of the village elders. The women would try to seek out Nazak or one of his staff. Though many tried to gain entry, most never made it through the front gate before being turned away. Those who did navigate the gate would shuffle to the side of the main district center office building and hunch down, waiting for Nazak to appear. Occasionally they tried to make their way past the guard at the front door and get inside to see him, but only once or twice did a woman ever make it into the carpeted hallways. It was not unusual to see the burqah-clad forms sit outside for hours.

The women were regarded by the guards as minor nuisances at best and annoying pests at worst. Occasionally someone tried to help one of them and asked who she wanted to see, but they were usually ignored. Every once in a while someone would yell at one of the women and tell her to leave. Women possessed no status in rural Afghan society. Any woman in Dand who spoke with a male without having a male relative present ran the risk of being condemned as a moral hazard.

Afghanistan is a patriarchal society, especially in the southern provinces. While women in Kabul worked in ministries and as teachers or studied at the university, women in rural Kandahar Province led a very different sort of life. In Kandahar one might often see a woman riding to the bazaar behind her husband on his motorcycle. She would be fully enveloped in a burqah, the black or blue fabric fluttering in the breeze. On patrols in villages soldiers could hear women behind high mud walls, but respectable women were never seen without male relatives.

Nazak occasionally spoke with the women at the district center, usually when he walked outside to his car and passed the waiting figures. He felt exasperated by these women because they usually asked for money. He had no money to give. There were too many for that to be a viable option. The Afghan government subsidized the district center in small ways, such as with a small allowance for gasoline for his car. But he received no state money or support to help these women. Other district staff or interpreters occasionally gave money to them. It was an ad hoc, inadequate, and neglectful system that filled us with dismay.

Many of these women were impoverished widows. Afghan society's strict rules governing women's lives were relaxed somewhat with widows, whom society valued even less. But while widows gained the right to travel unaccompanied outside the home without threat of condemnation, they often lost the attention and care the family might have been expected to provide. Distressed widows quickly became nonentities to society.

The national government ran a pension program for war widows, but the women seen at the district center rarely fell into that category. The Afghan government also operated a Department of Women's Affairs (DOWA) in Kandahar City, but it was a small department and few of its officials ever went into the villages. The DOWA offered little help for these rural widows.

In Afghanistan when a woman is widowed, she is generally taken in by her late husband's family. His brother might marry her if she is still young and desirable or offer charity and provide for her if she is not. But if neither option appeals, the woman is out on her own.

Many women fall through the cracks of this family system because they are elderly, have too many children, or the family spurns them for other reasons. Even if they are taken in, the food given to them and their children might be insufficient. Many widows relied on alms from villagers and, if they were lucky, their families. Many of the women who came to the district center had run out of food for their children and were in desperate straits. So the widows in Dand had no reliable safety net provided by either their families or the government. They eked out a living, often isolated on the margins of village life, and their children went hungry.

Often the women who came to the district center positioned themselves outside the entrance and waited until one of the foreigners came by. The foreigners, potential sources of handouts, were a much better bet than the governor. Luckily for the women, they had learned they had one champion in the district center compound.

Sergeant Sonia Blaha, from the Canadian military, had long dark hair, intense eyes, a tall, slender frame, and a purposeful manner. By the summer of 2011 she was at the tail end of her nine-month tour. In many ways it had been a frustrating tour, for she had witnessed how little had been done to help the women of Dand. She listened to the women's problems and saw that they had little recourse to alleviate them.

Sonia was not even tasked with helping women; she was a civil affairs soldier in charge of projects on the remote northwest fringe of the district. Her schedule would take her on patrols to the edge of the district, in the same sector where the Afghan army sergeant major had died in an IED strike. She returned to our base next to the district center to file her paperwork.

In fact Sonia had been told by her command to leave the women alone and to get on with the job of delivering projects to "her" villages. Characteristically and stubbornly she insisted on doing both. She found what assistance she could for the women and looked for opportunities to help them, scrounging around the base for care packages and donations.

But Sonia Blaha also had a plan. From talking with the women Sonia Blaha knew they wanted to learn new skills and open new businesses. And they wanted a way to communicate with the government besides skulking around the entrance to the district center. Sonia knew how to deliver. She needed a dedicated Afghan woman willing to serve as their conduit to the government and as a trainer to teach them new skills. She wanted to begin a completely new women's initiative that would bring training and jobs to women in Dand and would also help them to earn money in their village. Lack of income was, after all, the root of their problem.

Sonia Blaha collared me in early June about the women's dilemma. The Canadians were due to pull out over several weeks beginning in late June, and Sonia was frustrated that she had been unable to generate any interest in women's programs during her entire time in-country. Now, with a few weeks to go, in between her patrols in northwest Dand, finishing paperwork on a dozen old projects, squeezing in one more round of extra projects for the health clinics with leftover cash, and packing up her gear, she set out to help the women in Dand. There was a good chance we could get money for her initiative if Nazak wanted it. Matt Kotlarski, our reliable go-to man for support from the U.S. Army, would likely sign up for a good idea, which would go a long way to getting final approval from Lt. Colonel Payne, who trusted Matt not to pass stupid ideas his way.

Coincidentally that summer the Afghan government dropped off at the district center a large container that was supposed to house a DOWA representative. Forty feet long and made of white-painted steel, it held a desk, a conference table, and a bathroom because no female employee would ever be able to use the restroom used by men inside the district center. This separate housing/office unit was some headquarters wonk's notion of a good idea, but without Sonia's idea to ramp up a women's program the container would have been yet another U.S.-funded white elephant, because the provincial DOWA had no intention of sending a representative to Dand to work with the women. Maybe Sonia's plan could change that.

We spoke with District Governor Nazak about the idea. Nazak's first reaction was enthusiastic affirmation. He couldn't wait to begin. It turned out Nazak wanted to tie every segment of society to his government, and women were no exception. What began as a general idea to help local women soon became a district priority, and what was more important was that Nazak wanted changes similar to those outlined by Sonia Blaha.

Within two weeks Sonia had contacted three NGOs and invited their representatives down to speak with Nazak. The provincial DOWA director, Rokia Achekzai, also attended the meeting. One afternoon in late June a dozen people filed into the shura hall at the district center and settled into the plush couches. Some of the visitors perched on the sofas and presented an earnest appearance, while others relaxed and sank into the well-used cushions. Nazak outlined the problem and explained what he wanted done.

"Widows and poor women never went to school. We need to give them some economic help and some education. We need to get the NGOs in the villages to help," Nazak told the group. "We are the first district to start this process. We will make a website to announce that the NGOs and the Department of Women's Affairs are working here."

The NGOs then outlined their ideas. Not surprisingly, none of the NGOs had any money and would need funds from the U.S. government in order to proceed.

"With $10,000 we will try to teach tailoring," promised one. Others estimated that they would need in the neighborhood of $40,000 to get started. Everyone agreed that someone needed to come up with a plan.

"To get a solution we need to figure out the needs of the women," said Sonia. "Then the NGOs can work on it." DOWA director Rokia Achekzai said the NGOs needed to help the government implement the plan.

With that we were off to a good start. Nazak took the idea to the district's elders at the next weekly meeting. He reported that the elders had been happy with the idea. Within a week Nazak was sitting in his office and discussing Sonia's idea with our district team again.

"Women need a job, some kind of job," Nazak told us. "I told the weekly shura about this idea, and I asked the elders how many widows there are. I told them to call on the widows in their villages, and we will give them a helping hand. We'll get rice and flour, and the women will come and register with the DOWA here. We'll have a ceremony."

Nazak wanted to help the women in two ways: with humanitarian assistance and with jobs and training. DG Nazak thought helping women would improve his links with villages and his image with the Americans. Nazak had always planned to reach into every segment of society: farmers, elders, mullahs, teenagers, and now women.

Dand, in the heart of Kandahar Province, is one of the most conservative provinces in Afghanistan. Mullah Omar and the Taliban began there, working in districts outside of Kandahar City. Just nine months earlier Dand had suffered serious security issues, with rampant Taliban influence. It seemed an enormous leap to train women. So it was with some skepticism that Sonia Blaha received DG Nazak's enthusiasm. But Nazak was serious; his biggest concern was how soon the training could begin.

Who would pay for it? The DOWA's budget in Kandahar City was more than $700,000 a year, but according to the Americans in Kandahar City who dealt with the DOWA, the money was actually spent by the ministry in Kabul on projects in Kandahar City. Thus the Kandahar DOWA had no resources to assist the districts. Over time that might change.

Lt. Colonel Payne liked the idea of offering assistance directly to women, because it would strengthen the hold of the government over the people, and supporting Nazak was his priority as he shifted his forces to Panjwai. With that we received a commitment for our money, and our women's project was up and running.

But as yet no one had figured out what was needed to help each woman, or how many women were in need, or what in particular could be done to help them the most. Meanwhile the first group of Canadians pulled out of Dand. Within two weeks they would all be gone, including Sonia. We crossed our fingers that Sonia would be on the last lift out in the first half of July. Without her the women's program might just grind to a halt before it had even properly begun.

As the clock ticked down, Rokia Achekzai came to the district for another planning meeting. We faced the same issues, and we still didn't know how many women needed help.

"We are collecting information, but it is not the same problem in each village," Nazak explained. "It depends on the place. In one village the housing is good, but they need food there. We will have a plan. The women can come here to the district center. They can go to the DOWA trailer, and we will specify the day they can come. We will reach out to each village in Dand. Before you go to a village, I will call the village elder and they will hold a shura to tell everyone."

The meeting concluded with the idea that we would figure out what women wanted. Then the NGOs could come and do whatever needed to be done. At the same time the U.S. Army could distribute humanitarian aid (blankets and food) to the most desperate women. The village elders could coordinate what happened in each village.

This idea made sense until we looked more closely at the numbers. The cost of $40,000 for an NGO to teach tailoring to women in a village seemed excessive. We decided we'd be better off to empower the DOWA to handle the training themselves. We could pay for the trainers at a fraction of the cost, at most $500 a month. Adding in transportation and materials, we could probably do an entire three-month program for $10,000 to $15,000, a third of the money that the NGOs would charge us. And best of all we would have a program that could be locally controlled by Nazak and the district staff.

In the next planning meeting the district education director, who ran nearly thirty schools in Dand and was a Barakzai tribal elder, suggested we concentrate the training in one village at a time. Doing so would simplify monitoring, he said, and give us a test case to move forward.

"The women know embroidery," Abdul Ahad said. "If you provide cloth, the DOWA office in Kandahar City has a shop in which to sell it. And they have a shop in Kabul, too."

By the end of the day we had a plan to look at whether the DOWA could find us a trainer. We could do the embroidery program on the cheap, with maximum local involvement. The ideas came in the nick of time. Within three days Sonia was sent to KAF on the first leg of her journey out of the country. Given the convoluted methods of the military, it was an inevitable twist of fate when she spent the next two weeks at KAF with little to do while we carried on as best as we could without her organizational skills.

We figured out the budget and a start date for the first project. The elder for Ruhabad was pleased when his village was selected as the test case. Without his support the whole idea would have been stillborn, but he helped us find a place where the training could be held and the sewing machines and materials stored. He also gave permission for the first group of thirty women to congregate and learn in a single class. Despite the conservative Pashtun attitude toward women, it was relatively easy to find elders who would support the training as long as a few basic questions were settled, such as safeguards for the women's privacy and who would lead the project. Pressure from Nazak and the education director probably helped, too.

By the middle of July we had a rudimentary plan in place. The DOWA trainer would visit three or four villages and report back on the needs of the women. She would also double as the liaison to the district center, but the issue of staffing the trailer by the district center to receive women seeking help remained unresolved. Given the death of the female aid worker in Dand earlier that year, security was paramount. The DOWA hesitated to commit to specific times.

"Security is bad in Kandahar City," said Rokia Achekzai. "We can do two days a week in Dand. But security on the road is a problem."

Given that the Taliban had tried to kill Nazak more than half a dozen times alone on the road to Kandahar City in previous years, this concern for security was a significant one. As a measure of good faith, Rokia Achekzai traveled to a village that month and delivered the first bit of humanitarian aid to widows and poor women.

With Sonia gone, the U.S. battalion assigned women from its ranks to form a female engagement team to help out. This effort was not an immediate success since their first suggestion was to accompany the DOWA trainer into the villages in eighteen-ton armored fighting vehicles. The Afghan women from the DOWA were aghast, because their lives depended on keeping a low profile. They did not want the female soldiers even to visit the same villages they were visiting. The idea was quietly dropped.

Within six weeks the program began in Ruhabad, and it was the first district-led female engagement and training program in Kandahar Province. By sidestepping the NGOs, we had brought the idea of Afghans helping themselves to a new level. Afghans controlled the whole process while we monitored and advised. This idea of training women was old, but the notion of such projects being executed with full control by local Afghan government staff was, amazingly enough, brand new in the province.

NGOs often conducted job training programs for women. These had varying amounts of success and often cost huge amounts of money for each woman who attended. The long-term effects of these expensive programs were poorly measured. And because the provincial DOWA office tried sporadically to influence the districts, the idea of an official liaison officer who had resources to help women and serve as their spokesperson to the district government would be more or less revolutionary.

If we were lucky and it worked, we would branch out once the concept was tested in Ruhabad. The goal was to make embroidery that was good enough to sell in Kandahar City. Since embroidered goods sold for between $10 and $100 apiece, and the average monthly wage in rural areas was about $125, this project would improve family incomes quickly if done well.

The biggest fly in the ointment was ensuring the embroidered goods were sold. We would look into this in more depth in months to come. Our desired outcome—women's businesses—was simple but not easy. As time went on we realized we would have to teach the women and the village elders to market their products. Slowly the building blocks fell into place.

Ironically the person who had thought the whole thing up, Sonia Blaha, never saw the fruit of her labors. Worse, the Canadian military never acknowledged her work to help the women of Dand because it was not part of her job assignment. This sort of thing happened all the time in Afghanistan, where superlative performance was rewarded with brick-bats or nothing at all.

Still we were pleased. By the end of September we had a working women's program in Dand that was inexpensive, effective, and sustainable, because the Afghan government could easily cover the costs of such a low-budget program if they so desired. Given that the national plan was to spend more money through the Afghan ministerial budgets, the DOWA should be able to scale up its efforts in years to come. By involving the head of the DOWA in Kandahar from the beginning and getting her input in designing and carrying out the program, we figured we had plenty of leverage to ensure the women's program in Dand would be at the front of the line when her department received a boost in official funding from Kabul sometime in the future.

As the women's training in Ruhabad proceeded, we thought we were finally in a good place. It all began to get interesting, as events threw us some curveballs from a quarter we least expected.

# PART THREE

Dand in the Balance

# 12

## Stealing from Women

Although women formally have little power, they are informally quite
strong, not only in home-decision making, but often in extra-family
economic activities, such as the sale of homemade items. Women
have, in fact, always been politically strong in Afghanistan, as is
well illustrated by the following quote from Vigne (1840, 256–67):
"Muhammad Afzal Khan, the eldest son . . . I heard a very good account
of him, but he is motherless, and has fewer friends in the Zunana"
(i.e., harem or women's quarters), therefore he had less power than his
half-brothers. —**Louis Dupree**, *Afghanistan*, 1997

By late autumn a number of programs were ticking along nicely. For
instance, a new vocational education school opened in Dand in early
October. It was a major success for DG Nazak, who invited in the media
and some leading provincial figures. The school almost hadn't opened,
but the effort to do so had recovered nicely from dithering and delay that
spanned eight months.

Under the original ISAF plan the school would have cost $1.1 million,
but we had it up and running for $52,000. The school building was not
new; we used an abandoned concrete madrassa set in a high-walled
compound that was roughly two hundred meters square.

The idea of a vo-ed school had been cloaked with tension and animos-
ity for months. First, it was a mystery how anyone could spend a million
dollars in a space that size, because in Afghanistan a spare classroom
would cost only about $5,000 to build. A million dollars of new build-
ing would have been enough to construct Dand's version of the Empire
State Building.

What was worse was that the project had been delayed by months. By the time we looked at it with Lt. Colonel Payne's battalion in midsummer, the proposal had already been rejected by U.S. forces. (Perhaps predictably, USAID had no programs that we could apply to help with refurbishing and reequipping a building). Plans were rewritten and months passed. The ripples of these delays flowed into the district center. At one point the price of the original gold-plated plan dropped to $800,000, then $450,000. Nazak and his staff could not understand what was going on. Eventually we suggested that Captain Kotlarski and Lt. Colonel Payne could help with about $50,000 from their discretionary funding, which we figured would be plenty to open the school.

For one meeting in August Nazak invited the education director for all of Kandahar Province to the district center. Nazak wanted to strong-arm the provincial director into pledging money for teachers' salaries if we opened the school, and Abdul Ahad, the Dand education director, was there to help twist his arm. Ahad complained about the $450,000 option and the army officer in charge of the project.

"Last week this guy told me to sign the $450,000 proposal," Ahad indignantly told the provincial director.

The provincial director laughed. "If you get $450,000, give it to the Ministry of Education and we can spend that over five years," he replied.

Nazak explained the alternate $50,000 plan. "We started this process with the Canadians. They said that large amount of money is impossible. But if we spend $10,000 to $50,000, we need teachers for this."

"If we work well and cooperate, that would be good," urged Ahad. "I am disappointed in the $800,000 figure."

The provincial director gave way to the low-cost idea. "We can agree with this plan. I will provide the teachers, and I will get approval from the Ministry of Education in Kabul," he told Nazak and Ahad. They had their school. By extracting the blessing of the provincial authorities, they freed the U.S. military to assist as well, without USAID headquarters at KAF criticizing them for bypassing the provincial departments.

The upshot: the colonel who developed the big budget rotated home, Ahad found some teachers, and the school opened two months later, teaching motorcycle repair and plumbing. Places in the school were oversubscribed, and the opening made a splash in the local news media.

By late autumn our plan to finish the road network was coming along nicely, too. Our goal was to finish improving nearly all of the most important roads by using USAID money. Graveling these roads was possible now that brand-new asphalt roads that had opened in June ran across the top of the district from west to east, and another asphalt stretch pushed halfway down the district toward the south. Our extra improvements would enable 90 percent of the residents in Dand to reach Kandahar City within one hour or less, which would transform the lives of farmers in outlying villages. Previously it took people living in most of southern Dand up to four hours to reach the city, making day trips both difficult and expensive.

The improvements proved to be extremely popular with residents. Our next step would be to try to get government money for future maintenance of the road network. The road system would later prove to be a nationwide debacle, with relatively little money spent to maintain any part of it.

Nazak's push to spread his influence into all parts of society was boosted when he decided to support a new youth shura. He and Cip Jungberg spent hours mentoring several young men who wanted to set up a soccer league and build new playgrounds in villages. With the Taliban targeting disaffected young people as its prime demographic, the idea of connecting young people more firmly to the government held obvious attractions.

Despite Cip's patience, only so much could be done on this front. The youth organizer, Zahoor, made plans but took weeks to follow through with the simplest steps. The education director in Dand offered to provide computer training to the young people in the shura. When he brought up the idea, the teens, the majority of whom had grown up before most of the schools were reopened, just laughed.

"Nobody here can read or write!" one of them exclaimed.

The youth shura voted instead to build several playgrounds and fund some adult literacy classes in the villages to help the young men catch up on their lost years of education. This happened over the next few months under the watchful eyes of Cip and Matt Kotlarski, who originally pledged some start-up funds because USAID had no program that could help.

Our women's programs were also ticking along. The U.S. Army had sourced humanitarian assistance from its stocks at KAF, and the Afghans had given it to widows in villages after the provincial Department of

Women's Affairs director had gone to a village herself. Poor women had come to the district center, where Nazak distributed some of the packets, which included rice, oil, and tea. And the two women selected by DOWA to run our training program had distributed more in the villages. They also spent several days a week at the district center in their specially installed trailer where women could seek them out. Nazak directed the DOWA training representative to attend the weekly staff meetings held in the district center, which she did sporadically. She feared traveling the road from Kandahar City to the district center due to the ever-present insurgent threat.

The amount of money paid to the DOWA representative for doing the training was a constant source of frustration. The U.S. Army paid for the training with its discretionary funds, since no USAID programs had funds that would cover it. Because we preferred to let the district government handle the training, rather than an NGO, there was no way to apply for State Department grants either. But the DOWA representative's rate of pay was derived from Kandahar City private rates, which were inflated far above the government's standard pay scale by the hefty wages that NGOs paid to their staff. A common refrain at the district center was, "I can find a DOWA lady for less than that!"

Despite these concerns, by midautumn our pilot women's training program was into the second of three months of teaching embroidery. Thirty women in the village of Ruhabad were learning to produce items they could sell in Kandahar City. The women received a tiny daily stipend along with free materials. Including widows in the mix of students became a crapshoot, because the village elder selected the women designated to make up the lucky thirty. Besides receiving the stipend, the women could develop skills that could boost their incomes for years. Despite the conservative nature of local society, the village men, including the elders, supported this eminently practical idea more often than not.

We did experience some growing pains with the program. Selecting which village would undertake the program first and locating a private house where classes could be held required a month's work. We wondered if the embroidered items would be saleable. And Nazak presented an unexpected obstacle.

The women produced their first items in time to sell for Eid, a religious holiday that fell in late summer. DG Nazak put the sale of any items on hold. Instead he said he wanted a "business friend" to "help with the sale." The classes continued. The DOWA trainer kept visiting more villages, trying to find out what the women needed and how we could help them. Usually they wanted small animals such as chickens, tailoring training, or, if they could get them, female sheep so that they could sell milk. The DOWA trainer kept a running tally, which she occasionally shared with us.

The program ran smoothly for two months. Then the DOWA trainer left and the program hit a serious speed bump. It turned out the provincial DOWA director, Rokia Achekzai, had decided to help herself to some of the money destined for the women being trained in Ruhabad.

In setting up the women's program, Sergeant Sonia Blaha had envisioned that a district women's trainer would organize the women's teaching projects in the villages. This trainer would be in charge and handle the money that paid for the program every month. Each month ISAF paid the district trainer from DOWA the money allocated for transportation, the teacher, rental of the room, and materials.

Suddenly the money went missing.

We found this out in October, when Nazak fired the district trainer, because she did not visit the district enough. She had resisted doing so in part due to security concerns, and it was near Ruhabad, where the training took place, that a female NGO employee had been shot a few months earlier. Nevertheless the DG pressed the trainer to work more often, and she quit. We could hardly blame her and were sorry to see her go.

On her way out she mentioned problems with the program. When ISAF paid her the program money each month, she took it to the official Department of Women's Affairs office in Kandahar City. From there she took it to the village. Usually. She confided that this month the money had not made it to the village. Instead the provincial director of the women's department, Rokia Achekzai, had kept half the money meant for the women in Ruhabad.

The replacement DOWA trainer, also appointed by Rokia Achekzai, arrived the following week at the district center. She told us the money, when paid to the district trainer by Matt Kotlarski, did not go directly to the village. It went to the provincial office to be counted and then taken to the village. She confirmed that for the first two months this had gone smoothly, but in the third and last month of training Rokia Achekzai had decided to keep half of the cash. Apparently she fell prey to the temptation of seeing $5,000 pass through her office every month.

Mohammad Zahir, the cultural advisor and interpreter on our USAID district team, made a few calls to the old trainer and to Rokia Achekzai. The old trainer confirmed a few more details, and we took the entire story to Nazak.

While this was going on we were still looking to move forward with more training projects in other villages, and the DOWA trainer was still canvassing women across Dand. Some women wanted more tailoring instruction, while others wanted to can sauces and sell them in Kandahar City or use them at home in the winter. Still more women in another village requested training on raising and keeping chickens. A U.S. contractor, IRD, which handled a USAID agriculture program, agreed to help them.

For weeks the issue with Rokia Achekzai simmered. We checked with the village elder, who confirmed the money for that month had not yet arrived. The replacement trainer said the students in the village were asking for their money. But what to do about it? Even Nazak was flummoxed.

Rokia Achekzai responded by denying everything. The payments had been made, she claimed, despite the contrary tale presented by both of her own trainers, the village elder, and the village women themselves.

Meanwhile the replacement trainer refused to handle any more money. When it came time to buy more materials, she demurred, proclaiming, "We don't have the authority to buy stuff. If you guys in the district buy it, that is best."

Two weeks later she abruptly quit, caught between Rokia Achekzai on one side and, on the other side, Nazak and the Americans, who also wanted to know what had happened to the last month's rent for the room, which had disappeared along with the women's stipend.

So we soon had a third district trainer, also hired by Rokia Achekzai. Nazak demanded up-to-date lists of students. With more projects coming up soon, we ensured that the village elders were present when the money was handed over.

But annoyed as he was, Nazak was reluctant to call in the police. His relations with the provincial officials such as the governor were fraught enough already, and Rokia Achekzai was one of the few high-profile women in the province.

Keeping a closer watch on the money and urging greater involvement by the village elders, in December we began a second women's training program in another village, Kulchiabad. IRD, the USAID contractor, also began to train women, in another village, on how to keep chickens. Because of an unfortunate Canadian chicken debacle of previous years, when plans to grind feed in Deh Bagh village had failed, close supervision would be required. At least it was a limited project, with Nazak's oversight.

We never got the missing money back, and the women trainees never received their stipend for the final month. Rokia Achekzai remained safe in Kandahar City, and we could not travel there to confront her, nor did we possess any other leverage to get the money back. We asked the Americans mentoring Rokia Achekzai in Kandahar City to pressure her, but this came to nothing. Their follow-up was sporadic, and if they had pressured her they would have risked spoiling their relationship her. As the sole Afghan government point of contact for women in Kandahar Province, Rokia Achekzai was the only game in town. It made her invulnerable, and she knew it.

Instead we shifted to marketing items the women produced. Our marketing director made a tour of the markets and took some of the embroidery work with him. The shoppers made some suggestions for improvements, which we passed on to the DOWA trainer, who took that information back to the women. Often the items were not competitive with cheap textiles from Pakistan, so the feedback was vital to ensure that the students improved and produced things that did not compete head to head with cheap imports. The work needed to be decorative and attractive, but also cheap enough to sell. Without this feedback, the training would be much less effective. We figured that once we showed the village elders how to market the items and improve them, the villagers could take over in due time.

To top it all off, when we tried to account for all the embroideries it turned out that Rokia Achekzai had purloined a dozen of them, worth about twenty dollars each, and we pressed the trainer to get them back.

But Rokia Achekzai had taken them to Helmand. It was so bad it would have been funny if the women who had been deprived of their due hadn't already been so impoverished. The women were relying on the sales of their pieces to buy more material and continue their work. Losing their finished pieces represented losing their future capital.

The DOWA trainer promised, "We will get the pieces back, or we will get the money back." Surprisingly the purloined pieces were eventually returned.

We planned future women's projects, but we still avoided using NGOs. Pushing the projects through the Afghan government made the government work better, because the staff had to plan, monitor, and manage the projects. Using NGOs would have cut the Afghan government out of the business of helping its own citizens and reduced their skills over the long run, too.

Besides, avoiding NGOs saved a hell of a lot of money. Even the best-intentioned NGOs were terribly expensive. Our three-month women's program to teach embroidery cost $15,000. If an NGO had done it, it would have cost $45,000—what NGOs had bid the previous summer. Pushing projects through small Afghan NGOs threatened to be totally unsustainable once the Americans left with their money, because local NGOs generally had little money of their own nor any way to raise it besides relying on U.S. funds. (International NGOs, such as CARE or Relief International, are often huge international organizations with their own funding streams that can supplement government contracts.)

Our team's approach inevitably drove the people at KAF crazy. How, they wondered, could we justify helping the Department of Women's Affairs, or any Afghan government department, do things directly? What if the provincial government wouldn't pay for our project in the future? The message conveyed was that our idea was foolhardy and dangerous.

Our retort was, How would the provincial government know what to spend money on in the future if they never tried anything new now? At least now the Afghan government knew it could push projects into the villages without using NGOs and knew roughly how much doing so would cost. Women's training would always be a government priority. The DOWA would in the future receive more money to spend, but so far it had little experience actually doing anything in the districts. Our initiative changed that dynamic. Now that cooperation existed. And the villagers supported it.

In 2012 the DOWA in Kandahar City received an allocation of $750,000, with a staff of seven people. At some point the DOWA office would have to get its act together, even if Kabul controlled almost all of the DOWA spending for now.

Not every experiment would work, but we felt compelled to try. The Afghan government had thus far failed to provide almost any low-cost services that people wanted. In part this happened because there was no way for it to experiment with new ideas.

The vo-ed school had opened to massive enthusiasm in the district, although such schools almost never appeared in districts. The youth program was beginning. One of our goals was to help the Afghans figure out how to make a large impact for a low cost, and to make the right connections to fund it in later years, when the central government would have more money to spend. They should start now by working closely with the provincial directorates that would in time control the purse strings. This plan came straight from KAF's playbook, which we had been told to follow.

Our speed bump with Rokia Achekzai had cost us almost $3,000. Still, women had learned how to produce items for sale. It suggested that, though problems would occur, we were generally on the right path.

But that $3,000 rankled. The saving grace was that Rokia Achekzai lied not to the U.S. government but to her own—Nazak's government. Americans getting ripped off was more the rule than the exception in Afghanistan. That it had happened to Nazak, and that he had come up with a remedy by enlisting the help of the village elders, who would work with him more closely in the future to ensure this never happened again, put at least a partial silver lining in the cloud.

Our team was still learning, but tours in Afghanistan were short. Nine months was a typical individual stint, and our own little team in Dand would be broken up far too soon. As ever in Afghanistan, factors beyond our control would keep us scrambling.

# 13

## Still Starved of Money

The Amir once told me, when speaking of the unruly character of the people, and the difficulty of making them, by the example of others who were punished, become peaceful and law-abiding, that he had ordered over a hundred thousand to be executed since the beginning of his reign, and there were still others who thought they could set his laws in defiance.—**Frank A. Martin**, *Under the Absolute Amir*, 1907

When it is not corrupt, the bureaucracy is viewed as useless. People who have significant issues to discuss with the government will often go directly to the house of Ahmed Wali Karzai and wait for hours in hopes of getting attention for their problems. The proudly independent people of southern Afghanistan have traditionally lived without a strong central government, and they see no reason to accept a new regime in Kabul if this is all it has to offer.—*Kandahar Province Handbook*, December 2008

As the months passed, Lt. Colonel Payne's attention was taken up more and more with events in Panjwai as all his infantry companies, bar one, moved there from Dand. In the late fall the battalion headquarters shifted to Panjwai, too. The main base in central Dand closed. The battalion's three wooden buildings and many outbuildings were handed over to the Afghan National Police.

As the police moved in, they quickly stripped the place, leaving the three wooden buildings standing but taking almost everything that was portable. For several days after the last American pulled out, we watched a line of trucks pass the district center headed for the markets of Kandahar City, loaded with wood left behind by the battalion.

Then in early December Lt. Colonel Payne finalized preparations to close six bases in Panjwai and Dand. The battalion began to prepare for its return to Fort Lewis in Washington State; having arrived in March, its tour was near conclusion, and its final few months would be spent focused entirely on Panjwai. A new battalion would move into Dand at much reduced strength in late December and early January.

At the district center Nazak was heavily engaged with the village elders. He held meeting after meeting, and increasing numbers of elders waited to see him in the hallway outside his office. Presumably he assured them that the departure of most of the Americans would not affect his ability to govern. The village elders still referred disputes to him, which was a good sign. Foot traffic to the staff offices in the district center increased rather than dropping off, also a good sign.

Every day Cip worked with some of the line directors while I tackled others. The agriculture director, Abdul Rashid, still refused to send his men into the villages to train the farmers. He claimed his people were too busy, didn't have enough skills to teach, and had no money for gas to get there. Meanwhile most of the five men in his office continued to spend hours every day watching Iranian and Pakistani TV. Abdul Rashid kept busy by dealing with dozens of farmers coming in to discuss the next tranche of foreign assistance for farmers, including that from the UN and USAID.

Abdul Rashid and I had a sharp disagreement about all of this one day, and for about a month Cip took over mentoring him. Rashid's dark eyes and poorly trimmed beard were set in a scowl as we went back and forth over what could be done. Confrontation usually offers one little hope of success when dealing with Afghans, but there were limits to my patience when the other staff displayed a strong work ethic. Nazak chose not to get involved, and there was little else we could do to get Abdul Rashid to do his job. Any farmer training program run by Afghans, with training conducted by the district staff, remained a hope rather than a reality. Rashid let the USAID-funded programs operate using U.S.-hired instructors. He spent his time organizing distributions of seed and plants, paid for by USAID programs. His attitude bode ill for the day soon to come when the distribution programs would cease, and the district staff would have to work with the provincial government to help anyone. Could I truly blame him? Why not take the easy option? By doing the absolute minimum and riding on U.S. coattails, he was just doing what much of the government in other areas did every day. Luckily the agriculture director was an anomaly. The other line directors were as eager as ever to improve the villages.

As 2011 slowly ebbed away we found that we had done quite a lot. The women's program had trained women how to embroider items and sell them, and the women's trainer visited other villages to evaluate their needs.

The village well-repair program had chalked up some 350 wells repaired. The two-person repair team visited villages where wells had ceased to function. Usually there was nothing wrong with the water, and often it was just a few pipes that needed to be replaced or repaired with some glue or new mechanical parts. The project, which cost $125 per well, including labor, generated enormous support for the district government. The staff photographed the wells and wrote reports that Captain Kotlarski showed to Lt. Colonel Payne, who in turn extended the project every month. To Mohammad Naseem's relief, the provincial ministry vowed to continue to fund the program in the future, pending receipt of funds from the national level.

Using U.S. Army money, the health director worked with Matt Kotlarski to make additional modest improvements to clinics. And the district's vocational school, which taught plumbing and motorcycle repair, was still functioning after a fashion, despite problems in getting the teacher paid by the provincial education ministry, which had promised months before to support the school with salaries for teachers, money for books, and eventually maintenance, just like any other of the schools in Dand. The money to refurbish the vo-ed school had of course come from Matt because the education ministry had no funds.

We were still operating off the original U.S. embassy plan that 50 percent of all development money would go through the national budget by 2012; that is, half of new projects would be handled lock, stock, and barrel by the Afghan government itself, from planning to payment. This would be a sea change, since up until then only a fraction of the development money had been spent by the Afghan ministries. In 2010–11 only $1.9

billion of total public spending ran through the ministries—so-called "on budget" spending—and much of that went to salaries, not development.[1]

The bulk of development funding was spent by the international donors themselves, as USAID or the Canadians did when they spent millions of dollars on roads. They contracted the work directly. None of that money got near the ministries. This proved to be a problem, because when USAID drew down its spending the Afghan government needed to continue to push projects into the villages to motivate people to stay on board with the government. Without that money going to the ministries they would not be able to spend much money on new projects.

The plan called for the Afghans to quickly and dramatically improve their ability to spend the money they had been given. But the plan to push more money into official Afghan hands hit heavy weather. The Afghan ministries were having a difficult time spending what limited money they already had in their budget. According to an official U.S. Department of Defense progress report, in 2011 the ministries managed to spend only 39 percent of the millions they had received, and in 2012 that figure was still only 52 percent.[2] The rest languished in bank accounts, unspent, because the Afghan officials in Kabul could not make the system work. How could USAID hand over responsibility for even more money when the Afghans couldn't spend what they had already received?

As years passed this problem persisted. As late as 2015 only 25 percent of the Afghan government's development budget had been spent in the first six months of the year, an annual rate of spending that had changed little since 2012.[3] Consequently the government would eventually try to do an end run on its own system and let provinces spend development money directly, without waiting for ministries in Kabul to disburse it.[4] But at the end of 2011 we didn't realize that the problems with the development budget would persist for years to come.

The budget for operations and maintenance (O&M) money had its own issues. While the Afghans were having a tough time spending the development money they had received for new projects, their O&M money was insufficient to cover all their needs. They could spend it, but they had too little of it for everything that needed to be done.

Enter Matt Kotlarski. Using battalion money for maintenance and general improvements, he facilitated the repair of clinic roofs or funded new paint or added an extra classroom to an overcrowded school. The infrastructure in the district was under constant assault by harsh sun and wind in summer and by cold temperatures and damp in winter. Even small items like fixing broken windows was important to the village elders who looked to Nazak for help.

In Dand we received reminders of how bad the overall situation was each day, as line directors tried to respond to the villagers' requests. Staff at KAF criticized us, insisting we needed to push the district officials harder to ask the provincial officials for money. We had done so. Months earlier we had developed a system in which, before Matt sent a request to Lt. Colonel Payne, the line director would first send the identical request to his ministry, which would stamp that request and refer it back to us in the district, almost always because the province had no maintenance money to help paint a school, build a new classroom, or hand over a new solar panel to a clinic to run a refrigerator to preserve vaccines. The line directors grew accustomed to ferrying the requests up to Kandahar City, getting the stamp of rejection, and bringing them back to us. We had the letters and stamps to prove it.

Just how bad the situation had grown was driven home one day in mid-November. For weeks the Dand education director, Abdul Ahad, had asked Matt for funds to add space to a woefully overcrowded school in the northeast. Matt, Mohammad, and I had gone with a patrol to see the school in Kulchiabad. It was a low-slung, clean building with eight classrooms inside and two volleyball courts outside. The school director reported that his classes were jammed full, and he had four hundred more students than he knew what to do with. This was a high priority for us, because the school was so overcrowded, and for Abdul Ahad, because the school was in a Barakzai area and he was a Barakzai tribal elder.

That day Cip, Mohammad, Matt, and I walked into Nazak's office and found Abdul Ahad there with Nazak and a well-dressed man in his late thirties. We were introduced, and it turned out the man was the deputy education director for all of Kandahar Province. Perfect! Now was our chance to find out why the ministry could not pay for an extra classroom or for firewood to keep the children warm in the classrooms. This was the meeting at which the deputy director told Nazak he had $35,000 to fix all the schools in the fourteen districts of Kandahar and when he wrote out a chit asking ISAF to help maintain the schools. The chit read, "As you respectfully know, the government cannot reach out to all the problems as we do not have enough in our budget." The money was being spent only on schools in Kandahar City.

We had also heard unconfirmed reports that during the previous winter Abdul Ahad had sold some firewood that should have gone to heat classrooms, and we wanted to find out whether the persistent supply shortages came from problems within the district or from the more general funding issues at the province level.

As we settled onto Nazak's comfortable brown sofas, the governor and the two education officials resumed their conversation. They were talking about the winter. So far there was no firewood in the classrooms, and parents were threatening not to send their kids to school until the spring, which would extend the usual midwinter break by an extra month. Also some schools had leaking roofs that needed to be sealed. Fixing the roofs and windows might cost up to 800,000 Afghanis ($16,000).

The deputy education director was patient but firm. There would be no firewood this year.

"We don't have enough money for even one district," he told Nazak. "We cannot send it all to Dand. We have a budget for wood for the whole province of 460,000 Afghanis [about $9,200]." The visitor wasn't finished. "It is not enough. We have thirty-five offices for education," he continued. "That money is not enough to even cover firewood for our offices. Abdul Ahad needs one million Afghanis [$20,000] for wood in Dand. We have asked Kabul for help. But we rely on the district governors and ISAF in the districts for help." A few weeks later Kabul found some emergency money and provided a bit of firewood for the districts after all.

The discussion continued, with us asking questions and Abdul Ahad pressing for more resources. But the assistant director was adamant. Apparently the O&M fund for Kandahar Province would cover just about what was needed in one district. But there were fourteen districts in the province. We would never get what we needed.

Nazak said that what he really needed was an operational fund for Dand alone, so he could assign money to repair the roofs in the district and pay for other expenses, such as firewood. But there was no fund for each district; that was not how the system was set up. Districts did not control money. They could not tax residents. They could only make individual requests to the province for anything, whether it be a new school or the repair of a roof. All too often the answer was no.

The closest the United States had come to the idea of a district fund was a USAID program called the District Delivery Program, which set aside money for the districts to fund a little gasoline and some office incidentals such as printer ink. But it was not nearly enough to spread the benefits of government into the villages. The program, useful but limited, was habitually late in delivering what assistance it did send. There was no other reliable money for the district.

Nazak lamented that no one in the ministries was helping him maintain the district center either.

"I need the roof fixed, and they say to take the money from my own pocket!" Nazak exclaimed. He had received similar responses on all manner of requests to his higher command.

At the meeting the problem of repairing schools with Afghan money seemed unsolvable.

"We do not have a budget to do that," the deputy education director repeated. "If they increase the budget, it is still not enough for education. We still rely on the district governors to get support from ISAF to repair the schools. We have engineers to assess the project. We will put the signatures of the provincial education director and the finance director on the document of request."

Clearly that request would quickly come back to the Americans for action. The meeting wrapped up soon after on this less-than-hopeful note.

The information from KAF said that the current plan would push more money onto the official budget soon, and money should start coming through in about eight months, sometime in the summer of 2012. We shrugged and pushed on. Matt could channel military funding for some of the projects as a stopgap until the budget money started to come through.

Despite these problems, things slowly moved in the right direction, and most of the credit for this turnaround belongs to DG Nazak, who encouraged his staff, praising good ideas and criticizing poor performance. The line directors found they could make decisions, set priorities, and then see them through. This change of mindset—empowering the Afghan line directors and raising their expectations so they could do their jobs—was our main goal. The disillusionment among the Afghan staff I had seen when I arrived was gone. Things were hopping. Although the money at this time came from the Americans, we were also mentoring the Afghans on how to access money from their own budget in the future.

In spite of these improvements it was clear that the district center itself was going to suffer over time. In fact it would probably shut down because there would likely never be enough money to run the place. No one, least of all Nazak, believed the Afghan provincial ministries would ever send the fuel necessary to run the DDC generator or gas up the motor-cycles staff used to visit the villages. Repairing the roof or repainting the district center would also probably not happen.

Even if the Afghan government eventually paid for many of the activities we'd started in the villages, the district center itself would fall apart and the district staff would remain caged in offices that would slowly deteriorate, with no funds to visit the schools, clinics, and projects. I repeatedly relayed this problem to KAF, but I received little response except from the senior USAID officer, who considered the issue to be important and said it needed a higher profile. Unfortunately she left KAF and had moved to the embassy by the end of the year, so we lost an important advocate.

Matters came to a head in early November, when staff members from KAF and the provincial reconstruction team (PRT) in Kandahar City flew into Dand to discuss the eventual transition to full Afghan governance without American help. The staffers were a mix; some people had been in Afghanistan for years, while others were on their first tour and seldom left KAF. Unfortunately, as my predecessor Keith Pratt had earlier discovered, many of the people at KAF with greater Afghan experience had become set in their attitudes and opinions. Ironically it was sometimes the case that the longer they'd been there, the less interested they were in new developments. They already knew it all and had little use for more fact finding.

The staffers from the PRT were tasked with mentoring the provincial ministries, in the same way we mentored the district officials in Dand. They were easier to deal with, more helpful, and more interested in what was going on than personnel from KAF, perhaps because they worked more closely with the Afghans. A rivalry over turf and responsibilities had brewed between staffers at KAF and those at the PRT for more than a year. My sympathies generally lay with the PRT.

Cip had departed on well-deserved leave the day before the visitors arrived, and I faced a dozen civilian and military headquarters staffers alone. They came by helicopter and trooped over to the district center, where we sat in a dusty conference room on the second floor. Some of the staffers seemed happy to be away from KAF for the day, while others appeared to be along for the ride. I had not made much headway in my concerns over the future thus far.

I described the gains made in the district, talking about how the district staff were now prioritizing projects and completing them. They helped residents by running innovative programs. Things were getting better.

Then I ran through the problems, including the risk of the district center falling apart and how money from the official Afghan government budget had thus far failed to make much difference in the villages, except for the building of schools and clinics now scattered throughout the district. I explained that the Afghan system delivered on some things but not other activities the people wanted, and it was important to get this right in 2012 as the budget increased.

We discussed a list of issues in Dand, including setting and finalizing the border with Kandahar City, the political benefits we had accrued from the well-repair program, and the inability of our line directors to receive maintenance funding from the ministries in Kandahar City.

We then covered several of Nazak's issues. Nazak had no faith the Afghan government would ever pay for fuel to run the generator. Therefore, as soon as the Americans pulled out, there was an enormous risk that the lights would go off, the computers and air-conditioning would shut down, and the district center would cease to function. One idea to prevent this shutdown scenario might be to hook the DDC up with the Kandahar City electricity grid, which already brought power to within a couple of kilometers of the district center. This would potentially give a new lease on life to the district center, but it would cost about $50,000, according to U.S. engineers at KAF.

I finished by suggesting that Nazak was probably right in his concerns, and the district staff would need support from the provincial government in Kandahar City in the future to remain effective. The Afghan government was not likely to help them out in the year ahead because the priorities at the provincial level were seldom the priorities in the district.

We batted the issues around a bit. One of the KAF people suggested again we weren't trying hard enough to get money from the ministries.

"The district governor should take the line directors to their ministries to ask for money," the man said. He suggested that this approach would be more successful in getting the money.

Other staffers agreed. "Push the district governor to push the agriculture ministry to help the Dand line director for agriculture," said another.

At that time I didn't know about the gaping hole in the O&M funding at the provincial level; it would take the visit of the deputy provincial education director a few weeks later to hammer that home. The suggestions sounded better in principle than they could produce in practice, though I already suspected as much.

Instead I pointed out that the suggestion was unlikely to work because we already sent requests to the provincial directorates on a regular basis. The result: the ministries rejected the ideas by claiming poverty. I explained that we had no way of knowing whether or not these claims were true, because our district staff had no idea how much money the ministries had. I thought they probably were true. But it would help if the staff from Dand knew if the provincial branches had any money before they made a request, so they could not be so easily fobbed off.

The group agreed and said they would start looking into how much money the provincial ministries actually had. It seemed that no one had really nailed down these numbers before. And the PRT would try to follow up on any requests Dand officials sent to the ministries. But because the PRT had serious problems mentoring the provincial directorates, in reality this offer was not likely to be effective. (PRT officials were hobbled by a serious lack of transportation assets from the U.S. Army.) But it was worth trying. The PRT staffers were eager to help, and they later figured out what money was available to the provincial government.

If going through the provincial ministries did work, it would tie in with the plans to send more money through the official Afghan national budget.

I also wanted to make sure the staffers understood exactly what problems would likely sabotage the district in the future. Essentially the government needed to be run on the cheap. So I described the services the villages were receiving, such as well repairs and training for farmers. I said these types of services needed to continue in coming years, because they cost much less than expensive construction projects. After all, repairing a well cost a twentieth of the amount needed to dig a new one. In the future the government would want to show plenty of benefit derived from small amounts of money. This would require some creative thinking and a new willingness to fund low-cost services that generated the maximum impact in the villages.

The elephant in the room continued to be the district center. If the lights went off and the staff ceased to work, the district could easily slide back into Taliban control. I said there seemed to be no solution to the problem of running the district center. We needed an innovative solution.

Knowing that the districts received almost no funds directly, that they only received projects, I nevertheless took a deep breath and made a suggestion. I pointed out that if the district center staff had a discretionary fund of $100,000 to $200,000 a year, most of the usual problems there would all go away. The district center could maintain itself and also provide cheap services. This was an inexpensive and effective alternative that needed to be considered in 2012, and it would be a useful addition to the idea of getting funding from the regular provincial ministries using the regular system. After all, I knew there were numerous precedents in directing money outside the regular lines of the ministries. Donors had a history of directly funding projects they favored. The Kabul airport represented a striking example.

A grant to the DDC would be a low-cost and effective way to ensure the districts functioned well. I doubted the staffers realized it would cost $20 million a year to give the one hundred highest-performing districts $200,000 a year. Compare that amount to the $1 million the United States spent every year to keep a single service member in Afghanistan, and it paled to insignificance. The current system would allow the districts to steadily

atrophy over time. For the price of an understrength platoon of twenty service members, we would neglect the entire system of local government.

I also added that ISAF should organize training for the district staff so
they could understand the system they were expected to use. I made it
clear that no one at the district understood how the new, larger budgets
would work. Common sense suggested that, if the district officials had
a poor understanding of their own system, they would perform poorly.
This training idea was destined to be stillborn, however, despite several
efforts to get it off the ground at higher levels.

Except for the idea of training, these suggestions were not well
received. Three times the staffers said I should not "think outside the
box." They said the national budget plan was in place, and we all had
to follow the plan. Sure we could try to help the district staff know what
money was available at the provincial level, but if the whole system was
flawed, there was little recourse.

The meeting broke up. At least the staffers knew that Dand faced
serious problems going forward. I doubted the solutions they suggested
would work, but the idea of getting more information on the ministries
was at least a good step. Maybe the new information would give the
district officials in Dand more leverage to get support from the ministries. That hope took a big hit when we met with the provincial deputy
education director a few weeks later and we learned there was little
money anyway.

An unexpected upshot of the meeting was that I was branded as
unhelpful because I had floated the idea of getting funds directly into the
district. Still I warned about the danger of the district center going dark,
the need for low-cost services, and the inability of line directors to get
a positive response from provincial ministries. To the credit of the PRT
staffers, in coming months they worked hard to get the information on
what money the provincial ministries held. Rather than helping us get
more projects, though, it only proved that there was little money to repair
roofs, and the problem lay not at the district level but with the provincial
directorates and the entire system itself.

The last chance we had to personally present our problems to the
Americans at KAF came when the senior State Department civilian representative visited Dand toward the end of November. Andrew Haviland

was midway through his tour of almost eighteen months. Tall, lean, with gray hair and clipped gray mustache and invariably dressed in a blue Brooks Brothers shirt, Haviland was not a great listener and not beloved by staffers at KAF or in the field. He also alienated many military counterparts by his failure to coordinate his civilian operations with theirs as thoroughly as they wanted.[5] Knowledgeable but arrogant, he was not the chief of a happy ship. His eventual replacement in mid-2012 would be hailed as a radical improvement by most staff.

Andrew dropped in on the base in the late morning and walked the two minutes to Nazak's office, settling onto the couches in the more formal meeting room that Nazak kept for higher-ranking visitors. Andrew and Nazak exchanged pleasantries, and Andrew reminded Nazak that the war effort would be changing radically. He offered some advice.

Andrew told Nazak that district support teams such as ours would be going away and that the Afghan government would then have full control over everything. Kandahar itself would be handed over in two years, at the end of 2013. The finances of the districts would rely on the official process, which had the national government pushing resources to the provinces, where the district could access assistance. He advised Nazak to ask for money for pet projects from members of parliament.

This was the system that Nazak had spent half a year criticizing to me, the military, and anyone else who would listen, including visiting NATO delegations. He didn't hold back now.

"We don't care if the money comes from you or from the Afghan government," he told Andrew. "But with the Afghan government, if we ask them for something with a request, we need a response. We submit it and what we get is a no six months or a year later. My development plan is supported by USAID and the military. We are the only district with a plan. Can you push this plan and see that it is done? The budget for Kandahar Province does not have enough money."

He also told Andrew that if he knew how much money the province received, he would adjust his district plan to accommodate it. But no one knew anything about the province's funding.

Andrew sat close to Nazak, their two chairs only a few feet apart. The rest of us sat on sofas lined up along the walls. We waited for Andrew to speak.

"The province doesn't get much," he told Nazak. "No government does block grants to the provinces. Instead you need to say to them that you need an item and then you argue why you should get it."

Andrew seemed to be reciting details of the system for Nazak, who knew far better than he the system and its failings. As far as Nazak was concerned, this business-as-usual speech amounted to allowing the districts to fail, because their requests were seldom honored. Even worse, no one could get any information about what was going on. He told Andrew as much.

"The provincial director cannot see the minister in Kabul," Nazak explained in his high-pitched but authoritative voice. "Local services are important, and the only place for the people is the district."

A failing district would cause the entire government to fail, he added, and so the government was on course to fail because the districts were starved by the system.

Nazak continued, "If the budget is not spent, we need to ask why the money was not spent. We need to know how much money comes to the district and how much goes to the province."

This information was what was deemed vital in the meeting with the KAF staffers several weeks earlier. Nazak also believed getting that information would be a good way to hold the province's feet to the fire; it would be easier to do that if we knew how much money the governments had in their bank accounts.

Andrew reiterated that the provincial directors had little money and said the U.S. staffers would try to get the information on how much money was flowing into Kandahar.

"We will ask in Kabul, too," Haviland assured Nazak.

Nazak readily agreed. "The provincial director needs to know his subordinates and help the districts and monitor them to see they are doing their jobs," he said.

Andrew replied, "What we have been doing so far has not worked, and we need to do something else."

Nazak complained again that there was no money to fix the roof or run the generators. "We need an operational budget," he told Andrew. That was probably a step too far for Andrew.

"Tell Doug your ideas," Andrew told Nazak.

The meeting was over.

As I would find out a few months later when I moved to Maiwand District for a year to work with the district government there, other districts had similar views of the Kandahar Province government. Unresponsive, it made little effort to help the districts beyond providing salaries for the police, schoolteachers, and clinic staff. The points Nazak had made were the same elsewhere, to greater or lesser degrees.

I reiterated these concerns to Andrew in a side meeting held in a small conference room a few minutes later, and he told me again that the only way these issues could be resolved was through the established government system, which he had just heard, and well knew, was not working. I told him how an operational fund dedicated to the district, adding up to $200,000 per year, would solve all these problems, but he said this was impossible. So we discussed ways to find out how much money the provincial ministries had, which was information that might help when the district line directors went begging with their requests. The PRT and its budget wunderkind, Billy Woodward, could at least be trusted to do their best to dig up this information. Our meeting ended on a positive note.

Nazak didn't believe any of it. Within two weeks of Andrew's departure he complained again to the U.S. Army brigade in charge of Dand that there would be no money for generators to keep the lights on when the Americans left. The only way to avoid the loss of power would be if the army helped him string poles to connect the DDC to the Kandahar City electricity supply.

"We don't have fuel to run the generators," he told the U.S. deputy commander. He never trusted the Afghan government to do its job.

Nazak made one last try to find a solution to his problems when the PRT sent visitors in mid-December. Planning was under way to reduce the U.S. presence in the districts in 2013 and hand over to the Afghans. The PRT wanted the unvarnished truth on what the major issues would be. The PRT had a new civilian chief. She had not yet visited Dand, so we were pleased that she wanted to come and see the situation for herself.

Except for the twenty-eight schools and five clinics open in Dand, there were few signs of a government presence in any of the villages. Nazak pointed out to the PRT staffers that Dand received no money from the province to extend the presence of the government into the villages, and no one knew the amount or availability of funding at the provincial level.

"We need to know how much money the line ministries have to do things for Dand," Nazak urged the PRT staffers. "We expect the province to tell us what they can do for the districts and then do their plan. We can spend however much we can get from the province."

Nazak declared that, without an operational fund, he was very worried. He did not believe the province would send money for fuel. Only the district could be trusted to make spending a priority, but how could the district do that if it had no money? The district was legally forbidden to raise its own funds through taxes, and provinces never gave cash grants to districts.

"We need a fund to be used for our plan that is spent according to our priorities," he urged.

The PRT staffers were helpful, but the problem exceeded their power to address it.

"What did you get from the line ministries?" they asked.

"I got a letter from the province asking about the furniture," replied Nazak.

The military head of the PRT was not very impressed. He urged Nazak to continue his discussions with the provincial ministries. This was, of course, exactly the problem that Nazak complained about in the first place.

Nazak told the PRT staffers, "Even for the clinics and public health in Dand, the ministry does not have any money to help us."

This ended our best and only chance to push KAF into finding an imaginative solution to a system that everyone knew was not working. The PRT couldn't change the system that depended upon the province responding to requests by the districts.

In the coming months the promised extra money due to appear on the Afghan official budget failed to materialize again and again. We were told to expect extra money coming through in the summer of 2012. By the fall of 2012 savvy KAF staffers had despaired of seeing it. Planning began with the assumption that the money would be available in the next fiscal year, beginning in March 2013. That funding too was delayed. By early fall 2013 the big influx of on-budget government money to the provinces had not yet made its appearance.

In many ways this situation reflected the deep ambiguity in the relations between the Afghan central government and its regions. The only ruler in Afghan history to have securely subdued the regions was Amir Abdur Rahman Khan, who had ruled in the last twenty years of the nineteenth century. He systematically eliminated his regional rivals. He ruled mercilessly, killing thousands of his opponents. But since the days of the Iron Amir, the central government had struggled to keep its power.

In the words of one noted scholar, "Those Afghan leaders who would best succeed during the next century would apply a 'Wizard of Oz' strategy. They declared their governments all-powerful, but rarely risked testing that claim by implementing controversial policies."[6]

Nazak, told to rely upon the central government, found it had little ability or inclination to respond to the problems of the districts with innovative ideas. Nor, for that matter, did the Americans, despite evidence that the system wasn't working well. I wondered if other DSTs had made similar complaints. How could they not? Perhaps they worried more about not being a team player than giving due warning. National budget issues were certainly outside the scope of most DST members' daily concerns. It was understandable but very disheartening. I never knew the true answer.

Our solution was to wait for the official money while we also tried to keep services going with our own U.S. Army and USAID money. Without the official money getting to Kandahar, we could not transition away from reliance on the American funds. As each delay was followed by another delay, the wait felt like an eternity. Meanwhile the American funds dwindled more with each month that passed. We held our collective breath and worked to keep the district on the right path for as long as possible, hoping that the money would arrive in Kandahar City before the Americans left. In the end it would not even be close. We missed by a mile.

FIG. 1. Dand District Center was a magnet for village elders seeking an audience with its charismatic leader, Hamdullah Nazak.

FIG. 2. Hamdullah Nazak, sub-governor of Dand,
operating from his office at the district center.

FIG. 3. (*top*) Farmers crowd around a Dand District official for distributions of seed and fertilizer in November 2011.

FIG. 4. (*bottom*) A farmer and a boy on a tractor in southern Dand.

FIG. 5. (*opposite top*) An American Stryker armored vehicle patrols the chronically unstable northern fringe of Dand in November 2011. With the Taliban pushed back, DG Nazak had a short window of opportunity in which to cement the allegiance of the villagers by providing a working government.

FIG. 6. (*opposite bottom*) Elders gathered to speak with DG Nazak every week. He discussed what he expected of them and explained his plans for the district. Villages that failed to send elders to Nazak's meetings received no projects.

FIG. 7. (*above*) The USAID trailers on Combat Outpost Edgerton at sunset.

FIG. 8. One of the few working wells in the village of Nahre Shefe.

FIG. 9. Sewing machines used by women training to produce goods for sale. The women students waited inside the adjacent building for visitors to leave before resuming their training.

FIG. 10. DG Nazak addresses an assembly of village elders at an agricultural conference in Dand in the spring of 2012.

FIG. 11. Captain Matt Kotlarski served as Lt. Colonel Brian Payne's direct link to DG Nazak and as his eyes and ears for village improvements, ensuring the U.S. military funded critical projects, such as the highly effective well-repair program.

FIG. 12. An Afghan National Police outpost
in the middle of grape vineyards.

FIG. 13. (*opposite top*) A successful commercial chicken farm in Dand District.

FIG. 14. (*opposite bottom*) Farmers in the village of Karz prepare the ground for saplings provided by USAID.

FIG. 15. (*above*) Hills near Kandahar City seen from the window of a Sea Knight helicopter.

FIG. 16. (*above*) Salih Mohammad, sub-governor of Maiwand
District, meets with people outside his office, December 2012.

FIG. 17. (*opposite top*) A shura, or consultative council,
in the village of De Maiwand, December 2012.

FIG. 18. (*opposite bottom*) Leaving Maiwand District, with a
view of the bazaar, Highway 1, and fields, March 2013.

FIG. 19. U.S. and Afghan soldiers walk back to their base along a roadway inside the village of De Maiwand.

# 14

## Corruption of Many Kinds

However, it is not surprising that the Amir was chary of putting too much authority in the hands of his officials, for those who had the authority to judge minor cases invariably abused the authority given them, and the people who suffered through such abuse of authority, feared the enmity of the official too much to appeal to the Amir, and generally they were given cause to do so.—**Frank A. Martin**, *Under the Absolute Amir*, 1907

This year corruption is again the second most often cited reason the country is seen to be moving in the wrong direction.—**Asia Foundation**, *Afghanistan in 2011*, 2011

Two roads stretch like ebony ribbons from Kandahar City into the heart of Dand, past copses of green trees and wheatfields of brilliant gold. Every hour Toyota taxis, large trucks, and horse-drawn carts passed by, plying their trade.

These recently laid strips of asphalt were the arteries along which life in Dand pulsed. No longer did travelers from the southern areas of the district bump over rutted tracks to reach the bazaars of the city. Shoppers could purchase their weekly staples and farmers could sell their produce by making a quick and cheap day trip up to the city, moving most of the way on smooth macadam.

Roads generate commerce, and commerce sharply improves the lives of the people. Most farmers eking out a living on thin and sandy soil cared little about the government, except when it came to roads. Then they took notice, because their lives improved almost immediately when roads went in and taxi fares and travel times dropped dramatically.

The Americans and Canadians paid tens of millions of dollars for roads, because they translated into immediate support for the Afghan government. Better roads also allowed the security forces easier access into the remote villages. And roads of asphalt or hard-packed gravel were much safer than a rudimentary dirt track. Insurgents found it much more difficult to dig up hardened surfaces, and the villagers were more likely to inform on insurgents who tried to blow up "their" road. While critics contended that roads were both expensive and hard to maintain, the positive effects of a new road usually drastically outweighed the downside.

Over several days in early fall as we looked onto the roads running past the Dand District Center, we saw early-morning convoys of trucks hired by ISAF to carry cargo. They lined up cab to tail, always pointed south into Dand. Because the American battalion was shifting its bases, with some soldiers moving out of Dand and toward the fighting in Panjwai, the trucks had been hired from local contractors to carry equipment meant for new bases.

The trucks carried pallets of supplies, generators, and gravel used to keep down the dust on ISAF bases. Huge concrete T-walls, shaped like thick concrete slabs with a wide base, leaned drunkenly on the flatbeds; these T-walls would be lined up shoulder to shoulder like defensive linemen to protect camps from rocket attacks. The T-walls each cost $800 or more, and they were stacked six or seven to a truck.

The convoys of trucks followed a set pattern. They drove down from Kandahar City, reached the intersection, and stopped. They waited there for half an hour and then trundled off to the bases deeper inside the district or on to Panjwai.

No obvious reason existed for the trucks to halt in front of the DDC. There were no police checkpoints there, and the district center's gate guards expressed no interest in them because they never entered the district center. Yet there they were, morning after morning, lined up like school kids at recess, waiting for their morning milk. Stop. Wait a bit. Inexplicably drive on.

Several shops clustered around the junction. Our team was at the time administering microgrants to some of these small businesses. One day we went out for a short walk to talk to the business owners about these microgrants. That morning the trucks were lined up again.

We left the ISAF base and walked toward the bazaar, noticing a private security guard who carried an AK-47 rifle and stood about thirty meters from the district center's gate. He was thin, young, wore soiled khaki clothing, and had an open, friendly look. We asked him what he was doing. He matter-of-factly replied that his job was to check the toll receipts for the supply trucks hired by the Americans.

He said he worked for a private security company that ran checkpoints on three roads that led into Dand. Trucks carrying material bound for ISAF bases were required to pay a toll when they entered the district. The toll: $125 per load for large trucks and $75 for small trucks. The tolls were paid nearer to Kandahar City, and the drivers received a receipt. This guard checked the receipts when they reached the junction. This applied only to ISAF-hired trucks, he assured us, because they could afford to pay.

We walked back to the base, shaking our heads. The tolls were completely illegal. ISAF had become a milk cow for some well-connected resident of Dand!

Further investigation revealed the security company that extorted these illegal tolls was owned by Fatay Khan, the brother of District Governor Nazak. That connection made this corruption official, because it had to be government sanctioned.

Even worse, Fatay Khan's men were actually paid-up members of the Afghan National Police and counted as part of the official police force, although they did no work for the Dand police chief. This arrangement had been sanctioned by ISAF for some time, which made it transparent if not ideal. But the tolls were a new wrinkle on the problem.

In Afghanistan district governors were a mixed breed. Problem DGs could be categorized into three types. The first type were the absentee DGs, who rarely visited their districts because security was so bad. They preferred to spend their time in the provincial capitals and only visited their offices occasionally. It was hard to fault them when security was so poor and their salary so low, coming to only $400 to $800 per month.

Another type of governor tried to make as much money as quickly as possible from his position. He probably paid tens of thousands of dollars for the appointment and had little interest in improving the district. For him governance represented a money-making venture. Governors of this type were widely distrusted and generally ineffective. They might try to improve the district, but only if it didn't impede them from making money off the residents.

The last category included DG Nazak. Leaders of this type ran a moderately clean office but allowed members of their extended family and clan to profit without too much fuss. President Hamid Karzai adopted this model. These men were rich, with enough money for them to survive without resorting to obvious extortion. They personally refused bribes and asked little or nothing from contractors. They were dedicated practitioners of crony capitalism, and they were the best type of governors for the reality of Afghanistan. Their wealth allowed them to forgo much in the way of personal profit, and their administrations were often less dirty than the other types. That was why Nazak bragged about turning down a bribe from a contractor and using the money to refinish walls in the district center instead. This did not imply perfection; Nazak routinely overcharged residents receiving official government IDs and used the excess money for his own purposes.

In Hamid Karzai's case his brothers ran Kandahar Province. Extremely rich and powerful men, they grew steadily richer and more powerful. In turn they protected and assisted their brother in Kabul. Sadly, what was good for the Karzais was generally bad for the local people. When Ahmed Wali Karzai was killed in the summer of 2011, many Americans and Afghans figured it might be a chance to start over. Widely believed to be connected to the opium trade, to have Taliban links, and to have made millions of dollars off U.S. government contracts, Ahmed Wali Karzai was a key source of intelligence for the Americans and the man many Afghans turned to when they needed to get things done.[1] The wait to see him at his home was generally several hours long as scores of Afghan elders took their turn to see him.

This kind of corruption might have been useful for the Karzai regime, but the Afghan people resented it. The situation was worse in Kandahar, because many people considered the provincial governor to be corrupt as well. Earlier, in 2007, Governor Tooryalai Wesa had been fired from his job with a USAID contractor over allegations of mismanaging contracts and corruption.[2] In Kandahar corruption flowed through his administration. A nationwide survey in 2011 reported that when people thought the country was headed in the wrong direction, corruption was their second-biggest concern, after security.[3]

Another national survey in 2012 found that half of Afghans had paid a bribe to a government official that year. This figure was down slightly from previous years but still alarmingly high. Even worse for our fight to sway hearts and minds against the Taliban, 42 percent of the Afghans had paid off a police officer in 2012.[4]

This type of corruption alienated the people from their government. A 2009 study done for the British parliament found that only 6 percent of Afghans supported the government, noting, "Government corruption and partisanship at provincial and district level was consistently cited as a major reason for supporting opposition groups."[5]

A U.S. government report confirmed that corruption was undermining the government, stating that "limited progress toward improved governance at the ministerial, provincial, and district levels" was being countered by rampant corruption, unqualified civil servants, and the assassination of government officials.[6]

Corruption took many forms, from bribing sentries at checkpoints, paying off judges to dismiss cases or release prisoners, and bribing officials or guards to allow drug convoys to pass, all the way to more sophisticated methods such as skimming contracts. All of this activity caused Afghans to become cynical about their government.

But outright corruption was not the same as nepotism, often seen when leaders handed out offices or channeled contracts to relations or fellow tribe members and favored their businesses. Afghans elders were expected to assist members of their own tribes, and though Afghans grumbled when aid disbursements or contract awards were influenced by favoritism, they generally understood that it was outside the control of the office holder, who had a social debt to discharge. For instance, it might cost $5,000 or $6,000 for outsiders to buy their way into a government job. But connected people often appointed their sons or daughters to offices. The former practice was arguably seen as more insidious than the latter.

This nuance was important in dealing with Nazak's brother, Fatay Khan, who made money from a number of ISAF contracts, which made

Americans uncomfortable but was permitted because it worked and because the arrangement was a recognized part of Afghan life.

But now Nazak's brother had moved into pure highway robbery, which crossed accepted lines—both Afghan and American.

Money that Nazak made with Fatay Khan almost certainly helped pay Nazak's bills. Nazak had his own businesses, such as a land dealing company, but he jointly owned a car-import business with Fatay Khan, and it was highly likely that their commercial dealings were mixed together in a variety of ways. He might even have profited indirectly from the illegal tolls. And Nazak needed some of the money earned by Fatay Khan to survive because his monthly expenditure was vastly larger than his salary. While we seldom had direct proof of any arrangements between the two brothers, the circumstantial evidence of crony capitalism was overwhelming.

Normally projects went to Dand contractors who were connected to Nazak's family. To receive most ISAF contracts potential contractors had to be on a list approved by the DDC staff, and it was fairly easy for Nazak to rig the conditions to favor his extended family. At various times Fatay Khan ended up building a new school, adding classrooms, and digging wells, all of which were funded by ISAF. Other relations were awarded other contracts.

There was little we could do about it. Nepotism, hardly unknown in America, was the expected style of doing business in Afghanistan. Afghan society is based upon clans and families; favoring one's clan or family was ingrained into the very fabric of society, and it was impossible to stop favoritism when it happened.

However, the illegal tolls clearly crossed the line of what was acceptable, regardless of the cultural reference points. We nevertheless found ourselves hard-pressed to figure out how to stop the practice. The Afghan district chief of police and the district intelligence chief did not care, and ISAF had other things to worry about than policing roads for illegal toll stations.

Usually the companies paid and we heard nothing of it, which was why it took us so long to discover the problem. While we pondered the issue, it finally came out in the open one day when a convoy ran the tolls and Fatay Khan's men fired at the vehicles.

That day Fatay Khan's private security guards had stopped several trucks. One group of drivers refused the shakedown and drove off. In a rage Fatay Khan's men fired their rifles at the trucks, punching several holes in one of the vehicles. Luckily no one was hurt. The truck drivers drove directly to the DDC and complained to the Afghan police chief. Of course the police did nothing.

Mohammad Zahir and I were present in the DG's office when Fatay Khan came to talk to Nazak about incident.

Hearing the details, Nazak complained to Fatay Khan about the shooting.

"Don't take money from the ISAF trucks," Nazak urged his brother in rapid Pashtu he knew I could not understand. He said it looked bad when ISAF vehicles were extorted.

Fatay Khan just laughed. "But it's our district!" he exclaimed.

Mohammad related this later with a chuckle. Nazak probably assumed he would not tell me the full details.

Nazak's influence over his brother had limits. Fatay Khan was young and cocky. The illegal tolls continued even though it was politically embarrassing. As Hamid Karzai had also discovered, family can be an embarrassment when shady practices become entrenched.

Ultimately we could do very little to stop the illegal tolls. Our power was limited when we tried to award contracts to companies other than Nazak's clan, though we tried to get bids from all comers. Fatay Khan's companies multiplied faster than we could blacklist them.

We ended up writing several reports that detailed the stopping of the trucks. Sergeant Brian Hull distributed them to the military, while we pushed the story to the civilian side of KAF. Our reports dropped into a black hole. No one really cared.

To stop this type of extortion, pressure needed to come from the Americans. But the Americans also needed a governor who ran a smooth-functioning district, hence the need for Nazak. No one was about to rock the boat.

In coming years corruption would continue to plague the country. In a survey conducted in 2014 Afghans still labeled security, unemployment, and corruption as the largest problems in the country.[7] In 2015 the new governor of Kandahar Province admitted that for thirteen years the government had served the interests of the powerful rather than the people. He pledged to clean things up.[8]

In the end we were glad when the American military finally stopped realigning its bases and the convoys ceased. As the convoys of trucks carrying ISAF gear dwindled, the problem of illegal tolls dropped out of sight, though not entirely out of mind.

# 15

## Holding Back the Taliban

American military officers criticized the French—and later the South
Vietnamese forces—for their "outpost" mentality. But in an armed
insurrection, areas not controlled twenty-four hours a day by progovernment forces become, ipso facto, areas of insurgent influence,
if not dominance. If outlying areas are visited only in daylight by
occasional government security patrols, which flag flies over the area
at night?—**George Allen**, *None So Blind*, 2001

The U.S. counterinsurgency strategy (COIN) in Afghanistan calls on
the military to secure key areas—"clear" and "hold"—while USAID and
its counterparts follow up with the "build" and "transfer" phases. The
goal is to provide security, strengthen local government institutions,
and build critical infrastructure, such as roads, schools, and clinics.
In theory, these steps can improve lives and weaken popular support
for the insurgency.—**U.S. Senate Committee on Foreign Relations**,
*Evaluating U.S. Foreign Assistance to Afghanistan*, 2011

The simple mud fort was old and battered. Home to more than a dozen
members of the Afghan National Police (ANP), the "fort" had once served
as a family's home and was located in a green blanket of vineyards that
stretched in every direction. A dirt track beside the house led deeper
into the fields. Two hundred meters to the south, taxis, cars, donkeys,
and trucks swooshed by on a freshly tarmacked road. With easy access
in all directions, the house was a natural strongpoint for the ANP's use.

The police were posted there to keep the Taliban out of neighboring
villages. Every few days Lt. Colonel Payne's soldiers, who were based

up the road, stopped by to determine if the police had seen any Taliban or if they needed any help, and then they would do a patrol in the area. The U.S. patrol leader usually asked the checkpoint commander to send two or three of his men out with them to patrol. Patrolling helped to discourage insurgents from lingering in the area.

On this day when the American soldiers arrived, the police were being recalcitrant. Standing at the rear of the mud house, beside soot-encrusted cooking pots and a battered cot, the Afghan and American leaders glared at each other. The angry ANP officer thought the Americans came by too often and brought too little with them. He blamed them for his lack of supplies and fuel.

It didn't matter that resupply was the responsibility of the Afghan police commanders in Kandahar City and not this group of U.S. soldiers. All the ANP commander's frustrations poured out, built up over weeks of running a poor, ill-equipped checkpoint forgotten in some vineyards in the middle of nowhere. He chided and shouted.

"No!" he exclaimed. It was too much. "I will not go, nor will I send anyone else either."

There was more to it than that of course. There always is. The ANP and Americans at this checkpoint did not enjoy a great relationship. The police in this sector had been caught red-handed as they fouled up. Five kilometers down the road to the west lay the village of Bellanday. There the ANP moved into the village school, and they refused to move out again. They'd stolen furniture from the classrooms and then burned it for fuel or sold it.

Worse, the ANP checkpoint farther east had been caught hosting insurgents inside the post. Taliban fighters had spent time drinking tea with police working there.

This post also had problems. These guys were so busy swearing and shouting that they rarely did much patrolling. It was like pulling teeth to get them out for a few hours.

There was little the American captain could do. Not officially in charge of mentoring these police and solving their problems, he just happened to live at a U.S. base down the road. Lt. Colonel Payne's soldiers weren't official police mentors at all. That title belonged to a group of U.S. soldiers who lived at the base next to the district center about nine kilometers to the east. That unit's tour of duty was devoted to improving ANP's performance and logistics. They rarely made an appearance, instead spending most of their time trying to whip into shape the police leadership at the district headquarters and helping them to solve their logistics problems.

Lt. Colonel Payne had an agreement with the official mentors that his soldiers on the ground would help out the police, who were the only Afghan security forces in the district by late 2011. The soldiers followed some ideas sent along by the mentors and tried to train the police as best as they could, usually by patrolling with them or teaching first aid. But the soldiers were powerless to solve any problems of substance; only the official mentors had the connections to do that. A poor situation, it satisfied few of the American soldiers, who had responsibility but no power to help beyond occasionally bringing in a few supplies.

On bad days like this, it meant the patrol leader received the brunt of the police commander's misdirected angst.

The ANP supply chain left the police on this day in late November with too few winter clothes, too little fuel, and a sense of abandonment. All in all, it was a bad situation. The ANP adapted to their circumstances by sitting in the shade and smoking hashish all day.

These pathetic police were located just a few miles from the turbulent and hostile fringe of Dand District, which made matters worse. No one could afford to have these guys not doing their job.

This was not a new problem, nor was it limited to Dand. The ANP had been underperforming across the country for years. Everyone knew the ANP logistics could often barely deliver food, let alone other necessary items such as ammunition, fuel, winter coats, blankets, and clean water. Logistics consistently failed to deliver what was needed, where it was needed. Part of it was cultural; warehouse staffers preferred to keep items on the shelves rather than dispense supplies. An Afghan supply officer considered himself powerful if he had a full warehouse, because his services and assistance were regularly solicited by Afghan officers from many different bases. The supply officer who kept an empty warehouse felt less powerful, because no one would seek his help if he had nothing to offer. So he avoided empty shelves at all costs. Dispensing too many items cut directly into his opportunity to increase his personal power and prestige.

Problems also arose from the poor quality of police officers higher up the chain, the ones who often could neither read nor write nor were immune from corruption. The system, which gave a new meaning to the word cumbersome, depended in large part on handwritten records, and few items could be released without forms making their way through several offices. Nor was the system designed to be responsive to emergencies, and outposts under attack could not be sure their supplies would be restocked later.

In this case it turned out the ANP had no winter clothing, because four months before, in July 2011, the U.S. Army command in charge of assisting the Afghan police stopped supplying uniforms, including winter coats, and had handed off the responsibility to the Afghan government. The ministries couldn't handle the task. When the ministries did order winter clothing, the contract had to be torn up because the clothes didn't come from the United States; they had to be made in America because that was the rule set by the Americans who paid the bill. The winter-clothing football was kicked back and forth between the U.S. side and the Afghans for the next few years, and in the fall of 2015 the Office of the Inspector General for Afghanistan Reconstruction, or SIGAR, found that the security forces would lack adequate winter clothing "for the foreseeable future."[1]

The upshot of these supply problems was that many of the Afghan police, even those assigned to high-risk rural outposts, had no winter coat and little more than a single magazine of thirty bullets, sometimes even less. In turn that meant the police were less willing to take actions that could disrupt the Taliban, who might then attack. This was no imagined threat; the police took the heaviest casualties of all the security forces. The system was flawed at almost every level, despite the considerable bravery shown by individuals at many police outposts.

The Afghans' problems with equipment covered more than beans and bullets. Afghan forces lacked basics such as night-vision goggles, enough helicopters to move around the battlefield for a few high-risk missions, and mine detectors to find the IEDs littering the roads.[2] And on this morning at this outpost in Dand they lacked fuel and winter coats as the cold weather set in.

These issues were widely known in the U.S. community. About this time, in January 2012, SIGAR recommended "improving ANSF logistics, enhancing the capacity of the ministries of Defense and Interior, and sustaining infrastructure" (ANSF, the Afghan National Security Forces, includes both the police and the army).[3] Police training and morale were also key issues. The Afghan police had for many years taken advantage of the people they were meant to help. Ambassador Richard Holbrooke, the U.S. representative to the region, had called the police "an inadequate organization, riddled with corruption."[4]

Also notorious was the way the foreigners had addressed the problem. For years police training was neglected as NATO failed to provide meaningful instruction.[5] Yet the situation was routinely summarized as "significant challenges remain but progress is being made." Like the end of the rainbow, solutions to the problems were always near at hand but never quite realized. In mid-2015 a top-ranking U.S. general in Afghanistan conceded to a reporter that the logistics system for the army and police still had "capability gaps." But he claimed the Afghans "conducted deliberate, planned operations that are well resourced and they've performed very well."[6]

In 2012 one courageous U.S. Army officer described his dismay at the misinformation concerning Afghan forces in an article published in the *Armed Forces Journal*, a heavyweight magazine of commentary published for U.S. military leaders. Lt. Colonel Daniel Davis wrote of his tour in Afghanistan,

What I saw bore no resemblance to rosy official statements by U.S. military leaders about conditions on the ground. Entering this deployment, I was sincerely hoping to learn that the claims were true: that conditions in Afghanistan were improving, that the local government and military were progressing toward self-sufficiency. I did not need to witness dramatic improvements to be reassured, but merely hoped to see evidence of positive trends, to see [Afghan] companies or battalions produce even minimal but sustainable progress. Instead, I witnessed the absence of success on virtually every level.[7]

In response Lt. General Curtis Scaparrotti issued a familiar-sounding rebuttal, insisting that Afghan forces could eventually look after themselves, though he "acknowledged that Afghan army and police still had a way to go."[8]

For years I had seen the poor performance of the police in a number of places where people had complained that their local force extorted money and didn't pursue insurgents. The problem existed nationwide.

In 2007 I was reporting in Khost Province on the eastern fringe of the country, on the border with Pakistan. I joined a team of U.S. soldiers who were mentoring an ANP unit that patrolled some of the worst areas of an unstable province, where insurgents routinely crossed the border in large numbers and bypassed small police outposts. Villagers stayed strictly neutral. Many had entirely forsaken the government. Once while patrolling the main highway connecting Khost to provinces farther inside the country I asked a U.S. mentor if he felt outraged that the police he risked his life to help were extorting money from travelers.

"No," he replied wearily. "The police only get paid about seventy dollars a month. If they didn't take the money, their families would starve."

To him the system that paid the police too little was a bigger problem than the resulting corruption. This too was a nationwide problem, and once corruption crept in it became very difficult to stamp out.[9]

Now, at this outpost in Dand, the ANP were resentful because they saw Americans with plenty of gear and boxes of ready-to-eat meals and cases of water on their armored trucks. The ANP had enough food of the most basic variety, mainly rice and vegetables with a little chicken and not much else, nor any real hope that with winter coming things would improve anytime soon. Of course they were annoyed.

As for the American soldiers, what could they do? Their platoon wasn't part of the official police mentor team for Dand; they had no real control over the police in this outpost nor any way to help them besides reporting their problems. The soldiers couldn't offer more supplies for the ANP. They wanted to improve security and keep out the Taliban. They needed local beat cops to walk with them through the fields, which would be difficult if the local cops refused to leave the run-down mud house that served as their outpost.

Eventually the American captain tired of arguing. He walked away from the police outpost and headed down a dirt path deeper into the vineyards, his men hefting their weapons and walking after him. In some sort of face-saving gesture a couple of ANP detached themselves from their mud house before the Americans turned out of sight. They tagged along behind the Americans like an unwanted kid brother. It wasn't pretty, but in this context it represented success.

Luckily for Dand, the police in other parts of the district were better than this group in the northwest sector. Elsewhere the ANP were also reluctant to patrol; the lack of fuel and winter clothing was universal. But this particular area was notorious for its police consistently doing the wrong thing. The district police chief eventually tired of the constant issues with this group and switched them out, sending them farther south into a quieter area and replacing them with police brought up from the south. This tepid effort to solve the problem only shifted the issues to another location. At least some action was taken, which meant progress of a sort.

One indication that security in the northwest was bad was because it was so quiet. Insurgents regularly passed through the area and were known to stage nearby—to the west, just over the border in Panjwai, and to the north, closer to Kandahar City. If the ANP were doing their job you might expect to see some firefights, IEDs, or other activity as the two sides jostled against each other. There were none, which suggested that the Afghan police were ignoring the problem. Paradoxically in a counterinsurgency even good areas can have a trickle of violent events. This trickle might last for years, as it did when an IED exploded in late November in northern Dand. Another went off in eastern Dand in March 2012, when a suicide bomber detonated his three-wheeled motorcycle in the middle of a U.S. patrol, wounding half a dozen Americans. These developments were not good, but they were the cost of doing business. And it was probably better than absolute silence, such as in the northwest, where we had a genuine problem.

As autumn faded into winter in 2011 the ANP were almost the only game in town as the bulk of the Americans steadily pulled out of Dand and shifted to where the action was, in Panjwai District. But although

Lt. Colonel Payne was leaving Dand with only one infantry company in the south of the district, he wanted to ensure Dand remained stable and able to defend itself.

With insurgents constantly coming from Pakistan into Panjwai and Kandahar City, Dand could easily become a target again. The Taliban might push back into villages no longer covered by daily or even weekly patrols. Pulling out U.S. and Afghan soldiers from Dand was an enormous gamble. Just a year earlier the Taliban had been very active in Dand. A year prior to that the government had had little influence in many areas. Amazingly, not much happened as the Americans left in 2011.

The major reason for that quietude was that Nazak kept a tight rein on his village leaders. Under their influence the villagers continued to support the government. Without their support the Taliban could filter in without anyone informing the police. One of the measures Nazak used to figure out how well he controlled the villages was whether they grew poppy or not. Nazak took pains to ensure this did not happen. It was sometimes harder to tell which he opposed more—the Taliban or poppy. He took any poppy planting as a personal affront.

At most of the twice-monthly meetings he held with village elders, he reminded leaders they needed to work together and avoid poppy, especially in the fall, when farmers decided what they would plant.

At a typical gathering in mid-November Nazak drew about twenty elders together in the district center's long meeting room. The men sat along the sofas lining the wall, and the chief of police sat beside Nazak. A handful of Americans squeezed into one of the corners. We never took center stage in Nazak's meetings; our best position was in the corner—if not out of the minds of the assembled elders, at least not conspicuously in sight. Nazak didn't need our help to run his meetings, nor any reminder of our indirect influence.

Opening the meeting, Nazak said, "The last time we met we discussed poppy, and we're going to talk about it again."

He and they knew this was the decision time for farmers. Poppy would be in the ground by early December, and the poppy seed in Kandahar would push out its first tendrils within a month. By March the poppy flowers would blanket some unfortunate districts such as Zhari, Panjwai, or Maiwand. In May all fighting and other farming came to a halt as the Taliban and itinerant farmers pitched in to harvest the crop at the princely wage of eight dollars a day. The time to stop the cycle was in October and November.

"When I first got here, I went to one village and eradicated all the poppy with a tractor," Nazak reminded his audience. "In Nakadak," he said, referring to a village near Panjwai District where poppy growing was rampant, "you guys need to be careful not to plant poppy. You maliks own a lot of land there. You can tell tenants they need to plant wheat. If they want to plant poppy, don't give them a lease."

Some of the elders objected.

"Last year you eradicated my poppy and it was a small piece. But you left some other places inside their compounds," one complained.

"If they grow just half an acre of poppy, they will go to jail," Nazak replied. "The more land, the more jail time, and the bigger the fine."

Another elder objected. "Last year you eradicated my poppy. My people went to prison. But in the next village over they planted poppy. That was in Niko Karez, and this year too they are planting it."

Nazak held up his phone. "I'll call the chief of police and give the order to get rid of it if someone tells me what is happening. I need you to inform me, and I'll get it sorted out," he said.

The police chief shifted in his upholstered chair. Short and wide, Major Rahmatullah had run the ANP in the district for more than a year.

"I have intel that Mard Qalah and Rawanay are also growing poppy," Rahmatullah said. "People will plant or decide to plant poppy. I will prepare fifty ANP to go to these villages where people plant it. The maliks need to let me know which villages plant poppy. I have the authority to destroy the poppy. If maliks do not let me know, the maliks will be held responsible."

Nazak turned from the chief of police back to the elders. "Five people are responsible. The police checkpoint commander, the malik, the farmer, the tenant, and the owner. You all should let the chief of police know."

One of the maliks piped up. "I'll give you all the information about Niko Karez."

"I'll call the commander of the area to go get it fixed," replied Rahmatullah.

Echoing New York City's zero-tolerance policy, Nazak and the maliks worked toward a policy of complete prevention. The policy aimed to be

100 percent effective in eliminating poppy, and it represented a cornerstone for security in Dand. Poppy attracted the Taliban, who were known to fund farmers, provide them with seed, and cooperate with the drug networks that grew and transported the crop. The Taliban made millions of dollars a year from poppy. Nazak considered it a political and a security issue that he could not ignore if he was to maintain control.

Nazak also sought to solidify his hold over the villages by getting the mullahs on his side. He considered the mullahs to be the most important group of people in the district, and he wanted them working for him. Even a medium-sized village might have up to five mosques in it, with each mullah leading prayers five times a day. Should mullahs preach every day against the government, there could be catastrophic effects on his plans to keep villagers on his side, especially as security forces left the area.

Nazak told us soon after I arrived, "If the village is progovernment but the mullah is against the government, then the village will be against the government."

He said the mullahs were resisting his efforts to register them, and they feared this would be the first step to being co-opted.[10]

Ideally Nazak wanted to pay the mullahs, but he quickly ran into trouble getting money to do so. Instead he tried to reach out to them directly, either through phone calls or through the village elders. He closely monitored them. The village maliks who worked with Nazak kept close tabs on the political leanings of the mullahs. He knew, for instance, that some mullahs in eastern Dand sympathized with the Taliban and probably helped their operations. It proved difficult in practice to displace them, because they were installed by the village elders and it risked an offense against Islam to move one out without extraordinary cause. Mullahs routinely played upon the ignorance of the people, who were generally poorly educated and vulnerable to manipulation.

Many mullahs also hesitated to talk with the district government because, as high-profile leaders of their villages, they were subject to Taliban intimidation. That was why Nazak had been happy to have the ANP pretend to rough up a mullah who visited him at the district center. No mullah could be sure whether a display of a progovernment attitude would be reported back to the Taliban, with potentially fatal results.

Nazak's used this strategy with the mullahs for months. At a meeting in October hosted by the Afghan army at its large base near KAF and attended by district governors and chiefs of police from the three districts flanking Dand, Nazak recommended bringing the mullahs on board with the government, as he claimed he had been doing for months.

"The mullah registration process is about done in Dand," Nazak told the audience, seated in rows of folding chairs. "ISAF should register mullahs too. We have been most successful."

Despite Nazak's exaggerated claims, his premise was sound, though it was unlikely ISAF would focus on bringing mullahs into the fold.

But Nazak kept hammering at the issue. When American members of the provincial reconstruction team came to see Nazak in mid-December, he complained to his visitors, who were seated on the sofas and chairs in his office with steaming cups of green tea in front of them, that his mullah strategy needed money but that there was no money at the provincial level to support his efforts.

"We don't have funds to get the mullahs to be integrated with the district center," he told them. "Mullahs are a sustainable move for Dand."

A cheap investment, they would provide a lot of security for years to come. But the PRT had no money to offer. In the end Nazak relied on a carrot-and-stick approach for the mullahs. Even as he continued his personal overtures, in the autumn of 2012 he deported thirty of them to Pakistan, accusing them of fomenting rebellion against the government.[11]

One of the reasons Nazak pushed the mullah idea for so long was that he was concerned about the future. Security and assistance were changing.

As Lt. Colonel Brian Payne pulled troops out of Dand in the latter half of 2011, he made sure the government had plenty of economic support lined up from the battalion's discretionary funds for development projects and incidentals, named the Commander's Emergency Response Program (CERP). On top of that, in the fall USAID pushed in more than a million dollars in projects.

But all that began to recede as 2011 ebbed. Lt. Colonel Payne's outfit, the 1-5 Infantry Battalion, was rotating fully into Panjwai before it headed back to the United States. In late December it was replaced by a new unit, the 5-1 Cavalry Squadron, which would be headquartered in Dand but whose focus was mainly on stopping the rocket attacks on KAF, fifteen miles to the east of the district center. The attacks came from villages outside KAF that were mainly on the border with Daman District, a no-man's-land that no one had spent much time trying to control.[12]

That meant the military force focused most of its attention on the villages in eastern Dand along its border with Daman. This eastern fringe had been somewhat neglected by Nazak, both because the villages were dispersed and also because he'd feuded with the most powerful elder there, a man called Haji Hayatullah, who did not recognize Nazak's authority. Reconciling the political situation and patrolling near KAF to cut the number of rocket launches would take up much of the new unit's energies in coming months as it pivoted the bulk of its military and civil efforts eastward.

Aid money from the new squadron was considerably less than that provided by Lt. Colonel Payne and Matt Kotlarski. It would be increasingly difficult to keep projects going, such as the women's training initiative and the mobile well-repair program. Creating new projects that affected the entire district soon became almost impossible. Meanwhile we waited for any increase in official Afghan government funds. In early 2012 our USAID-funded programs became almost the only game in town to help the villagers.

Luckily USAID continued to improve roads and distribute seed to farmers. Some U.S. programs, such as agricultural support programs with acronyms like AVIPA, CHAMP, and later S-RAD, were helpful, even though others, involving legal training, a microcredit initiative, and the training of the district council, produced little impact. For now the money available propped up the security situation. Security held, though the expected trickle of violence continued.

As a result, even as the security forces thinned out, the villagers kept their bargain with Nazak. People still felt safe enough to talk freely with the district government, and they received enough projects to make the risks of cooperation worthwhile.

The danger was that, as U.S.-Afghan patrols ceased, people would feel unprotected, so when insurgents knocked on their door, they might not feel safe telling the government. Warning calls to the police and DG

Nazak could dry up. The risk was very real. For years the Taliban had been killing influential people, with a twofold purpose: to stop them from working with the government and to intimidate other people. Over the previous ten years five hundred prominent individuals across the province had been killed, including the deputy provincial governor, the mayor of Kandahar City, and hundreds of tribal and village elders.

As 2012 began, some worrying trends developed. The trickle of insurgent attacks rose slightly and then plateaued. The village of Karz, the home of the Karzai family, became a major insurgent staging area, where bomb-making materials destined for Kandahar City could be hoarded and assembled. In March 2012 Karz was the site of a roadway suicide bombing that wounded a half dozen U.S. soldiers. The number of IEDs ticked upward. A police subcommander was shot dead near the district center while riding his motorcycle. Maliks were abducted and intimidated. But the village elders still cooperated with Nazak.

The security situation was stable for now, but what would happen to it as the amount of money we spent on projects steadily diminished? USAID funding was on a sharp downward trend. Because projects underpinned the political system and security, would the system weather a drawdown in money for development projects too?

The chief of police vigorously lobbied the province for more police to augment his 340-member force, but he had little success. He said the number of ANP personnel allocated to Dand might be cut in coming years.

As winter set in, with freezing nights and sunny but chilly days, we faced a number of fresh hurdles. We couldn't help but wonder if the money promised from the Afghan budget, and the projects it might bring, would ever arrive in Kandahar Province.

# 16

## The Economy Misses

Yeah, . . . and that comes out of another sickness, and that is the worship of *charts*. It gets to the point where that's really the whole war—fucking *charts*, and where they're supposed to go up if you can make them rise, and where they're supposed to go down if you can push them down, and by just about any means whatsoever, instead of really thinking what the whole thing's about, and what really has to be done. Yeah, all these guidelines and objectives and so on—you can't fault them, and that ought to be *part* of it. But then we get wrapped around the axle watching these charts, and it becomes—somehow the chart *itself* becomes the whole damn war, instead of the *people* and the *real* things!—**General Creighton Abrams**, quoted in Lewis Sorley, *A Better War*, 1970

MACV [Military Assistance Command Vietnam] labeled its weekly situation report the Headway Report. [General Paul] Harkins' operations chief was put in charge of its content and carefully edited the intelligence input so as not convey any lack of "headway" in the war effort. Enemy developments or activities that might reflect adversely on U.S.-Vietnamese progress in the war were carefully reworded, discounted, or simply omitted.—**George Allen**, *None So Blind*, 2001

As 2012 began, the district encountered a trifecta of problems caused by bad fortune and U.S. missteps.

The weather turned cold. I woke up one morning to find ice covering the puddles left by the previous day's rain. Walking to the district center, we skirted shallow ponds and slithered through thick mud. We hopped across large puddles from one wooden packing skid to another, the wood slapping the water as we passed.

Inside the district center the carpets were pulled up and the concrete halls were covered in mud. Shoals of muddy shoes left by fastidious Afghans stood at the door of meeting rooms; the Americans tracked their muddy boots across the ornate red rugs in the offices.

The chill hurt our plans to begin new businesses in Dand. Governor Nazak wanted to boost the economy by developing new chicken businesses, but young chicks would perish in cold weather. We would need to wait for warmer temperatures.

After four months of planning we'd discovered poultry businesses would be ideal for Dand, because Kandahar City represented a huge and untapped market for chicken and eggs. Most of the chicken eaten by city residents came frozen from Pakistan. Aside from our own research about the chicken industry, we'd been flying blind. USAID headquarters at KAF didn't know what kind of chicken businesses might work. Nor did they know much about the kind of small agribusinesses that would work best in a rural district.

We conducted our own market study in Kandahar City to pinpoint what consumers there wanted. In October I flew to Helmand Province to visit a headline USAID project dealing with chickens. No one else in Kandahar had collected the information, and we needed to know what was possible. USAID had spent $6 million to create a poultry farm in Lashkar Gah, the capital of Helmand. A large, well-constructed facility of about eight buildings, including a warehouse, breeding sheds, and a feed-corn mill, it offered chicks and feed for sale. At that point it dealt almost entirely with about sixty farmers around Lashkar Gah. We wondered if it could offer competitive prices for feed and chicks for chicken farmers in Dand, who normally bought these items from Pakistan.

The lack of information was surprising. After all, USAID, the Canadians, and an alphabet soup of aid agencies and NGOs had spent nearly a decade distributing chickens to farmers and their wives. Despite this effort, no one could say for sure which model worked and which didn't. Was it best to give a woman a dozen chickens or ten dozen? Did you distribute cages and feed or encourage the people to pay for these items themselves? How did you ensure that the chickens given to the people wound up as the basis of a working business and not a series of meals? No one knew, because no one had evaluated the projects after completion. Distributions of goods were commonplace; data on results were an unknown. Most of the projects we heard about in Dand had sunk without a trace; few people could even recall what had been done, let alone who had benefited or whether any businesses had opened because of them.

We found a few reports on previous distributions across the country and determined their cost, but because no one made follow-up visits to the project sites we lacked information on whether they succeeded or failed over time.

In Dand we found plenty of anecdotal evidence that suggested previous distributions had not worked. We called a half dozen people who'd received chickens from the Canadians, and we discovered that after a year most of these chickens were dead. The birds died of disease, starved, or were eaten. The Canadians had also provided a milling machine to make chicken feed; the mill now reportedly stood idle a few hundred meters from the base.

Distributions like these were counted by the agencies as successfully completed, but "success" was derived from the item having been given, not from any assessment of the impact or long-term benefit. No one checked on the creation of a business or even if the chickens had survived. The chickens were supposed to provide people with new businesses, usually women selling eggs. But did they? Without follow-up, no one knew. Talking to farmers, we found that usually when forty to sixty chickens were provided to someone, about a dozen chickens remained alive a year later. It seemed a dozen chickens could forage for themselves in the yard of a house, but sixty could not, because that number required the farmer to sell eggs and buy grain to keep them alive. The returns on sixty chickens didn't justify the effort.

We knew chickens could work. The agriculture director told us about a very successful commercial chicken farm in Dand, where three thousand chickens produced thousands of eggs a day. We visited one day. A man was making mud bricks next to a small shed stuffed with feed bags and empty egg crates ready to be filled and taken to market. Nearby a large shed made of mud housed the chickens. Inside, two long rows of chickens extended down the hall, their heads sticking out of individual wire cages. Long steel trays where eggs were collected ran the length of each row of cages. The owner said people in Kandahar City were happy to buy his eggs, and he described in detail the economics of the operation. When I reported the information up to KAF, I was told by headquarters that the chicken farm could not possibly be economically viable. But the owner had proudly told me that he made so much money, he planned to double the size of the operation over the next year.

So after months of investigation we knew pretty well what would work. We should concentrate either on large commercial operations, with fifteen hundred or more chickens, or small household operations, with just over one hundred chickens. Fewer than one hundred birds would not create a workable business selling eggs; the profits were too small to interest farmers who were busy with other things, and a farmer's wife could not realistically run a successful egg-selling business in conservative, rural southern Afghanistan without her husband's help. Most of the chickens from such a small operation would soon go into the pot. We found women were likely to be good recipients at the one-hundred-plus scale, while male farmers excelled at the commercial level.

We wanted to know more. How could we expand this idea to include selling chickens for meat rather than just selling the eggs? In January I intended to head out to Helmand a second time, to get more information. Promoting meat sales seemed to be something we could manage over time.

I booked my helicopter flight into the embassy's automated system. But I soon received a curt message from headquarters at KAF. Why was I, who was assigned to Dand, going to Helmand to look at chickens? I was ordered to cease and desist pending approval from headquarters at KAF.

Unwittingly I became caught up in KAF's game of musical chairs. The previous senior USAID representative, Patti Buckles, loved new ideas and new methods, and she was a strong supporter of our efforts to squeeze more success out of fewer dollars. In October she'd responded positively to my trip to Helmand to investigate best practices. She wanted to see good ideas implemented in places such as Dand.

But Patti moved on, to the embassy in Kabul, and her successor proved less open to new ideas. In fact in this case the senior State Department man at KAF, Andrew Haviland, caught wind of my trip and vetoed it without asking for an explanation. The USAID chief relayed the bad news. But it did not end there.

Soon he mandated an entire chicken review. He called a halt to any plans for chicken businesses and said the idea would need a full market evaluation to be conducted by "all interested parties" at KAF and the provincial reconstruction team in Kandahar City, even though it was only a minor pilot initiative costing about $20,000. Yet despite the ban on pursuing the program in Dand, USAID continued to distribute chickens in Kandahar City.

The ban spelled almost instant death to our ideas. Time was of the essence, because baby chicks dislike intense cold or intense heat. Given that Kandahar's desert climate swings rapidly from winter to summer, we had a very narrow window of time for mild temperatures. Young chicks could handle the stress of transport, but to survive they would benefit from several weeks of mild weather as they grew larger before having to withstand summer temperatures. It was vital to get this project started by mid-March at the latest, because April could be a very warm month.

Due to the review we missed that window of opportunity. We wrote the market study, but January passed with no review from KAF. Then February passed, and then it was March. The people at KAF got off to a slow start. They did not know why the review was necessary, and they made it a low priority. Finally in late March KAF sent back a plan they had developed in answer to our own, but it proved to be very complex and totally unworkable. It ignored the lessons we'd uncovered during our months of field research about optimal project size and other factors.

Ultimately we discounted the official report and tried to move forward, two months late, but in late March I received notice I had to leave Dand. I was being sent off to a different rural district, Maiwand. I was deflated and felt KAF had piddled away our chance to create new agricultural businesses.

The problem with chickens was not an isolated case of headquarters wasting time, opportunities, and resources due to flabby thinking. Waste and torpor existed in a number of USAID programs. For instance, the USAID-funded microfinance program for Dand was effectively moribund, yet the program sucked up millions of aid dollars.

Another case was Checchi. USAID had spent $9 million on a program run by a consulting company called Checchi. It was designed to teach village elders and district staff how to resolve disputes and other legal issues. Checchi's efforts were wildly popular at headquarters, in large part because the program tried to teach women their rights. Successful women's programs were few and far between and consequently always welcome back in Washington.

Unfortunately Checchi had serious flaws. At the end of 2011 Checchi's contract had expired but then been renewed and extended. However, the new contract essentially required the company to redo training it had just spent nine months delivering.

It seemed an awful waste. Soon enough we had a chance to dig into the details of the program. Checchi officials came to the PRT base in Kandahar City to discuss their projects with some of the district officers who would oversee them, and I was invited to attend.

One worry was that with the contract extension the company would just repeat its training, giving the same lessons to the same people. When the program was extended, it was supposed to give classes either to new people or give new information to the same people. The Afghans who attended the training received a payment for coming and a free lunch, so even if they didn't learn anything they were very likely to show up anyway for the fringe benefits. The Afghans had no incentive to confess they had already received the training.

So scrubbing the list of attendees was key. But in our meeting at the PRT the company told us it had inadequate records to ensure the same people did not get the same training all over again. In the rush of the extension all the old records detailing who had attended classes over the previous iteration had been lost. When pressed on this point, the Checchi officials admitted they simply had no lists to compare the first run of the program with the second. Because they had expected to close the program down they had let their staff go, they said. They didn't really know who had received training on which subjects and could not therefore exclude anyone from coming to the new sessions.

In practice the majority of the training remained the same from one year to the next, so it was likely that most of the same elders in Dand would again receive the same training.

Checchi also did not know what sort of impact their activities had. Would people who were trained change their behavior when it came to resolving disputes? Could such change in fact be measured? The company admitted it would take at least three years to measure the impact of this sort of training, which was a period longer than their program would run.

"We don't expect to see an improved level of effects in our timeframe," one of the managers said.

Checchi had an elaborate monitoring and evaluation plan, but it basically assessed whether the training sessions had taken place. It was too hard to gauge the impact. In this matter Checchi's program was hardly alone; the same evaluation problem was mirrored in all of the eight USAID programs I monitored in Dand in 2011.

Perhaps no one at USAID had previously asked these difficult questions about program effectiveness. But we did. Our inquisitive approach throughout the session with Checchi officials at the PRT apparently ruffled feathers. Prior to the next scheduled session several of us were quietly told to cease giving the Checchi people a hard time with questions they found difficult to answer.

Avoiding hard questions manifested itself in other ways over time, such as in reporting. The official report used to gauge progress across the southern region of the country was grandiosely called the RSSA, or regional south stability assessment tool. It gave a brief summary of how a district was doing on several fronts, including governance, health, the economy, rule of law, education, infrastructure, and security.

Each RSSA was a spreadsheet made up of text and a series of colored squares that would indicate how a district was progressing. Red was "bad," while green was "very good." Amber and yellow were in the middle. The point was for us to devise ways to move the district out of red and toward green; once progress reached yellow, then the district was "good enough" and the Americans could safely go home.

The RSSA was a very basic way to report progress because it comprised a series of short descriptions for each sector of effort, plus some bullet points on what needed to be done next, plus the colored squares for that section. Consequently it was difficult to show how one sector affected another. For instance, would the lack of education affect the economy? Would fragile security affect governance? The report wasn't set up to tell us, and the reporting in the sections was narrowly stovepiped, so discussing other topics was not allowed outside of each section beyond a short introduction at the beginning.

In the autumn of 2011 the RSSA was simplified and the security section was dropped. At the time security was marginal in most areas of Kandahar. According to one official at KAF, the security section was dropped from the assessment because "security was covered elsewhere in reporting." But dropping the section coincidentally cleaned up the look of several district charts.

So even though the RSSA had flaws, district officers could instead use the weekly reports to describe the interrelatedness of problems and the major hurdles. Weekly reports were the best way to communicate to headquarters what was going right and what was going wrong.

But in early 2012 the field officers were told to change the weekly reports. These would no longer explain what was happening but rather would show how the district was progressing toward the goals identified in the RSSA. The RSSA identified three actions in each sector as priority tasks; we were told the weekly report should show what we were doing to get these tasks done.

The changes were supposed to ensure district officers concentrated on the things that would lead to transition. Our goal at the time was to transition the districts to full Afghan control and cut direct American involvement back to occasional visits. The effect of simplifying the weekly report inadvertently made it more difficult to pinpoint the potential points of failure. Highlighting progress in our reports could lead us to downplay the obstacles we faced and potentially emphasize good news at the expense of balance. To make the transition to Afghan control meant we had to identify all the obstacles and then deal with them in a holistic manner. Simplified reports would miss a lot of useful context and potential issues that weren't being dealt with in the RSSA.

We quickly sent in a complaint and were told that bad news would be welcome in the weekly report. We were happy to get this message but worried that the complaint was necessary at all. The whole episode suggested that no one put a premium on understanding the bad news over simply receiving the good.

This was probably just the natural state of bureaucracy asserting itself. People at headquarters at KAF worked long hours and were dedicated to their jobs. But I wondered whether they engaged in critical thinking and foresight. Did staffers lack curiosity about Afghanistan just outside the perimeter fence? Did they also worry that dumbing down reports could lead to trouble over the long term, or were people too busy dealing with the daily churn of paperwork to even care?

Civilians assigned to these "embassy" jobs were eligible for five vacations a year, and many people took all five, which meant they would be away for up to sixty-four days every year. KAF was universally acknowledged as being exhausting, but where did all that hard work lead?

A lack of critical thinking led inexorably to distributing chickens that soon died or USAID paying for entire programs with marginal impact or even no impact that could be measured. It led to missed economic opportunities just as the war wound down, and each day grew more precious as the departure date loomed.

We worried about the way things were going. And we worried about whether anyone at KAF or the embassy would care enough to act if it looked like we were getting fundamental issues wrong, especially since the consequences for the Afghans we were trying to help would be potentially devastating.

# 17

## Solutions Made in Washington

Excepting in the Government workshops there are very few trades carried on in the country. . . . The bulk of the commerce of the country is confined to dried fruits, which are exported to India and Russia.
—**Frank A. Martin**, *Under the Absolute Amir*, 1907

Most villagers cannot believe that central governments, provincial governments or individual local and foreign technicians want to introduce permanent reforms. Previous attempts have generally been of short duration and abortive, for once the "modernization" teams leave, the villagers patch up the breaks in the "mud curtain" and revert to their old, group-reinforcing patterns. Most villages listed in governmental records of the developing world as "developed" have never been revisited or rechecked, and the "development" only exists on paper.—**Louis Dupree**, *Afghanistan*, 1997

As winter passed the rains tapered off, falling only once a week or so and then not at all. In fields and orchards buds of grapes and pomegranates flourished under the bright spring sunshine and winter wheat sprouted pale green stalks.

Once a week Mohammad Zahir and I would accompany the soldiers on their visits to villages. As spring advanced we saw farmers working outside, channeling water into fields that were divided into sections with small ridges of dirt. The chug of diesel pumps driving irrigation water filled the air. By late spring the farmers had begun to cut wheat by hand and feed it into small threshing machines that sputtered under the hot sun. Red Massey Ferguson 240 tractors carrying plows trundled by on the roads, preparing to sow the next crop.

One day we turned into the village of Nakadak, where Nazak had once confronted the Taliban. The village elder invited us into his white house. Made of mud bricks, it was the only one in the village that had been painted, and his white Toyota Corolla sat in the driveway. We sat on rugs in a small room with decorative curtains. A son of this elder served us dried fruit, nuts, and tea. We discussed the growing season and this year's harvest. As ever, the elder complained that the farmers needed more water. Drought had come to Kandahar Province ten years earlier and stayed, and no real solution to the problem had been found.

Much of the irrigation water came from wells, supplemented by water from a lake north of the city. Water from Dahla Dam flowed through a complex and delicate network of canals that stretched across two districts before it reached Dand. Less water flowed than farmers needed, and the Americans and Canadians planned to spend $275 million to raise the dam and increase the draw.

Because many farmers pumped water from wells, they paid for a lot of fuel. The diesel pumps often cost more than the crops were worth, but the farmers needed the wheat to feed their families. Each pump cost up to $150 per month to operate, and only grapes and pomegranates made any real profit. The wheat was picturesque, but most of the farmers lost money by growing it, though they lacked the cash to buy wheat in the bazaar. Many fields outside the villages lay fallow.

The water discussion we had with the village elder was difficult. He asked us what we were doing about it. In truth neither the Americans nor the Afghan government could do anything except hope for more rain. The Canadians paid for some of the main irrigation canals to be dredged, but their outlay was not enough to help every village.

In this as in so many other things Afghanistan found itself betrayed by its history, geography, and inclinations. As a landlocked country, it has limited access to the outside world and thus poor access to the world's markets. This isolation made Afghanistan poorer and far more likely to fail as a state.

Historically the rulers of Afghanistan had forbidden the building of railroads. They watched the British presence in India creep steadily closer, steadily annexing the land that is now Pakistan, pushing railroads up to the Afghan frontier, and even staging two major invasions into Afghanistan proper that lasted for years. The Afghans grew wary of more imperial ventures.

Without railroads Afghan exporters currently rely on the fragile road network. Many of the overloaded trucks head east toward the delay-ridden docks of Karachi in southern Pakistan and west to the border crossing into Iran.

Afghanistan is a nation of farmers. It lacks manufacturing, processing, and large-scale operations to exploit its rich seams of minerals and vast oil and gas fields. For centuries these resources were exploited poorly, if at all, with the Afghan rulers wary of being plundered by their neighbors. So Afghans rely on farming and trading, and the country's fields and roads are its greatest assets. Years of war, followed by a drought, have hammered the farmers of Dand with a particularly harsh double whammy.

The Americans helped the farmers in some ways, but many other things were not being done. USAID and its partners relied on a limited number of tried and true methods of assisting the farmers, usually with mixed results. USAID distributed seed wheat, fertilizer, tractors, trees, and animals; it trained farmers, built demonstration farms, greenhouses, and so-called farm stores; it cleaned clogged canals and operated a micro-credit program.

Some ideas were spectacular successes, such as improving roads and a few canal dredgings. Most were political successes, which drew people to the district center but provided limited economic benefits over the medium term. Others failed both economically and politically. People didn't care if they received the project benefits or not (beyond the money received for attending daily training sessions). Once the training or project ended, the impact or legacy disappeared with barely a trace.

Some things that could have been done inexpensively and sustainably were not brought to fruition, such as introducing new crops, developing new sectors of agribusiness, or assigning NGOs to coordinate those efforts and thus boost farm exports. Eventually in late 2012 USAID diverted an existing program into improving the processing and marketing of produce, an effort that was a bit late given that this was the province's major activity.

The task of boosting farmers' output, opening new lines of production, and improving their access to markets was not easy, especially because farmers resisted change and clung to outdated methods. Farmers were generally taught what they would easily accept, such as pruning techniques, which offered marginal benefits to farmers who had pruned trees for generations.

But teaching other basic techniques, fundamental but outside the experience of the average Afghan, could have gained the greatest results. For instance, farmers irrigated by completely flooding their fields, which wasted water and was very expensive given the cost of running irrigation pumps. Soil that was overwatered became rock hard and salty when minerals leached out of the ground, a situation that grew worse every year, unbeknown to the average farmer.

Afghan farmers were also unaware of the dangers of tilling twice a year and failing to preserve the structure of the soil. They would take their small tractors out into the fields and plow up the soil for planting. After the harvest they collected the straw from the wheatfields and took it home to burn, leaving the field untouched until planting began a few months later. Little emphasis was placed on teaching farmers to help the soil to maintain its structure with organic material, as American farmers had learned to do. With careful preservation of the organic material in the soil, the ground retained pockets of air and crops could grow better. Instead the Afghan fields baked and hardened under the sun, and rain packed the soil down even harder, which in turn led the farmer to over-water the next crop.

USAID training didn't attempt to teach these simple tricks because farmers resisted, insisting, "My father did it this way." USAID and USDA and the other agencies never really tried to sell the new methods. Good ideas need selling, especially in rural societies with ancient traditions. The district's Afghan agriculture staff often made the problem worse; they sometimes displayed woeful ignorance, making the job of selling new ideas even harder. Even so, there was almost no effort to train them on new techniques rather than minor incremental improvements to old ones. In the end no one came up with a plan to popularize new techniques; whether this was due to cultural chauvinism, a lack of time, or a sense of hopelessness about changing historical practices we never knew.

USAID did distribute seed wheat and fertilizer while demanding a small copayment from the farmer. The USAID contractor handed out two thousand of these packets at a time in Dand. This distribution was meant to raise yields across the district, because now farmers would use better grades of seed and fertilizer. It was impossible to tell if this effort worked because two thousand was too low a number to produce measurable impact in a district of seventy-five thousand people. It certainly lowered the market price of seed wheat. The political effects proved tremendously positive, although the economic ones were more doubtful.

Some ideas cooked up at KAF were hard to fathom. U.S. officials spent most of 2011 working to send agricultural exports to Dubai by an air bridge out of the civil airport co-located at KAF. USAID would subsidize the costs of transport to make the shipments economical as the idea got under way. The concept slowly got off the ground, with a handful of shipments from Spin Boldak District being flown to Dubai in 2011 and several more in 2012. One major issue was whether the transport would prove to be too costly when the American subsidies ended in 2014. In 2012 the United States doubled down on the idea and built a cold-storage facility at the airport. We hoped that a previous report by a U.S. agricultural expert, which detailed how the building of cold-storage facilities by donors had turned out to be an expensive failure across Afghanistan, would be wrong in this instance.

KAF planners also tried to bring processing plants to KAF or Kandahar City, which would allow grapes and pomegranates to be processed and packaged for export. But this idea saw delay after delay, well into 2012. The related idea of a juice factory eventually faded entirely, while the raisin plant struggled to open all through 2012. Even by late 2014 the idea had still not worked because problems with assuring a consistent supply of electricity and the inability to find investors overwhelmed the initiative.[1]

Mobile processing "plants" were also tried on a limited scale but with the same result. Each mobile plant cost $75,000 and was built inside a tent. The idea of such plants was thought up at KAF and pushed into the districts. Few of these top-down ideas worked very well in practice. As a result of these shortcomings, the big-picture ideas from KAF never had any impact on farmers in Dand.

We grew frustrated in Dand. Planners did not facilitate practical and achievable goals, such as clearing away red tape to enable traders to massively increase their exports to India, a traditional market for Afghan produce. The Pakistanis refused transshipment of goods across their country that would allow Afghan traders access to New Delhi. Solving this puzzle over the space of a decade would have boosted farm incomes immediately. Instead the planners messed around with costly air bridges to Dubai. In July 2012 the Afghan commerce and industry minister noted that Afghanistan's exports to India were "insignificant." He too sounded frustrated.[2]

As all these ideas percolated, 2011 turned into 2012, and we encountered major problems with the economy in Dand. We faced a black hole in terms of funding. The drawdown of money from USAID projects loomed, with nothing to replace the funds that fueled Nazak's political system.

We would lose hundreds of thousands of dollars every month when the main USAID agricultural program, S-RAD, came to an end in mid-2012. This program affected most of the villages. The maliks, elders, and farmers wanted to work with the government to receive free seed and fertilizer and to build roads and culverts.

To compensate for the scheduled end of the S-RAD program we needed to make real gains in the economy. It would bolster the political system if, when we departed, we could point to initiatives that continued to bring benefits to more than a handful of villages. The construction of many roads helped, but we needed something more. Agribusinesses would fit the bill perfectly to shore up the political system. Meaningful farm training that would have a positive impact on inputs and output, such as teaching techniques to substantially cut the use of irrigation water, would also demonstrate value.

We repeatedly pointed out this looming shortfall of money, and the KAF planners identified a solution. The senior USAID advisor at KAF duly told us we should fill the shortfall by applying for U.S. embassy grants for Dand.

Grants from the embassy are like grants from any other organization. You identify a need. You help an organization that wants to address the need. The organization writes a proposal and applies for the money. You wait. The proposal might be approved, or it might not.

Grants required time, an outside organization (which we lacked because no NGOs worked in Dand) to implement the idea, and the idea itself. This combination made grants suitable for a very small number of villages, if the money came through.

Consequently the suggestion to substitute a massive program like S-RAD with grant applications lacked credibility. The previous summer a woman working for a Kandahar City–based NGO had been killed in Dand, and the effect was chilling. Even if there had been NGOs operating in Dand, the number of projects that could be approved was relatively tiny and the grants themselves not very large. The notion of grants replacing the pool of USAID-S-RAD funding was a nonstarter on the grounds of scale alone.

To substitute for the loss of USAID money, what would be needed was a funding stream from the Afghan government's upcoming budget. That was unlikely to happen until well past the spring of 2012, if at all. Grants would certainly not compensate for either S-RAD's end or the Afghan government's failure to push its funds through official channels.

As 2011 turned into 2012 we heard a great deal from KAF about developments designed to help the Afghan farmers, but S-RAD had been one of the few programs that actually delivered. The other schemes would have little or no impact in Dand throughout 2012.

In the end there was no answer for this problem of evaporating funds. It simply happened. It was like watching two vehicles approaching a crossroad at top speed. The crash inevitably occurred, and one could not turn away from the ghastly sight.

By the time we identified the problem, in late 2011, it was too late anyway. USAID works at a glacial pace. Short of boosting the army's funding, interim funding could not be acquired in time to make a difference. The system could not respond quickly.

So the S-RAD program would conclude in Dand. There would be no near-term follow-up to fill a substantial gap in funding that would last until official Afghan money came online. The political system would come under even greater strain. District Governor Nazak would avoid the stress of this problem and begin to search for another job. Even at the critical moment when S-RAD ground to a halt in the summer and the flow of money stopped almost completely, Nazak took a month off to vacation in Germany. A new USAID program would kick in months later, but at a much reduced level.

When Governor Nazak returned from Germany his largest task was to keep his political system functioning with fewer resources, a problem we had identified a year before and had worked to solve. Had we done enough to keep the engine running? Or had too many opportunities been squandered, thus digging the hole too deep? The jury was out on whether he would succeed or fail.

# 18

## Dand in the Balance

If in 1879 we secured a predominant influence for India in Afghanistan, without risking hasty and dangerous annexations, we are now in the position of having spent thousands of brave lives and fifteen millions, to gain exactly—nothing.—**Charles Gray Robertson**, *Kurum, Kabul and Kandahar*, 1881

In mid-July 2012 District Governor Nazak held a press conference and announced his resignation. The district staff and residents were alarmed and deeply unhappy. For them this was the end of an era and the beginning of an unsettling time in which nothing was certain anymore.

I didn't call to commiserate or congratulate Nazak. I figured he had his own thoughts and worries. Nothing I could add would make much difference. His announcement reminded me of the day he'd told me that when the Americans left, he'd be going too. I could imagine why he had resigned.

By then Nazak had been attacked by the Taliban twelve times. One of the worst attacks came in March 2009, when a suicide bomber made his way up to the second story of the district center and detonated his vest. Eight people died, six were wounded, and the entire floor was devastated.[1]

The threat level against Nazak was so high that continuing attacks became an almost macabre joke. But he showed no fear. The Taliban targeted him four times in 2010 alone, the final time in December. During an August attempt a suicide bomber tried to blow up Nazak's armored car when he was on his way home. Six children playing nearby died instead. A second blast wounded two more children and a police responder a few minutes later.

"I saw the children playing by the edge of the road, and they are still in my mind," Nazak told a reporter about the explosions. "I will not be deterred from the campaign I have launched against the militants. I just wish that it were me or one of my policemen who were killed. It was painful that innocent children have been killed."[2]

But Nazak didn't resign because of the threats. Those would continue. At the press conference he complained about the district staff not being paid extra money to top up their salaries; the District Delivery Program that handled the money was being quietly killed by the embassy. He expressed anger that U.S. Army Special Forces had conducted a night raid that targeted the compound of a tribal elder who had made it possible for him to win over the people. And he pointed out that the official status of the district had never been resolved; Dand remained an "unofficial" district more than six years after it had been formed.

Nazak also noted that, despite all of the open schools in the district, the government ignored the district when it came to additional projects. Clearly he believed that outside support for the district was slipping away. That spring the flow of projects was at a reduced rate, down from $400,000 a month in funding to $200,000. Then, within the next few months, the funding dropped to a tiny fraction of that.

We had hoped that several USAID projects would continue for at least six months, which was when we estimated the Afghan government money would begin to kick in. This is what Nazak asked his high-level visitors from KAF to arrange. He explained that if USAID funding ended before Afghan government resources arrived, the villagers and maliks would be less inclined to engage with the government, which would spell deep trouble in terms of security.

Our district team was splitting up too, which added to the sense of uncertainty in the district. I wasn't there to see Nazak's announcement. On April 11, 2012, I left Dand for the last time. The sun shone brightly, the day practically cloudless—a powder-blue replica of the day on which I'd arrived more than eleven months earlier. Cip and my replacement, Lulu, saw me off at the landing zone, helping me run my boxes into the belly of the big CH-46 helicopter. After smiles all round, a quick handshake from Cip, and a hug from Lulu the helicopter rose with a whirl of dust.

In August, after a year in the district, Cip departed too. Lulu represented an unknown quantity for Nazak. She had worked in Panjwai prior to arriving in Dand, and she knew how to move USAID programs along. But her playful practice of making balloon animals during meetings in the district center and giving them to staff to take them home to their kids probably did not endear her to Nazak, who had a serious fight on his hands to keep his district together.

The previous winter and spring Nazak had seen his warnings about the district center coming unglued go unheeded. This neglect was demonstrated by a long-running but ultimately futile battle to bring electricity to the district center. Nazak lost, even though he did everything right and followed every instruction from ISAF.

Nazak had conceived the idea of stringing a power line to the district center the previous autumn. He hoped that with an electricity hookup, the staff would no longer need to run a generator to power their lights and computers. In order to connect to the Kandahar City power grid, a line would need to be extended six kilometers from a village named Spin Ziarat, located on the southern fringe of the city. Our district team agreed to help Nazak investigate the idea. It turned out to be feasible, but with caveats.

American technical officials at KAF estimated it would cost about $50,000 to string the line. A project of that size required the approval of the local U.S. Army brigade, since USAID lacked the money. It was too large an outlay for the battalion to handle. The brigade commanders said they would support it and provide the money if the necessary authorities, both U.S. and Afghan, did too. Several USAID officials at KAF, hearing the idea, immediately tried to quash it, because the electricity grid was already overburdened and there was little chance of demand easing in the future. But other USAID officials and the army indicated that, if the Afghan company in charge of distributing electricity in the province approved the idea, then they would consider it too. In fact extending power to one building would have little impact on the long-standing problem of giving power to neighborhoods across the entire city, but it could be a game changer for Dand.

In February 2012 Nazak convened a meeting at his office to hash out the issue once and for all. All the local players were present, including the brigade deputy commander, the district team, and the technical officer from the PRT in charge of electricity. Nazak said he had the approval of the state-owned power company, known as DABS, as well as the approval of the provincial governor, the brigade, and the district team. We had told him he needed to get these signatures on paper, which he had done. Could he get approval from everyone in the room to go forward?

The technical officer from the PRT remarked that the primary DABS engineer had told him that the agency hadn't approved the idea. Nazak promptly telephoned the engineer, Wali, who told the group via speakerphone, "I can give electricity to the district center, and this line is no problem."

The technical officer then commented that the head of DABS, Haji Sultan, had told him the project was not possible.

"He said there is no extra power, and if I took power for this line I would be taking power that is in short supply," the PRT officer explained.

"I'll call Haji Sultan," Nazak answered, again reaching for his phone. "Engineer Wali and I already went to see Haji Sultan." Nazak waved the signature sheet. "This is Haji Sultan's signature and this is Provincial Governor Wesa's."

Haji Sultan answered the call. Nazak explained the purpose of the meeting and held up the phone so everyone could hear.

"I approve the power for the district center building but not for the village," said Haji Sultan. He then added, "Probably this is a misunderstanding."

The PRT officer shrugged. "He said yesterday to talk about it in the future. I'll send a letter saying DABS was in on the meeting and that they approved it."

The brigade deputy, a smart and dedicated soldier, stated the obvious— that everyone in the room needed to agree. They did. With that the final decision on the power line was pushed up to KAF, where it awaited the signature of the brigadier general responsible for all large U.S. Army-funded projects. He was very likely to sign, since everyone now approved.

By an ugly twist of fate Nazak's electricity project died. The general whose signature was needed went on vacation in March before he could sign the final papers. During his absence a female captain on his staff confessed to their superior that she and the brigadier had engaged in a years-long affair. The army took a hard line, and Brig. General Jeffrey Sinclair never returned. In the turmoil of the moment, which coincided with our local U.S. Army brigade leaving the country at the end of its tour, Sinclair's hastily appointed replacement never signed the paperwork. The power line was never extended to the district center—one in a string of disappointments for Nazak.

A sense of futility probably weighed heavily on Nazak, and he simply decided it was time to go. Nazak's very public resignation stirred a response from the provincial governor and the U.S. headquarters at KAF. Words were had. Nazak was persuaded to stay on, which he did reluctantly. His tenure in Dand limped on for another six months, with foreign correspondents coming to Dand to see the miracle at work.[3] He continued his push to bring mullahs into the fold. In October he expelled thirty clerics he had decided were under Pakistani influence.[4]

Nazak still kept one eye on the exit, and in December word filtered through that he was finally leaving for good. His ties to the extended network of Gul Agha Sherzai continued to pay dividends, his sterling stewardship of Dand being a useful rung on the ladder of progress. He soon moved to Zabul Province for a higher profile government job that entailed handling the provincial security service. After a year in Zabul he took over the security service in Helmand Province, one of the highest-profile jobs in southern Afghanistan.

As Nazak's final chapter played out, I'd left Dand and settled into a new assignment in Maiwand District, a rural area forty miles to the west. I was not happy to leave. About a month before I left, headquarters had asked me to move to KAF to "make use of my experience" and to "let others have a shot at a DST." I declined that offer because, I explained, I had come to help Afghans in a district, not to ride a desk. Then, three weeks prior to my departure, headquarters phoned and told me I was to leave Dand for Maiwand. The second phone call did not offer a choice. I was told to leave within ten days, even though the American unit that owned Dand, the 5-1 Cavalry Squadron, was also switching out that same week and their replacements had not yet arrived. The brigade in charge of the whole area was also leaving, as was the mentor team assigned to the Afghan police in Dand. No one except Cip would know what was going on, and he was on leave and due to return the day I would have departed.

It was a typical headquarters screwup. I wangled an extra eleven days to hand over to the incoming units as best I could. It would take time to explain how the district operated, what the future plan entailed, and what needed to be most urgently pushed forward. The normal army handover lasted two weeks, and I would use every minute.

Now, as we lifted off and flew away, my mood hardly matched the sunny sky. A single side gunner hunched over an M240 machine gun on the starboard side, his face hidden behind a green plastic wind mask. The big chopper made its shuddering way into the air, flying slightly crabwise under the influence of its big rotors mounted fore and aft. I gazed out the side windows as a second Sea Knight helicopter followed to the side. Behind it the jagged hills bordering Dand receded. We passed the green rectangular fields of Panjwai on our right, and the brown desert floor etched with erosion marks of long-past streams flowed by on our left.

Leaving Dand, I felt uneasy. Some things had gone right. We had set up programs that were economical and easy to continue, and we had the attention and cooperation of the provincial officials. But the programs' continued success depended on the next step working out: Afghan government funds filtering into the district to support these activities. I knew it was a long shot that the situation would improve anytime soon.

We had also set up a number of programs to revamp local businesses, but we hadn't pulled the trigger yet because we were waiting for funds to be released. Some of these initiatives, such as new chicken businesses, had been opposed by headquarters for months. I doubted that Cip and Lulu would overcome the bureaucratic obstacles to get them done quickly. I wanted to stay for at least another three months to shepherd them through, but it was not to be.

As the baked sand of the desert rolled by, I reflected on the past eleven months. Personally I had enjoyed every minute of it. We had mentored the Afghan officials almost every day, working together with friendship and good cheer. Running USAID projects had also taken time, constantly requiring emails with updates or inquiries to write, time spent investigating how the budget worked, or writing reports. One of the hardest challenges had been to carve out time to think about the big picture of what needed to be done and then to figure out how best to work that into existing plans and programs.

Ultimately the war in the district was not rocket science. When I left Dand, it was much as I found it: reasonably quiet, somewhat prosperous, and with a fully developed political system. For all these things Governor Nazak and the ISAF units who served there deserved full credit.

Over the course of eleven months the U.S. Army had been pulling out, going from more than three maneuver companies to none as the 5-1 Cavalry left. The Afghan army had also departed, and only Afghan police remained. Of the U.S. forces, only the police advisors continued on, with the USAID officers living alongside them. Yet peace held tight through the drawdown of these units because the political system was strong.

When I left, I warned headquarters that simultaneously taking out troops and projects would risk security. Projects should be downsized incrementally and cautiously. Most important, almost all the activities should be directed by the Afghans themselves, especially those who knew how to extract the most impact in the villages per dollar spent. As I left, a sufficient amount of projects and services remained, but not for long. Within four months of my departure the main USAID program disappeared. Its replacement program would not appear until 2013. Our greatest fear, a gap in funding that was not filled by Afghan government money, was fully realized. The gap would persist for years, not months.

Nazak's grand bargain with the people persisted, but for how much longer? It was unfortunate that convincing KAF of the seriousness of this problem had been an uphill battle. When I first arrived, people in headquarters argued that Dand should be cut off from assistance "to see what happens." We lobbied KAF intensely to kill this idea, but the concept lingered.

Soon enough Dand experienced a string of events that threatened to erode the system, much as an incoming tide laps against and damages the pilings of a pier.

The DST was supposed to remain open until December 2012, or so Nazak had been promised. But that summer as Cip left, KAF slated it for closure. They reduced it from a seven-days-a-week presence to a day and a half. A few months later KAF closed it down completely, with occasional drop-in visits from KAF. These visits worked poorly, with limited coordination between the Afghan staff and the person assigned to drop in.

One of the Afghan staff reported, "It is like no DST, because when he comes he even does not see us and we don't know when he comes and goes."[5] The Afghans felt that they were on their own.

Nor had any way been found to fund the district center. Without enough money for district staff to do their jobs thoroughly, the staff would again work at a fraction of their potential. Headquarters at KAF took the strictly legalistic point of view that nothing could be done, though ISAF had a history of finding ways to push the government to do the unpopular but correct thing. On this the issue was conceded, and there didn't seem to have been much of a fight to find a solution. The problem was just assumed away; the district would simply make do.

And then we learned there would be no effort to train the district staff in how to use their own Afghan budget system. They were expected to figure it out themselves. The official line was that the district staff didn't need to know how the system worked, because they didn't handle money, just requests. That was hogwash. The more the staff knew about the system, the better they could make it work to their advantage. KAF had conceded as much when it said the district team should try to discover the amounts of money that the provincial ministries had to spend, because this knowledge would strengthen the arguments that district staff could make when submitting requests.

The district staff would continue to do the best they could. But there was another bleak omen.

In late fall 2012 the district chief of police, Major Rahmatullah, decided to go to Gorgan, a village in southwestern Dand. He mounted up with his men and drove south along an asphalt road that had been opened barely eighteen months before. They followed the road as it wound past vineyards, across the Tarnak River, and continued south.

The tires of the Ford Ranger whirred as it traveled south on the road that carried taxis, tractors, and motorcycles going to and from Kandahar City.

The police chief passed Nakadak, the scene of one of Nazak's greatest triumphs, and approached Gorgan. Six months previously an elder had been kidnapped in this village. The Taliban had bundled him over the border with Panjwai, just three kilometers to the west, and held him for ransom. The Taliban let him go after a dozen elders intervened and he promised to pay a $10,000 bounty.

But that was Panjwai and this was Dand. The last time anyone in this area had died from insurgent violence was a year earlier, when an American patrol searching for an IED got too close to it and a Stryker was blown up. That was two kilometers farther west, hard against the Panjwai border.

The day was bright and sunny, with a wind rushing in from the west. Major Rahmatullah didn't even know what hit him. Suddenly there was an IED blast and his life ended. The subsequent investigation suggested that one of his own men had fired a weapon during the incident and the bullet struck him, probably accidentally.[6]

Did his death mean violence was creeping back into the area or was it a random act? Major Rahmatullah's death probably marked the beginning of the end of the time when Dand could be considered mostly safe. In coming years it would be more difficult for government employees to commute between Dand and Kandahar City. In 2011 they covered their faces with scarves and commuted every day, keeping cautious and alert but not fearful. Within a few years the drive became a much more serious enterprise.

And in coming years the district staff would return to the lives they'd had before we'd started. With little money coming in and few projects there was far less they could do to influence the villages. The schools remained open, as did the clinics, which were run as they had always been—by staff hired by an NGO.

After years of extraordinary efforts by thousands of people to bring peace to Dand, and seeing it achieved to a large extent, we now contemplated how fast the district would progress downhill. Ultimately we could not fix national problems, such as dysfunctional budgets and faltering security, at the district level.

So we won. And then we lost. We failed to give the government the tools to consolidate and make a political bargain that would stick for years to come. As I flew toward Maiwand, twisting in the nylon webbing seats to look out the small portholes of the helicopter, I reflected that it had been a good year. We had figured out how to help villagers for small amounts of money. The district staff felt motivated and empowered.

They were set up for success. And every month Dand remained stable, residents grew more accustomed to good government. As long as we continued to avoid losing, we could win. If only the system wouldn't let them down. It was frustrating.

My experience in Dand would be good preparation for a year in Maiwand. But as I arrived in April 2012 at the new district, located on the western fringe of Kandahar Province, I quickly found that everything we had in Dand was absent from Maiwand.

# PART FOUR

On to Maiwand

# 19

## Two Districts

The State Department and USAID are spending approximately
$320 million a month on foreign aid in Afghanistan. In part, the
administration has been using aid to "win hearts and minds." For
instance, roughly 80 percent of USAID's resources are being spent
in Afghanistan's restive south and east. Only 20 percent is going
to the rest of the country.—**U.S. Senate Committee on Foreign
Relations**, *Evaluating U.S. Foreign Assistance to Afghanistan*, 2011

"If the generals had been allowed to sustain the early impact on
security and the civilians in charge had just focused on roads,
irrigation and electricity with governance being devolved to the
local level rather than too much held centrally, things would be
much brighter."—**General Sir David Richards**, quoted in Sandy
Gall, *The War against the Taliban*, 2010

The flying time from Dand to Maiwand was less than thirty minutes. The
nose of the old twin-engined helicopter surged forward, leaving Dand
quickly behind. We flew over the Arghandab River with its brown water
dividing the green fields of Panjwai and Zhari Districts. On our right the
desert hues of sand stretched farther north in northern Zhari District. We
flew past a line of burnt-umber ridges seemingly close enough to reach
out and touch with your hand. Barren, jagged peaks towered over the
helicopter. Suddenly the hills gave way to a flat and dusty desert floor,
the broad landscape of Maiwand opening out below.

The villages were widely scattered, and green fields lay in strips across
a broader mass of bare ground. Farther north a few jagged peaks rose

out of the haze. Twenty miles to the south a thin band of green marked the Arghandab River, known locally as the Dari Rud, as it curved westward toward Helmand Province. Across the river lay the high dunes of the orange-tinted Reg Desert.

Then the helicopter banked toward the base. We passed a large outdoor marketplace and skimmed over the inevitable wall of double-stacked HESCO gabions. The nose came up, and we bumped down onto the gravel landing zone. The ramp dropped. A soldier helped me move my bags and boxes out of the helicopter before it lifted off with a blast of air that blew the bags against the wall and peppered us with gravel. Welcome to Maiwand!

The base was tiny, the size of COP Edgerton in Dand, less than two hundred meters across. Dust-laden tents huddled between two hard-walled buildings, and a few single-wide trailers were scattered against the walls next to some plywood shacks used as barracks and a laundry. Guard towers were built at irregular intervals around the wall. The camp wore an air of great tiredness, as if it had been there too long. Unlike Dand, Maiwand was a bit of a dump.

The Maiwand DST was different too, with three men instead of two. One of the men was on leave and the other was about to go. Unlike in Dand, the district center was in a separate compound two hundred meters from the base. Instead of starting the day with a short walk to the district center, we accompanied a section of armed soldiers who never carried fewer than two weapons.

The team leader in Maiwand, Eric, was tall and thin with a gray-flecked beard. A veteran USAID employee, he had worked in a number of development jobs around the world. The other was Skip, a State Department surge draftee who had spent much of his tour at KAF. Getting out to a DST was a treat for Skip, who spent most of his time trying to figure out the personalities in the district, writing reports, and compiling the information into a document for future teams.

The feel here was different. The DST didn't visit the district center every day, and the close ties we'd enjoyed with the district staff in Dand were almost completely absent in Maiwand. Not just the physical space was different; trust and camaraderie were missing. They would need to be built up, almost from scratch. I got the sense early on that the Afghans regarded the Americans as being on a separate team, a feeling I had never experienced in Dand, where we all worked very closely together.

The district center was scattered; it wasn't really a district *center* at all. It was a district center complex, with offices spread over separate buildings. In contrast to Dand the hub of the Maiwand government was the building housing the police chief. On one side was a small graveled parade ground rimmed with small buildings used as barracks and offices. Beyond the parade ground and past a swing-up barrier stood a large meeting building where the district governor, Salih Mohammad, had his office.

On the other side of the police building stood an open patch of ground that was used as a demonstration garden and beyond that an agricultural center, built at great cost several years earlier. The agricultural center had five buildings, which were large, two-story affairs, now completely empty except for the agricultural director's office and meeting room. The district governor had taken over another one to use as a residence. A third would eventually be turned into a legal office where a judge could hear cases. During my time there the judge held court only two times.

The hub of the government was the complex, not the government staff, who were largely absent. The health director preferred not to operate out of the district hub at all. He kept a small office at the health clinic in downtown Hutal, the market village adjoining the base and the district center. He rarely appeared in the district, much to the annoyance of the district governor, even though he was well paid. I recalled Dr. Mousa in Dand, who toiled for free. One Maiwand District staff member who handled projects also doubled as the education officer and operated out of a nearby school. The rest of the civilian staff was made up of the DG's bodyguards and men who issued ID cards from an office near the inner barrier. In Maiwand issuing ID cards was big business, which I witnessed the first time I went to the DG's office building.

The DG sat on the veranda of the squat concrete building. A line of men sat against the wall, waiting their turn. Each man clutched in his hand a piece of paper that served as an identity card. The line began at an inner gate and snaked around the corner of the building, barely moving. The men sat for hours.

The line ended at the DG himself, where one man crouched in front of him. The DG held the man's identity paper, or *tashkira*, in his lap and spoke with short, jabbing sentences. The DG was irritable, and though it was only 11:00 a.m. he had been there for two hours, servicing the line of men waiting for his signature.

DG Salih Mohammad, a bulky man in his mid-fifties with a gray-flecked beard, was conscientious but lacked efficiency. His official stamp, needed for each identity paper, was a long time coming. The Taliban had a strong presence in Maiwand, and he wanted to be sure that each man was who he claimed to be.

"Who is your father?" DG Salih Mohammad snapped. "Who is here to vouch for you? Which village are you from?"

Snap, snap, snap. No time to waste with the men lined up for hours or sometimes for days; he had to get through them all. The pace was both hurried and slow at the same time.

In Dand DG Nazak had also issued ID papers, but via a much simpler system. His staff asked all the questions and brought him the identity papers ready to sign. The DG would stamp them, one after another—stamp, stamp, stamp—as his assistant or his police guard pushed the correct paper in front of him and whisked it away once stamped. DG Nazak hardly touched a piece of paper, spending no more than a few seconds on each. He trusted his staff to get the details right.

DG Salih Mohammed was not so fortunate. He asked questions, then scribbled on the application, signed it, and handed it back. Next! Amid this hurry the DG would squeeze in other business. As the line of crouching men sidled up, the DG would discuss district matters with a circle of elders in front of him.

It was scarcely surprising the DG was usually irritable. The phone also rang constantly, and newly arrived visitors would butt into the circle of elders to speak first. Life with DG Salih Mohammad while doing business was never restful. Yet each of the crouching men paid good money for his identity papers, perhaps $5 or more, and the DG kept some of it, perhaps a dollar or two or three. On his salary, not even $500 a month, he could not afford to turn the line of men away even if he'd wanted to. Poor security in the district necessitated that everything be carefully verified.

Maiwand was no Dand, in either the particulars of the district nor life in the villages. In Dand, after years of effort, the Taliban been kicked out of most areas. They skirted the fringe of the district, their movements exploiting a narrow, lightly policed area dividing the district from Kandahar City, but in general the insurgents were furtive and unwelcome

In Maiwand, however, the Taliban ran more of the district than did the district governor. In May 2012 the DG dared not enter most areas in the north or the far south. In most of central Maiwand the Afghan and American security forces routinely got into firefights if they ventured more than a few kilometers from the district center.

Only the daily routine was familiar. Each morning the sun rose from behind a ridgeline to the east. At about nine o'clock I headed over to the district center to make the rounds, talking with the DG and his staff, if they were there. Sometimes the other DST members joined me and sometimes they didn't.

All the advantages of Dand seemed to have been reversed in Maiwand. In Dand the district governor had already mastered the political arts, forging alliances easily and bending the elders to his will. This district governor lacked the political ideas and resources to persuade the elders to enter into a bargain with the government. A former officer in the Afghan police, DG Salih Mohammad failed to make the political calculations that DG Nazak in Dand had found so easy to produce.

Marginal security, absent district officials, and the inconvenience of checking their attendance all degraded the government, as did the overt corruption. The projects director for the district, the one who doubled as an education official, spent a great deal of his time trying to steal from the education account and to grab a share of the funds from the few projects paid for out of the official budget, which sporadically helped people in the villages.

Yet he couldn't be fired because no one would be foolish enough to replace him. He spent thousands of dollars a year paying off the Taliban so he wouldn't be killed. The money he made from corruption paid off the Taliban, making his illegal takings a life-or-death issue for him, according to the men he worked with every day. I soon longed for the cheerful face of Mohammad Naseem, who had singlehandedly managed a program that repaired five hundred wells in a little more than six months and who had also typed up the weekly reports on his computer.

In Maiwand only one official school was open, along with several more unofficial ones hidden away in mud houses in the villages. The Taliban killed teachers in the official concrete schools, but they turned a blind eye to teachers working incognito in the mud-house schools. The thirteen empty concrete shells of schools around the district testified to the power of the insurgents.

Even when the district staff did turn up, little could be accomplished. It was unsafe to operate in most of the villages. A small bubble of security extended out three miles from the district center. A small medical clinic operated in the bustling market located next to the district center. It was open about four hours a day and closed on Fridays. It was the only clinic in the entire district of about seventy-five thousand people. At least the provincial government paid salaries for several dozen teachers and medical staff, but almost no projects arrived. The windows in the school could not be repaired without American help, because there was no official money (a problem we had also seen in Dand). The district's monthly operating fund was tiny, and the official development budget was almost nonexistent.

Nor had ISAF made up for the shortfalls. Projects carried out in the villages were few and far between. The villages farthest from the district center received nothing. People in villages wanted wells, walls, and roads; none of these projects had been carried out except in the most sporadic manner. Meanwhile the concrete culverts that dotted the dirt roads in central Maiwand were dilapidated and stamped with markings such as "2004 Government of Japan." A USAID program had pushed a thousand parcels of seed and fertilizer into about thirty villages, but most of the other programs run by the Afghan government or U.S. military either didn't work or were clustered around the district center, where security was best.

It was not an auspicious start. Even worse, in April 2012 the district governor and much of his staff were on nearly hostile terms with the Americans.

The U.S. military and the civilians on the DST were in a war of words with the Afghans, accusing the district staff of being ineffective, milking projects for money, and generally being uncooperative and unimaginative in running the district. They argued the DG should hire more staff and criticized him for failing to place more employees behind desks at the understaffed district center.

The DG replied that no competent staff member would want to work for low wages in a district with such poor security. He faulted the Americans for failing to bring projects to any of the villages in his charge. Deadlock.

Both were partly right. It was hard to blame the DG for his attitude. In truth there was too little for the existing staff to do. No wonder they seldom showed up. In previous years ISAF had not pushed most of its limited budget into the villages scattered across the district. Instead projects were showered on the central hub near the district center, where security was tight. The villages were starving for projects.

And many of the projects they did do were not explained well enough, so the DG and his staff never understood everything that was going on. The Americans had fallen into the trap of thinking that one or two briefings would be enough to explain a project. Consequently the DG felt constantly surprised with the goings-on around him and not really in control of his district.

He often complained, "You don't tell me what is happening!"

But the Americans thought he had a problem listening to what they told him and so responded with equal vehemence, "You are just trying to control the projects!"

The Americans believed the DG worked only to line his pockets, by fleecing the contractors. The DG believed the Americans wanted to cut him out of the decision making. He assumed they lined their pockets too and thus wanted him out of the way to make it easier to take their cut.

This situation had turned from dysfunctional to acidic. ISAF officers in Maiwand routinely pushed complaints about the DG and other staff up their chain of command to headquarters at KAF. This stream of complaints spawned visits from the abrasive senior State Department official, Andrew Haviland, who descended by helicopter and threatened to pull all ISAF projects out of the district unless the DG reformed himself. After these visits the DG felt even more disempowered and under assault from the people who were meant to help him.

The DG grew angry when projects did not go where he wanted—in the villages—or had too little effect on the people. His criticism further incensed the Americans. For example, the Americans wanted to begin a training program near the district center to teach twenty young people how to pour concrete, which would help the Afghans get jobs. But the DG argued it wasted money because it took funds out of the villages, where projects were most needed. The project, run by an American NGO, went ahead despite his objections.

As another example, when I arrived a new USAID program started up that aimed to employ hundreds of local people. Initially the Americans decided where the projects would go, with a bit of input from the DG. These ideas soon proved unworkable, because security was poor and the Afghans who lived in the villages didn't want the projects, nor did the elders of the development assembly, a council charged with organizing projects in the villages. As I began to work with the Afghans of the assembly and the DG, we quickly decided to scrap these impossible ideas and put the onus instead on these key district players to figure out what they wanted and where. They soon developed a whole new list of projects that we used going forward.

In other ways what had occurred before I arrived was unsatisfactory. The USAID program known as S-RAD was winding down. We had used the same program in Dand with great success. Having S-RAD money available allowed us to gravel eight dirt roads and use hundreds of thousands of dollars for other projects needed in the villages, including large distributions of seed. The economic and political benefits for DG Nazak were enormous, giving him tremendously powerful leverage over the village maliks. This same program had produced little for Maiwand besides distributing seed wheat and fertilizer to almost a thousand farmers, giving villagers chickens that soon died, donating several tractors, and building a wall at the district center.

It took six months of work to straighten out this knot of problems. As in Dand, we operated on the principle of empowering the Afghans to help themselves. In this case, because the district staff was so small, we used the district's development assembly of elders (the DDA) in a much more proactive role than we had in Dand. They developed lists of projects and plans, prioritized them, and worked closely with the village elders, along with DG Salih Mohammad. The DDA became the de facto district staff, and they did almost everything.

First I tried to squeeze projects for villages out of the existing S-RAD agriculture program, and the Afghan staff quickly nominated several project ideas. But it was too late and the program folded too quickly to accomplish much more, even though we were promised an extension that would allow us to extract a few more projects, such as culverts.

Even though this effort failed the Afghans began to feel that their opinions mattered. Less sidelined, they took charge of the district. Our goal was to make sure that most ISAF-funded projects would henceforth respond to their wishes and come from their ideas. This simple proposition seemed to them quite radical. The situation mirrored the exact issues we had encountered when I arrived in Dand almost a year earlier.

We also streamlined the handling of projects. The DG and the district development assembly would henceforth approve all projects not related to security. Almost no project could go forward without the members' signatures. And we tried to push the district staff to figure out what they wanted to do and match those wishes to available funding. Once the projects began to flow, we turned to maximizing political impacts by demanding accountability from maliks and elders, just as DG Nazak had done in Dand.

The turnaround proved to be a quick one, and ISAF found that DG Salih Mohammad no longer held up projects. We instituted an official list of companies, so the district staff felt in control over who worked in the district. This trade-off, giving control in return for performance, was not foolproof, as it offered an easy way for the assembly elders to extort bribes. But over time it ended the bureaucratic skirmishing between the Americans and the Afghans, who previously had sent the police to stop contractors from working on projects when they felt blindsided.

Even the poisonous dialogue between the Afghans and the headquarters people at KAF stopped. The DST no longer sent up reports criticizing almost everything the government did, and the government had less reason to criticize the Americans. Peace broke out between allies.

This progress underscored a simple goal: get the Afghans ready to handle their own money. Our thinking was that if the Afghans could identify and manage projects now with American money and the DST's help, then they should be able to handle the projects that were sure to be funded soon by their own government. This idea was tied into some initially encouraging signs at the national level. America poured almost as much development money into Afghanistan in 2012 as it had in 2011. But in 2012 much more of it was being directed to the Afghan ministries.

This offered hope for a time that money would finally begin to flow from the budget to benefit the countryside.

Unfortunately this plan failed because most of the money sent to the Afghan ministries never arrived in the provinces and districts. It transpired that throughout 2012 the Afghans in Kabul sent only some of the official money down to the provincial government in Kandahar City because the national officials distrusted the provincial staff. Much of the money stayed in Kabul. Of course Kabul was too far away for the district officials to have any influence on how the money was spent. Our main goal—to bring the district officials to the point they could work with the upper levels of their own government—faded away. Yet, without the upper and lower levels of the government working together, nothing the government did would be sustainable in coming years. It was like falling at the final fence of the Grand National.

So much had been going so badly for the Afghan in Maiwand for so long that I didn't see how it could get any worse. Then for nearly six months almost no ISAF money came through. DG Salih Mohammad and the elders he worked with complained to us that they had promised more than they could deliver; their reputations had been undermined by the extreme shortfall in funding.

Finally, as 2012 drew to a close, some emergency USAID money arrived and we could begin to work on some projects. A good omen? As 2013 approached we hoped the new year would be a lucky one.

# 20

## Security Failing in Maiwand

Young love if you do not fall in the battle of Maiwand;

By God someone is saving you as a token of shame

—**Legendary cry of Malalai** at the Battle Maiwand, 1880

I 'eard the knives be'ind me, but I dursn't face my man,

Nor I don't know where I went to, 'cause I didn't 'alt to see,

Till I 'eard a beggar squealin' out for quarter as 'e ran,

An' I thought I knew the voice an'—it was me!

—**Rudyard Kipling**, "That Day," 1896 poem about the
Battle of Maiwand

Maiwand District occupies a special place in the hearts of the Afghan people, being the scene of one of their greatest victories over the British Empire. The defeat of the British at Maiwand in 1880, during which 969 British and Indian soldiers died, is the Afghans' second-greatest triumph after the defeat of the British army in the retreat from Kabul in 1842, when most of the invaders were wiped out.

During the Second Afghan War the British pushed into Maiwand, where they built a fort in the center of the district. In July 1880 the British dispatched a force of twenty-five hundred men led by Brigadier George Burrows to run down and kill the youngest son of the emir they had deposed the previous year.

Hearing that Ayub Khan was approaching fast, the British sallied forth to meet him on the flat plain of central Maiwand. Streaming out of a mountain pass from the west, Ayub Khan and twenty-five thousand men hemmed in the British on three sides. Pummeling the British with artillery, the Afghans charged the enemy lines under the exhortations of a young Afghan girl named Malalai. During the furious fighting the left side of the British line ran out of ammunition, crumbled, and broke, and the defense collapsed. Soldiers streamed back toward Kandahar City, forty-five miles away. Hundreds of soldiers were cut up as they ran; hundreds more died of thirst on the road back. The Afghan army laid siege to the city. Only when the great British general Frederick Roberts swept down from Kabul and drove them away from the city did the siege end.

In 2012 everyone who worked in Maiwand knew its history. The old British fort stood next to our base, adjacent to Maiwand's main market. We walked past it most days, uncomfortably aware that British troops were currently trying to stave off massive attacks by the Taliban only sixty miles west, in Helmand; history was repeating itself. This history would make it difficult for the Afghans to publicly root for the British, who were our very visible allies. Luckily most Afghans viewed the current insurgency as coming from Pakistan, which put the Afghans on our side against a different set of invaders.

We assumed the Afghans saw us as the good guys, but daily issues that cropped up made the situation not so clear cut. I arrived in April 2012. Every Monday I attended a security meeting, or *shura*, at the district police station. At one of these security shuras I saw how the Afghans stuck together and regarded outsiders with suspicion.

The office of the police chief was comfortable. A television that captured twenty channels hung near a window, the floor was covered with red carpets, and couches lined the walls. For the security shura a dozen folding chairs had been brought in. U.S. and Afghan soldiers and police and a few civilians filled the seats. In true Afghan tradition the most important persons, including the district governor, the American lieutenant colonel in command of the U.S. battalion in Maiwand, and the National Directorate of Security (NDS) chief, who ran the district security service, all sat beside the police chief. Lesser ranks and other Afghans filled in the open spaces.

Officers gave routine updates involving attacks, dispositions, and plans. What most interested the Afghans was the arrest of three men several days earlier. Several elders from the village of the suspects entered the room and said they wanted the men returned. The trio had been arrested after an IED went off nearby. The suspects were brought in—two older men and one lad in his late teens who was the son of one of the men. An elder declared the men were innocent.

District Governor Salih Mohammad replied, "We want to release the detainees. We are all Afghan. But if one of them has any relations with the enemy, I want him arrested."

The NDS man chimed in, "We need to have family guarantees that they will not do it again."

One of the elders insisted the men had done nothing. "If you had no evidence, why did you arrest them?" he asked.

The police chief, a large man with a heavy black beard and a deep voice, asked the elders, "Will you guarantee these men? And will you bring them back if we need them?"

One of the elders quickly agreed.

Another elder told the chief of police, "They were two kilometers away from the IED. The U.S. arrested them and said it was close to their house."

The NDS chief conceded that the men might be innocent. "We have no information on these three. We will release two and seek more information. We can ask for information at the Wednesday shura and decide then." Every Wednesday many village elders attended a general shura at the DG's office. "We'll release the two of them and keep the small guy," he concluded.

DG Salih Mohammad agreed, summing up for everyone. "Today is Monday. ISAF arrested them near Loy Karez," he said, referring to a village a few miles south of the district center. "ISAF did not know, so they brought them to us. We got some information that they are good. We will release the two guys. Two men from the bazaar are guaranteeing them."

The American lieutenant colonel kept quiet, reluctant to justify the arrest.

The DG turned to the detainees. "We brought you here and you are good guys, so sorry for that. We are all families. We are all Muslims. We have to help the young guy if I can get information about him. On Wednesday we will release the young guy. Until then he stays here."

The DG then gave the men a piece of paper with his stamp on it to show they'd been released.

Security in Maiwand was poor, and people were arrested all the time. Only a few villages were considered safe. From the district center a government official could work in an area two or three kilometers from east to west, plus a kilometer to the north and a kilometer to the south. I'd visited Maiwand in 2010 as a field researcher, and the size of this bubble of security had barely changed.

Security depended on the villagers cooperating with the security forces. But the villagers outside the security bubble were in a tight spot, squeezed between the Americans and the government on one hand and the Taliban on the other. It was risky to inform on the Taliban, who controlled most of the villages, and information was spotty.

When villagers were arrested, their families could ask the village elders to vouch for the men and get them released. But the Taliban could just as easily pressure village elders to vouch for guilty men. The security forces hoped that if they asked enough questions they could separate the good from the bad. It was an art rather than a science, despite the high-tech gadgetry the Americans used, such as the chemical detector swab pads applied to suspects' hands to check for explosive residue.

If security across Maiwand was bad, the worst area included the southern fringe, in a region named Band-i Timor. A long and narrow patch of ground stretching the length of the district, Band-i Timor followed the Arghandab River as it flowed westward toward Helmand. On the northern side of the river a series of villages lay in what was known as the green zone, a lush and irrigated strip with many poppy fields. Across the river on the southern side the orange dunes of the Reg Desert towered high. Band-i Timor was a place where drug smugglers followed the riverbed toward Pakistan, while arms smugglers and Taliban fighters followed it back the other way, deeper into Afghanistan. In late 2011 the Americans positioned two small firebases seven miles apart in the green zone beside the river. Patrols leaving the bases inevitably ran into firefights if they ventured more than five hundred meters from the front gate.

One day in April the American and Afghan soldiers held the first-ever government-sponsored mass meeting in the village of Pain Kalay, about five hundred meters from one of the bases in the green zone. Thirty-five elders showed up, a surprisingly high turnout. They squatted down in a long line facing the soldiers. Most of the men were old, with dirty *shalwar kameez* clothing—long shirts and baggy trousers. Years of eking out a poor living under a hot sun were etched heavily in their faces.

Merely holding this gathering was a major breakthrough for the soldiers. Every villager was vulnerable to Taliban reprisals for attending and publicly speaking with the security forces. The Taliban would later visit many of them, demanding to know what they'd discussed.

The men listened as the Afghan and American soldiers offered assistance. One officer said they could start a few projects and patrol more often in the village to keep out the Taliban. They might even bring the district governor to visit.

"We can hand out some seed," offered the American officer. "After the harvest we will meet and decide what to do."

But the people dismissed most of these ideas. One man declared that the village didn't need any assistance. Another said they did need help, but it was too risky.

"We need a school, seed, and a mosque, but we do not have security. When we get security, then we will get everything that we need," he said.

Another elder, old and thin with a full white beard, replied that it was too soon to talk about this.

"Every elder from the village is here," he said. "We are all scared of the Taliban. This is the life for us. We will work with you when it is safe."

Another elder complained that it was impossible to work with the government. Whenever they went to the district center, the auxiliary police stopped and arrested them and demanded money to release them.

"If we go there, they will throw us in jail," one elder explained.

The soldiers persisted, eventually persuading the villagers to accept two projects: two culverts that would be installed near the base, where an irrigation canal had washed out the road. Although the villagers agreed reluctantly, they pushed the start of work months into the future, explaining they were too busy with the harvest to work on them now. The culverts were never built.

Over the next few days I went with the soldiers on patrols in the area to talk to other farmers. They reported similar problems. When they went to the main market beside the district center, the auxiliary police took the opportunity to shake them down. A man talked to us for twenty minutes outside his compound, from which poppy fields spread into the distance along the green zone. His kids played nearby.

"We cannot go to the district center," he said. "They will detain us and charge 5,000 or 6,000 Afghanis to let us go." Equivalent to $100, this sum was a month's wage.

His village elder complained to the district governor, but it made no difference. The next day another man two kilometers away reported a similar experience. He said that the last time someone drove to central Maiwand to buy oil in the bazaar this person was arrested by the auxiliary police for no reason. It had cost 120,000 Pakistani rupees, or about $1,250, to get him and his car back. Four elders who had gone to retrieve him had paid 30,000 rupees ($315) each, a massive sum in a farming district. The man said the auxiliary police who controlled a checkpoint closer to the green zone used to take money from travelers, but one night the local Afghan army unit put a stop to it.

Another man complained that the fighting had grown worse since the base had opened in Pain Kalay six months earlier.

"We are sick of the fighting. If the U.S. and Taliban keep shooting people, we will have to leave the area," the man said flatly.

The police continued to regard the people in Band-i Timor as real or potential enemies, even when a few days later the district governor and the police chief went to the other American base in the green zone and held a meeting with two local elders. This trip marked the first real effort to get the government into Band-i Timor, and another shura would follow there the next month.

In Maiwand the Americans had an uphill battle persuading anyone to work with them. With so few Americans spread out over a large area, the soldiers couldn't adequately cover every village. Most villages rarely, if ever, saw any security forces.

The Americans and the government were sworn to stamp out poppy production, but almost every farm grew poppy. Everyone feared for the safety of their crop. The government periodically sent soldiers with tractors into a few fields to knock down the poppy plants, but it was common practice in southern Afghanistan for the landowners to bribe corrupt government officials to bypass their land and move onto the next farm.

To some extent it was a tribal problem. Some tribes opposed the government. Worst of all, the Americans had a dismal history in Band-i Timor, and they had yet to live it down.

When I arrived, the local U.S. battalion was raiding villages in the desolate western sector of the district. Soldiers would drive out to villages and search them, hoping to draw fire from lurking insurgents. The vehicles often met up with soldiers inserted by helicopters. The trips sparked frequent firefights. The Taliban were very good fighters, yielding ground grudgingly. Because the Americans left immediately after the firefights and seldom returned, security never improved in the villages. The Taliban could always replace their losses. The U.S. effort didn't produce long-term benefits, even if the Taliban stopped using an area for a few weeks.

Sometimes the soldiers pushed these raids south into Band-i Timor. In 2012 the area was a hotbed of the insurgency in Maiwand. Ironically the people in Band-i Timor in late 2001 had strongly supported the Americans.

The story of what went wrong in Band-i Timor at the beginning of the war started in Kandahar City. It's documented by the American author Anand Gopal. When Gul Agha Sherzai became governor of the province, he didn't just help Nazak. He turned on his enemies, among them the tribal chiefs in Band-i Timor.

The tribal elders had by this time turned against the Taliban. In early December 2001 the tribes in Band-i Timor had come together and decided to back the Americans. They'd previously supported the Taliban, but the extremists' time was up. The Americans would bring schools, health care, and roads. Even tribes traditionally opposed to Sherzai's Barakzai tribe signed up to support the government. It wasn't just in Kandahar City, where men cheered and shaved their beards, that people celebrated the end of the old regime.

The elders persuaded Taliban bigwigs to turn themselves in and even delivered guns taken from the Taliban to Sherzai's office. Sherzai saw Band-i Timor as a place where he could squeeze money out of tribal elders for whom he had little regard and could strengthen his control of the rackets that enriched him.

To do this he turned to the Americans. In December 2001, as the Taliban fled Kandahar City, many of them headed over the border to Pakistan.

Many others simply stopped fighting and returned home. The Taliban was a spent force, and it would be two years before Mullah Omar even thought about resurrecting his troops.

But the Americans had an ongoing mission: to catch and kill Taliban, who might lead the way to al Qaeda. Sherzai pointed the Americans at business competitors, tribal rivals, and those from whom he wished to extort money. Families would pay hundreds or even thousands of dollars to have their relatives released.

One night U.S. Special Forces arrived in Band-i Timor and stormed a compound owned by one of the top tribal elders, Haji Burget Khan. They detained fifty-five men in a village and took them to KAF. Several men were shot in the raid, including Haji Burget Khan, who died in custody. Those who survived were all later released. Sherzai's war had come to Band-i Timor, and it continued for months. Elders who had phoned Taliban leaders to persuade them to lay down their arms were accused of being Taliban supporters themselves.

As the arrests and raids continued, people in Band-i Timor turned against the Americans and the government. Influential elders who were pro-American were scooped up. People drifted. Over time the old smuggling routes prospered, the Taliban came back, and Band-i Timor supported them as they had before 9/11.[1]

In 2012 Maiwand suffered because Band-i Timor had suffered ten years earlier. It was tragic. The soldiers suffered alongside the villagers as they patrolled Band-i Timor and tried to win back what had been lost.

As 2012 slipped by, security in parts of Band-i Timor improved. Early one morning in November 2012 the Americans climbed into their Stryker armored fighting vehicles at the easternmost base in the green zone. They slowly pushed toward the other base, at Pain Kalay, setting up checkpoints guarded by Afghan soldiers as they progressed. They worked their way through several Taliban strongholds and put down a gravel road as they inched forward. Roads would give the soldiers access to the newly opened areas and allow the villagers to drive to markets more easily.

For two weeks they pushed along the road. Most nights they slept in abandoned mud compounds or in their trucks. The next day they rose early and pushed on. They uncovered caches of IEDs in undergrowth, in orchards, and along the riverbed. In one of the villages the Taliban had recently convened its district court, trying cases brought by the local people.

Progress eventually ground to a halt halfway to Pain Kalay as the soldiers finished a final section of gravel road. The Afghan security forces ran out of men. Without more they could not build and guard additional checkpoints.

A few days later another gravel road was built from the district center north fifteen kilometers to the village of De Maiwand, where U.S. and Afghan soldiers maintained a precarious hold on an outpost that anchored security for the entire northern sector of the district. The soldiers had found more than fifty IEDs in the south, and they had found another eighty while driving north. Four security vehicles were blown up along the way, but two weeks after the operation began the road to the village of De Maiwand was declared open after being closed for years. Seven new checkpoints were hastily built along the road.

The government was revitalized. In the course of a month the Taliban had lost control of about a third of the district. Of the five important population centers in the district the security forces now controlled three.

Soon after the northern road opened, Afghan and American soldiers from the base at De Maiwand called the village elders together. They sat in front of a large concrete mosque with domed shapes cut below the eaves of the roof. The soldiers told the elders that life was improving, and it was time to support the government.

One elder answered warily, "We want peace and security in the village." His beard was very white against his wide, dark brown face. "You make promises, but you never do anything."

The soldiers replied that the elders had asked for the road to be opened and now it was. But this did not satisfy them. Every day the Taliban shot at the checkpoints along the road within a mile or two of the village, reminding the villagers that they remained close by.

Worse, the Taliban had banned the villagers from using the newly built road and threatened to kill them if they did. Now local people had to use an older, bumpier road, and the travel time to the bazaar in central Maiwand had jumped from half an hour to an hour. One man complained the operation was making life worse, not better.

Yet the villagers made a partial opening to the soldiers. They wanted projects and were willing to work with the government to get them. Drinking water was a particular problem.

The elder with the white beard said, "We want many more wells, like hand-pump wells. If we got five more wells that would be good."

The soldiers replied that the elders needed to go to the weekly shura and ask the district governor directly.

That was impossible, the elders insisted. The Taliban would surely hear of it and kill them the same day. They said the district governor had come a few weeks earlier and made promises and left. They received nothing. So what was the point?

Time proved the elders right to stay on the fence. The Taliban remained strong in the area and fighting raged on for years.

The U.S. Army closed its main base in Maiwand but left its soldiers guarding the scattered outposts. The drawdown continued. Soon only a mix of police and auxiliary police held the district, with periodic help from Afghan soldiers operating out of the neighboring district of Zhari. The Maiwand DST closed in mid-2013. By the end of 2014 all of the Americans were gone. That December an elder in Maiwand complained about the intense fighting.

"The security situation is really bad, with constant fighting between drug smugglers, the Taliban, and security forces," said Malik Din Mohammad, one of the primary elders in charge of Pain Kalay in Band-i Timor. "The government is not powerful enough to contain the situation," he told a reporter.[2]

The agony of Band-i Timor would continue well into 2015. As the year began, heavy fighting was reported as the government battled to regain control of the area.[3]

In Maiwand the close cooperation among the civil government, the villagers, and the security forces never really got off the ground. Unlike in Dand the security situation failed to reach escape velocity. Without security the civil government couldn't use its persuasive power to get the villagers to work on its side. When I arrived, the Americans were poised to leave, with about a year remaining. With time about to run out, we tried to salvage something from our long-running effort there.

# 21

## Drugs, Not Jobs

As of March 31, 2015, the United States has provided $8.4 billion for counternarcotics (CN) efforts in Afghanistan since 2002.—**Office of the Special Inspector General for Afghanistan Reconstruction**, *Quarterly Report to the United States Congress*, 2015

Many ordinary Kandaharis believe the government's counter-narcotics programs are also corrupt. Villagers do not believe the government genuinely wants to curb the opium industry, but instead wants to damage the farmers and dealers who do not serve the government's own cartel. This impression breeds resentment; when police are dispatched to insurgent-controlled districts to cut down poppy fields, their actions are seen as hurting the poor, weak, and tribally disenfranchised. As a result, such actions often result in violence. —***Kandahar Province Handbook***, 2008

Every Wednesday morning District Governor Salih Mohammad walked across the district center compound to his office building and met with the elders assembled in his conference room. On alternate weeks they discussed different subjects, so some village elders only came every other week. On some days a dozen would show up, and on other days thirty-five would come. They talked about projects, or about security, or about the problems of the villages. In the fall of 2012 the DG spoke often about poppy.

In a country that is the world's number-one producer of opium poppy, particularly in the southern tier of the country, Maiwand District was notorious. Poppy fields lined both sides of the main river channel coming from the mountains to the north. Over the previous ten years the poppy problem had grown worse, not better. Eventually Afghanistan was producing 90 percent of the world's poppy crop. The resulting oversupply drove down heroin prices in America, where drug use skyrocketed.[1]

Because poppy needs relatively little water to grow compared to wheat and vegetables, Kandahar's ten-year drought had pushed more farmers into planting it. Security had been so bad for so long, the Taliban also pushed farmers into growing poppy; the insurgents taxed the trade and relied on it for perhaps 40 percent of their funding.[2] To make money many landowners imported sharecroppers into the central valley of Maiwand to grow poppy under contract. It was cultivated almost everywhere, including Band-i Timor. The problem expanded every year, feeding a vicious cycle. The more poppy fields bloomed, the more water the farmers pumped from the aquifer below the desert floor. The more the traditional wells and water sources dried up, the poorer the people became. So they grew more poppy to compensate, and the cycle began again.

In his weekly meetings the DG consistently called upon the elders to stop poppy production. Fall was the time farmers began to plant the crops that would appear the following spring. By April the bright flowers would be replaced by the ugly, bulbous seed pods from which farmers would extract the milky opium fluid. The DG stepped up his pressure on the elders. In late November 2012 he told them that there was an alternative to growing poppy.

"The U.S. made a commitment that no one can grow opium," he told about twenty elders one day in November. "We have wheat and fertilizer. I want farmers to use wheat. Bring letters from farmers to the people's shura and then they can get it."

For years the U.S. government had tried to shift farmers away from poppy and into other crops. The Americans had tried small-scale projects to grow saffron, cumin, and other crops. But those scattershot ideas had failed to solve the problem. They also offered the stick; every year the Americans paid hundreds of millions of dollars to knock down the poppy plants before they could be harvested. In 2013 the government in Maiwand planned to knock down a thousand acres of poppy. In 2011 the former chief of police and the district governor had charged farmers a fee to keep them off the list of fields targeted. Now the old police chief had left, so that scam was unlikely to reappear. But piecemeal eradication efforts failed to halt the scourge.

It wasn't just Maiwand; the counternarcotic effort was failing nationwide. Farmers across Afghanistan cultivated 131,000 hectares of poppy in 2011, even more in 2012, and in 2013 they grew 209,000 hectares.[3] Almost 3,000 hectares grew in Maiwand alone.

Given a general lack of seriousness about stopping the poppy, we knew nothing would change in Maiwand. We received multiple reports that the district chief of police accepted bribes when his men intercepted smugglers in the southern half of the district, though the U.S. soldiers didn't think the allegations were fully proven. Assertions about corrupt Afghan officials were nothing new; even Hamid Karzai was accused at one time.[4] In Kandahar Province, though, the allegations were very often true. The Americans regarded the Maiwand police chief as an effective leader and were loath to lose him.

At the DST we tried to persuade the staff at KAF to lay out an alternate crop that might work for us. They refused. Cotton was not viable, they said. Even though Helmand, fifty miles to the west, had a thriving cotton industry in the 1960s, attempts by USAID to revive it had faltered badly. Saffron was apparently too fragile, of inferior quality for world markets, and of too small a scale. Cumin, too. Beyond that there were no options. Instead headquarters offered subsidized seed wheat and fertilizer, which had also been sent to Maiwand the previous spring. But the basic economics of growing wheat in a drought zone made no sense to the farmers. They would grow it to eat but not to sell, because the cost of running the irrigation pumps was more money than they could get by selling the wheat. Nor would these commodity distributions reach most farmers in such a large district. Distributing subsidized seed and fertilizer was a Band-Aid approach that appeared to solve a problem but in reality masked it, unaddressed, for years.

As time went on the district fell into a listless state. The farmers barely made ends meet, the water supply continued to shrink, and no one could think of a solution. Some of the elders and soldiers said darkly that the only long-term solution would be to completely clear out the population of the district.

The government couldn't offer answers to the farmers because it lacked answers. We saw the malaise on our patrols.

One day we approached a group of farmers seated outside a mosque in a village a kilometer south of the district center. The police had just shooed the men out of the mosque so our patrol could speak with them. Prayers were finished, so the men were in an agreeable mood as they sat in the dust along the wall surrounding the mosque. The men opened tins of low-grade hashish and put the green powder in their mouths as they talked. Some sat in the shade of the wall and others sat in the sun, but no one cared about the glare. They were weather-beaten from decades in the harsh sun, their eyes bright beneath the mahogany of their skin.

"The government gives us nothing," one man grumbled good-naturedly.

"It's been twenty years!" exclaimed another with a laugh.

Sure, they conceded, the government provided polio shots this year to their kids, who also went to the single official school open in the district, a thousand meters away. But they received no help with water or seeds or new crops.

"It's not just the water that's the problem. There are no crops that will work anyway," an elder explained, absentmindedly drawing circles in the dust with a stick. The economics of farming simply didn't add up.

I had heard similar opinions in 2010, when I visited the district as a field researcher for the U.S. Army. Back then we had walked the fields south of the district center on a bright, sunny day in February, the poppy leaves sprouting about four inches out of the ground. In the fields farmers hunched over their poppy plants, weeding. In spots the ground was damp from being irrigated the day before. In field after field men tended the crops. We stopped to talk to them.

One farmer explained that every day he watered his fields he used thirty liters of fuel. Each liter cost at least a dollar, which he bought on credit.

"At the end of the year we have to pay the shopkeeper," he told me. "But we still owe at the end of the year." He said he still owed his shopkeeper $2,000, because when he sold the poppy the previous year it hadn't earned him enough money to pay all of his debts.

Another farmer a few fields away agreed.

"At the end of the year we still owe," he complained. He said farmers could hold off selling the poppy resin until they could get a good price from buyers who came to the village, but it still wasn't enough.

"So we also work at the bazaar," he said.

The problem was intractable because there were so few options. The regular economy was overwhelmingly rural. The bazaar near the district center was a thriving hub, with hundreds of shops that serviced the district and the traffic on Highway 1. The roadway, which was part of the national ring road that connected Kandahar to Herat in the west, passed between the market stalls and was a shopkeeper's dream. But most people didn't work in the bazaar. They worked in the fields.

The national government was having almost no effect. By the end of December 2012 the province had spent half of all its development money for the ministries, about $20 million, and not a single project had reached Maiwand. Nor had any projects gone to the rural districts in Kandahar Province, according to the people at KAF. The ministries in Kabul didn't trust the provincial staff, so Kabul-based staff spent the money, and they funded projects near Kandahar City. The system had almost completely seized up, both isolating the villagers from the government and reducing their chances of finding employment by working on the projects.

Worse, we discovered that a major Afghan government program to bring projects into the districts, the National Solidarity Program (NSP), was a hotbed of corruption in Maiwand. The program, designed to push projects into the villages, had been functioning for years. The villagers would elect a council, which work with the NSP officials in Kandahar City and with the district development official to get projects it nominated.

Unfortunately in the few villages in Maiwand where the program existed the village councils were controlled by a small number of corrupt men who colluded with the NSP officials in Kandahar City and the district development official to steal the money. They simply filed phony plans for projects and pocketed the money sent from the province to pay for work that was never done. The money was then split among all of the officials. The corrupt village council members closed off membership from anyone not in on the scheme. The scam had been going on for so long the villagers forgot a council even existed.

We discovered the scheme by obtaining the NSP list of projects from the Kandahar Provincial Reconstruction Team, visiting the villages, and asking the local people about the projects on the list. They knew nothing about any projects. DG Salih Mohammad was furious when he heard about this, and we spent five months trying to track down the responsible officials. By March of 2013 the DST was closed, with only occasional visits by USAID officials based in a neighboring district. We ran out of time to bring the offenders to justice.

The last option to boost employment was to rely upon the Americans. USAID instituted a major project to build sidewalks in the bazaar and beautify the place, and almost two hundred men worked on the project. We tried to put in a road-graveling project to the village of Loy Karez, a few kilometers south of the district center. But again the Americans could do little to affect most of the villages. USAID contractors would not operate farther than three kilometers from the district center. The villagers in the district were largely left to their own devices. Gold-plating the area around the district center was not the answer, and the larger problem remained.

By the spring of 2013 we'd run out of time. If we were lucky, one last USAID agricultural program might show up in late 2013. By then the DST would be closed. One of our last initiatives was to distribute chickens to women who lived near the district center. Pushed hard by KAF, the military, and my DST teammate, this plan gave women forty chickens each, along with some feed to keep the birds alive for a month. Run by an NGO, the project cost more than $30,000. This was the chicken-farming model that had failed in Dand, yet here it was again. There were too few chickens to make a viable business. Half the chickens were almost certainly dead within the first week. I tried to find out what happened to them, but, like so many other projects, few traces remained. Several women told us after a few days that the chickens were mostly alive. We could not contact the other women, because the NGO neglected to take their husbands' phone numbers so we could call and check. The entire enterprise was a farce.

Then we received word in February that the DST would close the following month. Over the previous year we'd managed to set up a system that could continue into the future. There was a fully functional district development assembly of elders, who served as a point of contact for village elders who wished to request improvements for their villages. The elders on the assembly could select projects, handle the oversight of the contractors, and provide reports on finished work. But now the Afghans were aghast that the DST would close, and they appealed the decision to KAF, because they saw their only funds going with it. They were right.

When we left, nothing replaced us. As in Dand we had built the system with the expectation that the official budget system would kick in and there would be projects flowing from the province down to the districts. In the spring of 2011 KAF informed us all of this would happen in the fall of 2011. In the fall of 2011 we were told it would happen in 2012. In 2012 we were told it would happen in 2013. The passage of time showed these assurances to be the triumph of hope over reality.

In 2015 the situation was sufficiently bad that the central government authorized the provincial ministries to receive 40 percent of their development budget directly, as a block grant, without the need to check with Kabul first for spending decisions. In the first five months of that year the national ministries had managed to spend only 17 percent of the budget for projects. The promise of block grants seemed like a single bright spark in a dark constellation of unfulfilled expectations. The minds of the central mandarins were probably focused on budget problems after two thousand staff members in the president's office were not paid for six months.[5]

Left to fend for themselves, the Afghan farmers simply adapted as best they could and carried on. The pumps watered the poppy, and life continued as it had for decades. There was nothing at this point the district government could do to stop poppy cultivation. It was impossible to hold back the inexorable tide of green, white, and pink that filled the desert plain as far as the eye could see.

As the DST closed, my final day in Maiwand was March 11, 2013. A small contingent of soldiers from the battalion remained at the base. Within months it would be turned over to a U.S. Special Forces team.

The rotors of the gray helicopter sent to pick me up were audible a minute before it appeared as a dot against a brilliant blue sky. It flew alongside the base and swooped onto the landing pad, blowing dust against the gray HESCO walls. My DST teammate would stay for another few days. I loaded up my bags and boxes, waved good-bye, and the chopper jerked into the air, nose down, passing over the bazaar as we turned for KAF and headed for home. After a week at KAF I was back in the United States. Within the next week, after stopping in DC to sign some paper-work and have a mission debrief that lasted twenty minutes, I was home in Massachusetts.

In Maiwand and Dand we had tried to make changes that would sustain the Afghans for years to come. In Maiwand I felt happy that we had changed the way the district government worked so that villagers were involved and the district had a functioning government. Again, as when I left Dand, I had deep forebodings about the future of the district. Preserving the gains made at our low level in a rural district depended on forces at the upper levels, beyond our power to change or even influence. If the upper levels didn't work, the lower ones wouldn't last.

I suspected the U.S. civilian effort to help Afghanistan had been set on autopilot a long time before my service there. Whether the system that remained after its ministrations worked or not would hardly matter to the American bureaucrats now leaving the country and heading home. We were drawing down, and the civilian war in the countryside was all but over.

# Epilogue

Throughout this extensive area he was able, as British Representative, to settle outstanding quarrels, allay animosities, and make tribal warfare cease—winning, at the same time, the affection of the Khan and chiefs and tribesmen, over whom he exercised commanding influence till his death.—**Thomas Henry Thornton**, description in *Colonel Sir Robert Sandeman*, 1895

The Taliban now controls more territory than at any time since 2001.
—**Office of the Special Inspector General for Afghanistan Reconstruction**, *Quarterly Report to the United States Congress*, 2016

The British successfully ruled the tribes along the edge of the North-West Frontier Province and Baluchistan for a hundred years, from 1848 to 1947. The regions of direct rule were known as the Settled Areas. Just beyond, in the true border regions where the British had influence but no direct control, lay the so-called tribal areas, which even today are outside the full control of the Pakistani government and hotbeds of extremism. Four British officers who spent their lives on the frontier stood head and shoulders above the rest: John Nicholson, James Abbott, John Jacob, and Robert Sandeman. Two Pakistani towns still retain the names of these officers, Abbottabad and Jacobabad, as testaments to the enduring influence of the men.

Each officer improved his area of the frontier and altered its very nature. They settled disputes among the tribes and dispensed justice. They collected taxes and built roads and canals. They created a government that worked. To do this they relied upon the power of persuasion rather than the sword. Backed by small security forces, each one built a culture that rested on predictability and the rule of law, replacing feuds and isolation with prosperity and trade.

James Abbott quelled the Hazara areas north of Peshawar by mediating between rival clans. Robert Sandeman settled decades of strife between the khan of Khelat and his subordinate chiefs in Baluchistan by negotiating a lasting compromise between them. Once John Jacob and John Nicholson had stamped out highway robbery, trade flourished and towns grew. Villagers were so impressed by Nicholson that they started a religion that took him as their god. He whipped the adherents for this offense against his own strong Christian belief.

In Afghanistan the central truism of counterinsurgency is that you cannot kill your way to victory. Despite years of killing, the official numbers on the Taliban battle rolls hardly changed at all: between twenty-five thousand and thirty thousand. Nor was killing the goal. Better security, paid for by the hard fighting that went with it, provided a breathing space into which the government could step and become effective. That in turn improved security in a virtuous circle.

This dynamic worked both ways, and without an effective Afghan government our efforts were doomed to fail. People would turn away from the authorities and security would steadily erode, making government even less a part of people's lives.

From the perspective of the average Afghan, the occupation since 2001 has failed. In some respects the average person's life is better. There are schools in some areas, the ring road is drivable, and medical clinics operate in almost all districts.

Each of these achievements has its dark side. Almost half of children receive no education at all. Schools are typically open for only three hours a day. Thousands of ghost teachers on the books do not teach, wasting millions of dollars. Those who do teach give lessons at a level that will not afford students sufficient learning to boost their job prospects.[1]

Lacking maintenance, the ring road is deteriorating, with potholes seldom fixed and security incidents proliferating. Nor does the highway yet extend around the entire country. Clinics operate in districts, but many districts have a single clinic for seventy-five thousand or a hundred thousand residents, and the health-care system is fragile, even though it is farmed out and administered by NGOs (and thus is not quite a government achievement). That is the story of U.S. "wins" in Afghanistan.

The failures include a predatory justice system of the police and judiciary, the nonperforming system of local and provincial governments that fail to affect the lives of rural people in a meaningful way, and a security situation that deteriorates with each passing year, with rising numbers of attacks and civilian casualties and more territory lost to insurgents.[2] The economy stagnates, with a lack of real trade access to India and other partners, which pushes the unemployment rate to levels Americans would consider another Great Depression.[3]

Despite these problems, the people have no great love of the Taliban, which they perceive to be a creature of Pakistan and a cruel movement bent on tearing their country apart. People are suffering with little hope for the future. How did this happen after $1 trillion in assistance?

In many respects we were behind the eight ball from the very beginning. When the Karzai government took over in 2002, aid trickled down sporadically to the districts, affecting too few villages. Instead of seeing an improvement in their daily lives people saw lawless police and corrupt officials running roughshod over them, their elders, and their future. This legacy effectively doubled the task the Americans faced, because years of ineffective governance and high-handed official brigandage steadily eroded public support. By 2009 a good government that provided security and responsive civilian officials was the best, and possibly only, way out of what had steadily become a quagmire of our own creation.

This is what General Stanley McChrystal reported to the president. In his words we had "an urgent need for a significant change to our strategy" that would "improve the effectiveness of the Afghan National Security Forces and elevate the importance of governance."[4]

A government that ruled effectively could allow the U.S. forces to exit with honor, while an ineffective one would doom the country to more war and a return to chaos. Nothing in the character of the Afghan people predetermined the outcome of this struggle. The future hinged on our performance working with the Afghans to create a government that functioned.

For years the United States made all of the right noises. Security patrols were nominally "Afghan-led," when even a casual observer could clearly see they were not. Trying to get a few Afghan police patrolmen or soldiers to accompany Americans as they walked through a few villages could be comical. Over time this situation improved, especially with the Afghan army. But the sham persisted for more than a decade.

But the United States failed to make an equivalent effort on the civil side. There, too, we made the right noises. We spent hundreds of millions of dollars in the districts and made it appear that the Afghans handled the money and decided which projects went to which village. In reality we offered them a narrow palette of projects from insufficiently flexible programs designed in Washington. We controlled the money. Starved of responsibility, resources, and often of any choice in the matter, Afghan local government at the district level existed on handouts from the Americans. When we left and U.S. money dried up, the system already rotten from the inside withered to a husk. Because security went hand in hand with projects, that too faltered. In September 2015 the Taliban captured its first city, Kunduz, and held parts of it for two weeks.

We could have pulled out all the stops to institute a vibrant system of local government that could support itself and function at an acceptable level. Whether doing so meant sending small block grants to the districts (as our federal government sends block grants to U.S. counties and states, and states send block grants to cities and towns), nothing in our civilian effort ensured the lowest level of government in the districts did not fall apart once the Americans left. Instead we instituted half-baked ideas such as the District Delivery Program, which delivered items to the district center if the Afghan staff went through sixteen different steps, including getting competing bids from three different vendors for each item. Expectations were out of sync with reality. Advice from the embassy regarding DDP concluded, "If the DST doesn't engage in this it is NOT going to work"—as if the DST could force the Afghans to follow rules that would be unworkable anywhere else.[5]

A basic problem: many, if not most, districts possessed too few resources to ever pull themselves up to an acceptable level of operation. Unlike Dand but similar to Maiwand (or worse), the districts lacked the security forces and the money to do much more than hunker down behind the walls of the district center and hope their periodic supply runs would arrive on time. In 2015 these runs often didn't arrive at all.

Far-flung district centers were being overrun by Taliban massing outside. This bunker mentality was seen by the embassy as proof that the Afghans were not capable of governing. But that analysis was self-fulfilling; no district governor could govern with no resources.

Our policy toward the districts stemmed from our rock-bottom expectations of them. It assumed most would fail if they did try to help the people and instead relied upon a bureaucratic, top-down official system that was clearly failing by 2011 and 2012. Under this policy it was helping the national, provincial, and city officials who counted. It didn't matter if the system worked badly in the districts or not at all. We never tried to alter our strategic course, despite the warnings that the districts would likely fail once we left, even though they were the only thing keeping the rural people on the side of the government.

One of the great tragedies of our intervention is how we deluded ourselves for so long that districts could survive after we left, with projects parceled out at a tiny rate from a palsied national system. As General Creighton Abrams warned when commanding in Vietnam, the graphs that showed progress took precedence over the reality, and we stopped asking ourselves if the important things were really getting done. Our military and financial might was obvious, so we thought we couldn't lose, when in the countryside we were weaker than we imagined. So it happened that even where we won, such as in Dand, we then began to lose when we left, because we failed to give the government the tools it needed to maintain a political bargain with its people for years to come.

\* \* \*

To understand the American mindset requires only that one stroll across KAF at night. To do so is to step into a science fiction movie. Dust hangs in the air, kicked up by thousands of vehicles constantly crisscrossing the vast base. Few streetlights exist, while the beams of headlights of cars bouncing along the roads jerk sharply and skitter through the dirty air.

A journey by foot is tortuous, with many dead ends and turnarounds. Shipping containers ringed with chicken wire and large concrete T-walls topped with razor wire form individual yards. For mile after mile the pedestrian dodges and weaves, cutting this way and that, trying to find paths between the thousands of self-contained compounds that carve up the base. The base is constantly being reconstructed; a pathway open yesterday is closed today. Thousands of massive concrete T-walls protect metal accommodation sheds and office blocks from rocket fire.

T-walls symbolize of the mighty U.S. effort here in Afghanistan. T-walls are poured in a factory near Kandahar City, loaded four or five to a truck, and delivered by the thousands to bases across the province. T-walls come in a variety of shapes and sizes, and the utilitarian concrete is often transformed by amateur artists taking a break from their day job. Units paint medieval knights, attack helicopters, rifles, and shields on them.

T-walls are throwaway items to Americans. Like guardrails on an American highway, you see them but they don't register. But they are emblematic of the American effort. In 2011 the average Afghan person's share of the national economy, or GDP per capita, was $1,000, according to the CIA. A single gaily painted T-wall cost $900. One of these throwaway items is worth almost as much as an Afghan person's work for an entire year.

On KAF, with its enormity and solidity, the prospect of actually losing seemed remote. On a firebase in a remote valley such as in Daechopan District in Zabul Province, on a hill once occupied by the Soviets, where thirty Americans and seventy Afghan soldiers and police constitute the sole authority over a district of forty thousand people, the prospect of losing is much more real, especially when the previous unit tells you the Taliban attacked for two days straight and the soldiers almost ran out of ammunition because choppers couldn't fly through bad weather to resupply them.

The American effort is massive. Most of the trillion dollars the United States has spent in Afghanistan paid for security—T-walls and bullets, along with pens, tents, and the salaries of U.S. soldiers, all serving to keep the Americans in the game. It costs between $500,000 and $1 million to keep a single American soldier in Afghanistan for one year.[6] In fiscal year 2011 the United States spent $118.6 billion in Afghanistan, mostly on its own forces.

With this massive capability and outlay, how could we lose? The prospect seemed inconceivable. Our instinct defied our own perceptions. As Ambassador Ronald Neumann told us in training at the Foreign Service

Institute in April 2011, every three-year plan that he'd seen had failed. Yet we always assumed the next one would succeed.

We could have altered course, but we didn't. We passed the buck. When Afghans complained about the system the United States helped to build, we told them it was their fault for building such a lousy system in the first place, as if we had no hand in it. Many Americans forgot that foreign advisors originally arrived in 2002 to help set up a national system. In the words of a British ambassador to Kabul, spoken only half in jest, the constitution was "designed by a Frenchman and imposed by an American."[7]

Foreign advisors promised the system would be bottom-up. A key advisor to the Afghan finance minister from mid-2002 onward was British national Clare Lockhart. She said the system they created was a good one that would restore the faith of the people in their government. "We designed national programs as the key instrument for fostering citizen trust in its capacity to govern," she later wrote.[8] The Afghan finance minister she advised, Ashraf Ghani, was elected president in 2014 and began trying to dismantle large parts of the faltering system he helped to create.

Already we see the Afghan government trying to reform itself. More anticorruption governors are being appointed. The broken budget system is being cast aside where it doesn't work, and new approaches are being tried, such as sending block grants to the provinces. What the Americans hesitated to do—wholesale reform of a system that didn't work—is being forced upon the Afghans, who cannot continue to settle for a nonfunctioning government if they hope to avoid oblivion. At its heart the national government is finally trying to empower the people at the lowest levels—something we failed to do all along because we lacked the awareness to admit it was both necessary and possible.

Afghans are a hardy, fierce, smart, and patriotic people. If they learned anything from the Americans, they learned cynicism. They learned that the powerful are rewarded with what they can grab and their enemies (Pakistan) are rewarded by their friends (the United States). There is no sign the Taliban will let up their attacks for years, until the government proves it can survive under pressure. But it must adapt to survive.

After the Afghans spent years preparing to take over a system that failed to work as soon as the switch was pulled, they must now and in the future rely on the resilience of their own people. This is the surest path to success. The Afghans are now adapting in order to stave off a determined enemy. We could blame the precarious nature of the current situation on the failings of the national government or the culture, but any reasonable reading of the record suggests that it is we outsiders, just as much as they, who should shoulder the blame for the current chaotic state of affairs in Afghanistan.

# NOTES

### Introduction

1. U.S. Agency for International Development, *U.S. Foreign Aid by Country: Afghanistan*.
2. World Bank and Islamic Republic of Afghanistan Ministry of Finance, *Transition in Afghanistan*, 18.
3. Shakeela Ibrahimkhail, "Afghan War Costs Country $9bn a Year," *TOLO News* (Afghanistan), October 19, 2015, http://www.tolonews.com/en /afghanistan/21960-afghan-war-costs-country-9bn-a-year.
4. Office of the Special Inspector General for Afghanistan Reconstruction, *Quarterly Report to the United States Congress*, January 30, 2012, 4.
5. Saleha Soadat, "Education Minister Says Predecessor Falsified Data on Active Schools," *TOLO News*, May 27, 2015, http://www.tolonews.com/en /afghanistan/19727-education-minister-says-predecessor-falsified-data-on -active-schools.
6. Obama, "Remarks by the President in Address to the Nation on the Way Forward in Afghanistan and Pakistan."
7. U.S. Agency for International Development, *Results of USAID's Spending*.

### 1. The Train-Up

1. Office of the Special Inspector General for Afghanistan Reconstruction, *U.S. Civilian Uplift in Afghanistan Is Progressing*, 13.

### 3. Settling In

1. Although officially a district sub-governor, Nazak was always referred to as the (district) governor or DG.
2. Office of the Special Inspector General for Afghanistan Reconstruction, *U.S. Civilian Uplift in Afghanistan Is Progressing*, 14.

### 4. Ousting the Taliban

1. "These issues may be related to food security, subsistence agriculture, agricultural production to address market demand, or income generation activi-

ties within the context of community demand." Agriteam Canada Consulting, *Afghanistan Villages Development Project Number A-033707, Mid-Term*, 1.

2. Gopal, *No Good Men among the Living*, 192–98.

3. Recovery and Development Consortium, University of York, *Strategic Conflict Assessment of Afghanistan, Final Report*, 2.

4. Recovery and Development Consortium, University of York, *Strategic Conflict Assessment of Afghanistan, Final Report*, 3.

5. McChrystal, Commander NATO International Security Assistance Force, Afghanistan, *Commander's Initial Assessment*, 1–2.

6. Grau, *Bear Went over the Mountain*, 84.

7. Liaison Office-Afghanistan (TLO), *District Assessment—Dand District, Kandahar Province*, 28.

### 5. Nazak's Grand Bargain

1. Eric Slater, "These Spies Called the Shots in Strikes against Taliban," *Los Angeles Times*, February 24, 2002.

2. Tomsen, *Wars of Afghanistan*, 531–35.

3. Tomsen, *Wars of Afghanistan*, 533.

4. Gopal, *Battle for Afghanistan*, 6, 9.

5. Farmer in the Baghtu Valley, interview by author, Shah Wali Khot District, Kandahar, February 12, 2010.

### 6. Priming the Economy

1. Richard W. Stevenson, "As U.S. Withdraws Troops, Fears That Afghan Aid Will Dry Up," *New York Times*, February 14, 2013.

2. James Petersen, "Was $73B in Aid to Afghanistan All for Naught?," *Bakersfield Californian*, January 14, 2012.

3. Norris, "Crucible."

4. Addleton, "Dust of Kandahar," 26.

5. Abdul Rashid, in discussion with author, Dand District Center, Kandahar, July 12, 2011.

6. Asia Foundation, *Afghanistan in 2011*, 25.

7. Ladbury and Cooperation for Peace and Unity (CPAU), *Testing Hypotheses on Radicalisation in Afghanistan*, 4–5, 29.

8. Office of the Special Inspector General for Afghanistan Reconstruction, *Quarterly Report to the United States Congress*, January 30, 2012, 3.

9. Office of the Special Inspector General for Afghanistan Reconstruction, *Quarterly Report to the United States Congress*, January 30, 2012, 15. ANSF refers to the Afghan National Security Forces.

### 7. Waiting to Work

1. U.S. Department of State, "Refining Our Governance Orientation in Light of Transition," 2–3.
2. U.S. Department of State, "Implementing a New Governance Orientation," 4.
3. U.S. Department of State, "Implementing a New Governance Orientation," 4.
4. Recovery and Development Consortium, University of York, *Strategic Conflict Assessment of Afghanistan, Final Report*, 47.
5. Dobbins, Jones, Crane, and DeGrasse, *Beginner's Guide to Nation-Building*, 73 (emphasis added).

### 8. Kick-Starting the Staff

1. World Bank and the Islamic Republic of Afghanistan Ministry of Finance, *Transition in Afghanistan*, 5. See also World Bank and the Islamic Republic of Afghanistan Ministry of Finance, *Executive Summary, Transition in Afghanistan*, 1.
2. World Bank, *Afghanistan Economic Update*, 9.
3. World Bank, *Afghanistan Economic Update*, 9.
4. World Bank, *Afghanistan Economic Update*, 8.
5. World Bank and the Islamic Republic of Afghanistan Ministry of Finance, *Transition in Afghanistan*, 13.
6. World Bank and the Islamic Republic of Afghanistan Ministry of Finance, *Transition in Afghanistan*, 13.
7. District Governor Hamdullah Nazak, in discussion with author, Dand District Center, Kandahar, July 4, 2011.

### 10. Security Holds

1. Gopal, *Battle for Afghanistan*, 36.
2. "Afghan Taliban Seize Humvees for Sneak Attacks and Propaganda," *Reuters*, September 22, 2015, accessed at http://news.yahoo.com/afghan-taliban -seize-humvees-sneak-attacks-propaganda-104212488.html.
3. Waldman, *Sun in the Sky*, 1.
4. Waldman, *Sun in the Sky*, 14.
5. McChrystal, *My Share of the Task*, 345.
6. Lawrence Bartlett, "Afghan Forces Deaths Outstrip NATO's 5–1: Officials," *Agence France-Press*, July 29, 2012, accessed at http://www.muscatdaily.com /Archive/World/Afghan-forces-deaths-outstrip-NATO-s-5-1-Officials-1lfb.

### 13. Still Starved of Money

1. World Bank and the Islamic Republic of Afghanistan Ministry of Finance, *Transition in Afghanistan*, 6–7.

2. U.S. Department of Defense, *Report on Progress toward Security and Stability in Afghanistan.*

3. Zabiullah Jahanmal, "Finance Ministry Irked at Under-Spending of Budget," *TOLO News*, July 16, 2015, http://www.tolonews.com/en/afghanistan/20488 -finance-ministry-irked-at-under-spending-of-budget.

4. "Provinces Being Authorised to Spend Budget," *Pajhwok News* (Kabul), May 6, 2015, http://www.pajhwok.com/en/2015/05/06/provinces-being -authorised-spend-budget.

5. Chandrasekaran, *Little America*, 183–84.

6. Barfield, *Afghanistan*, 164.

### 14. Corruption of Many Kinds

1. Lynsey Addario, "Assassination in Afghanistan Creates a Void," *New York Times*, July 12, 2011.

2. Joshua Partlow, "Afghan Central to U.S. Push in Kandahar Faced Allegations in Job with Contractor," *Washington Post*, May 26, 2010.

3. Asia Foundation, *Afghanistan in 2011*, 21.

4. United Nations Office on Drugs and Crime and Islamic Republic of Afghanistan High Office of Oversight and Anti-Corruption, *Corruption in Afghanistan*, 5.

5. Ladbury and Cooperation for Peace and Unity (CPAU), *Testing Hypotheses on Radicalisation in Afghanistan*, 180.

6. Office of the Special Inspector General for Afghanistan Reconstruction, *Quarterly Report to the United States Congress*, January 30, 2012, 17.

7. "Public See Corruption as a Major Problem: Survey," *TOLO News*, August 12, 2015, http://www.tolonews.com/afghanistan/public-see-corruption-major -problem-survey.

8. Bashir Ahmad Naadim, "Past Kandahar Rulers Only Served Powerful: Azizi," *Pajhwok News*, August 12, 2015, http://www.pajhwok.com/en/2015 /08/12/past-kandahar-rulers-only-served-powerful-azizi.

### 15. Holding Back the Taliban

1. Office of the Special Inspector General for Afghanistan Reconstruction, *SIGAR Alert Letter to the Secretary of Defense.*

2. Kevin Sieff, "For Afghan Troops, Donkeys Are the New Helicopters," *Washington Post*, November 9, 2012.

3. Office of the Special Inspector General for Afghanistan Reconstruction, *Quarterly Report to the United States Congress*, January 30, 2012, 19.

4. Miller, Hosenball, and Moreau, "Gang That Couldn't Shoot Straight." See also Hosenball, "Afghan Cops."

5. David Isenberg, "The Contractors That Couldn't Shoot Straight?," *Huffington Post*, April 18, 2010, accessed at http://www.cato.org/publications /commentary/contractors-couldnt-shoot-straight.

6. "Afghan Troops Doing Well but Still Need Coalition Support: Shoffner," *TOLO News*, August 14, 2015, http://www.tolonews.com/node/11013.

7. Davis, "Truth, Lies and Afghanistan."

8. Quoted in Dan De Luce, "Afghan Forces Will Be 'Good Enough' to Take Over: US," *Agence France-Press*, February 8, 2012, accessed at http://english /alarabiya.net/articles/2012/02/08/193469.html.

9. Soldier of the Iowa National Guard, interview by author, Khost Province, October 2007. See also "Afghan Police Delayed for Years," *Doug Grindle: Journalism Worldwide* (blog), October 7, 2007, http://www.douggrindle .blogspot.com/2007_10_07_archive.html.

10. District Governor Hamdullah Nazak, in discussion with author, Dand District Center, May 10, 2011.

11. Tahir Khan, "Over 30 'Pakistani Clerics' Expelled from Afghanistan," *Express Tribune* (Pakistan), October 10, 2012, http://tribune.com.pk/story /449394/over-30-pakistani-clerics-expelled-from-afghanistan/.

12. Geisler, *5-1 CAV Operations in Kandahar* (video).

### 17. Solutions Made in Washington

1. Mohammad Ibrahim Spesalai, "Afghan Raisin Producers Hope for Sweeter Future," *Institute for War and Peace Reporting*, December 2, 2014, https://iwpr.net/global-voices/afghan-raisin-producers-hope-sweeter -future.

2. Gyanendra Kumar Keshri, "Afghanistan Keen to Trade with India via Wagah-Attari Border," *The Nation* (Pakistan), July 2, 2012, http://nation .com.pk/national/02-Jul-2012/kabul-keen-to-trade-with-india-via-wagha -border.

### 18. Dand in the Balance

1. Agence France-Press, "Afghan Suicide Blast Kills 8," Australian Broadcasting Corporation, March 30, 2009, http://www.abc.net.au/news /2009-03-30/afghan-suicide-blast-kills-8/1635776.

2. Taimoor Shah and Rod Nordland, "Car Bomber Fails to Reach Afghan Governor, but Kills Children at Play," *New York Times*, August 2, 2010.

3. Bernard Smith, "Haji Hamdullah Nazak Defying Threats on Afghan Taliban Turf," *Al Jazeera*, November 12, 2012, accessed at https://www.youtube.com /watch?v=OobjTiKMwtI.

4. Tahir Khan, "Over 30 'Pakistani Clerics' Expelled from Afghanistan," *Express Tribune*, October 10, 2012, http://tribune.com.pk/story/449394/over -30-pakistani-clerics-expelled-from-afghanistan.

5. Communication to author, December 2013.

6. "Bomb Kills Police Chief in Afghanistan," *Al Jazeera*, November 4, 2012, http://www.aljazeera.com/news/asia/2012/11/201211382432216938.html.

### 20. Security Failing in Maiwand

1. Gopal, *No Good Men among the Living*, 101–17.

2. Ben Sheppard, "Conflicting Loyalties among Afghans at Mullah Omar's Mosque," *Agence Press-France*, December 19, 2014, accessed at http://news .yahoo.com/conflicting-loyalties-among-afghans-mullah-omars-mosque -104804351.html.

3. "Afghan Forces Capture Taliban Bastion in S. Afghanistan," *Xinhua News* (China), February 7, 2015, http://news.xinhuanet.com/english/2015-02/07 /c_133977643.htm.

### 21. Drugs, Not Jobs

1. Elizabeth Chuck, "As Heroin Use Grows in U.S., Poppy Crops Thrive in Afghanistan," *NBC News*, July 7, 2015, http://www.nbcnews.com/news/world /heroin-use-grows-u-s-poppy-crops-thrive-afghanistan-n388081.

2. Mirwais Khan and Lynne O'Donnell, "Afghanistan's Poppy Farmers Say New Seeds Will Boost Opium Output," Associated Press, May 5, 2015, accessed at http://www.huffingtonpost.com/2015/05/05/afghanistan-opium_n _7216756.html.

3. Office of the Special Inspector General for Afghanistan Reconstruction, *Quarterly Report to the United States Congress*, April 30, 2015, 117.

4. Anthony Boadle and Hamid Shalizi, "Ex U.S. Official: Afghan Leader Shields Drug Trade," *Reuters*, July 24, 2008, http://www.reuters.com /article/2008/07/24/us-afghanistan-drugs-IDUSN2444215920080724 #gcRddLFFCscw0TQE.97.

5. "Provinces Being Authorised to Spend Budget," *Pajhwok News*, May 6, 2015, http://www.pajhwok.com/en/2015/05/06/provinces-being-authorised -spend-budget. See also "Ministries Only Spent 17% Budget in 5 Months of Fiscal Year: MoF," *Ariana News* (Afghanistan), May 31, 2015, http:// ariananews.af/latest-news/ministries-only-spent-17-budget-in-5-months-of -fiscal-yearmof/; and Shakeela Ibrahimkhail, "Presidential Palace Employ- ees Have Gone Unpaid for Months," *TOLO News*, July 28, 2015, http://www

.tolonews.com/en/afghanistan/20646-presidential-palace-employees-have
-gone-unpaid-for-months.

### Epilogue

1. "UNICEF Finds 40% of Afghan Kids Out of School," *TOLO News*, January 12, 2016, http://www.tolonews.com/en/afghanistan/23263-unicef-finds-40 -of-afghan-kids-out-of-school. See also Saleha Soadat, "Education Minister Says Predecessor Falsified Data on Active Schools," *TOLO News*, May 27, 2015, http://www.tolonews.com/en/afghanistan/19727-education-minister -says-predecessor-falsified-data-on-active-schools.
2. Javed Hamim Kakar, "Taliban Scorn UN Report as a Propaganda Campaign," *Pajhwok News*, August 5, 2015, http://www.pajhwok.com/en/2015 /08/05/taliban-scorn-un-report-propaganda-campaign.
3. Zabiullah Zhanmal, "Unemployment Rate Spikes in Afghanistan," *TOLO News*, October 2, 2015, http://www.tolonews.com/en/afghanistan/21676 -unemployment-rate-spikes-in-afghanistan.
4. McChrystal, Commander NATO International Security Assistance Force, Afghanistan, *Commander's Initial Assessment*, 1-1.
5. Unclassified email from IPA/SNG, U.S. Embassy, Kabul, July 2011.
6. Larry Shaughnessy, "Cost of Keeping One Soldier in Afghanistan Is Rising," *CNN*, February 28, 2012, accessed at http://security.blogs.cnn.com/2012/02 /28/one-soldier-one-year-850000-and-rising/.
7. Sir Sherard Cowper-Coles quoted in UK House of Commons, *Oral Evidence Taken before the Foreign Affairs Committee regarding the UK's Foreign Policy Approach to Afghanistan and Pakistan*.
8. Lockhart and Ghani, *Fixing Failed States*, 205–6.

# BIBLIOGRAPHY

Addleton, Jonathan. "The Dust of Kandahar." *Foreign Service Journal* 92, no. 8 (October 2015): 25–31.

Agriteam Canada Consulting. *Afghanistan Villages Development Project Number A-033707 Mid-Term Report*. Calgary AB, November 2009. http://www.agriteam.ca/projects/profile/afghanistan-villages-development-project/.

Allen, George. *None So Blind*. Chicago: Ivan R. Dee, 2001.

Asia Foundation. *Afghanistan in 2011: A Survey of the Afghan People*. San Francisco, 2011.

Barfield, Thomas. *Afghanistan: A Cultural and Political History*. Princeton NJ: Princeton University Press, 2010.

Campbell, Sir George. *The Afghan Frontier*. London: Edward Stanford Publishers, 1879.

Chandrasekaran, Rajiv. *Little America: The War within the War for Afghanistan*. New York: Knopf, 2012.

Davis, Lt. Colonel Daniel L. "Truth, Lies and Afghanistan: How Military Leaders Have Let Us Down." *Armed Forces Journal*, February 2012. http://armedforcesjournal.com/truth-lies-and-afghanistan/.

Dobbins, James, Seth G. Jones, Keith Crane, and Beth Cole DeGrasse. *The Beginner's Guide to Nation-Building*. Santa Monica CA: RAND, 2007. http://www.rand.org/content/dam/rand/pubs/monographs/2007/RAND_MG557.pdf.

Dupree, Louis. *Afghanistan*. New York: Oxford University Press, 1997.

Elphinstone, Mountstuart. *An Account of the Kingdom of Caubul and Its Dependencies in Persia, Tartay, and India*. Volume 2. Rev. ed. London: Richard Bentley, 1842.

Forsberg, Carl. *The Taliban's Campaign for Kandahar*. Washington DC: Institute for the Study of War, December 2009. http://www.understandingwar.org/report/talibans-campaign-kandahar.

Frere, Sir Bartle. *Afghanistan and South Africa: Letters to the Rt. Hon. W. E. Gladstone*. 1881. 5th ed. Pretoria, South Africa: State Library, 1969.

Gall, Sandy. *The War against the Taliban*. London: Bloomsbury, 2013.

Geisler, Pfc. Andrew. *5-1 CAV Operations in Kandahar* (video). 1st Stryker Brigade Combat Team, 25th Infantry Division Public Affairs, February 4, 2012.

https://www.dvidshub.net/video/136650/5-1-cav-operations-kandahar#
.Vi6ANCuq2VA.

Gopal, Anand. *The Battle for Afghanistan: Militancy and Conflict in Kandahar*. Washington DC: New America Foundation, November 2010. https://
www.newamerica.org/international-security/policy-papers/the-battle-for
-afghanistan.

———. *No Good Men among the Living*. New York: Metropolitan Books, 2014.

Grau, Lester, ed. *The Bear Went over the Mountain*. Fort Leavenworth KS: U.S.
Army Foreign Military Studies Office, 2005.

Hosenball, Mark. "Afghan Cops: A $6 Billion Fiasco." *Newsweek*, March 18, 2010.
http://www.newsweek.com/afghan-cops-6-billion-fiasco-69333.

Intelligence Branch, Division of the Chief of Staff, Army Headquarters, India.
*Frontier and Overseas Expeditions from India*. Volume 1. Simla, India: Government Monotype Press, 1907. https://ia902608.us.archive.org/16/items
/frontieroverseas01indi/frontieroverseas01indi.pdf.

*Kandahar Province Handbook*. Arlington VA: IDS International, December 2008.

Kaplan, Fred. *The Insurgents*. New York: Simon & Schuster, 2013.

Kipling, Rudyard. "That Day." 1896. Accessed at PoemHunter.com, http://www
.poemhunter.com/poem/that-day/comments/.

Ladbury, Sarah, and Cooperation for Peace and Unity (CPAU). *Testing Hypotheses on Radicalisation in Afghanistan: Independent Report for the Department of International Development (DFID)*. Kabul: CPAU, August 14, 2009.
http://webcache.googleusercontent.com/search?q=cache:oDVl0PjClOcJ:
d.yimg.com/kq/groups/23852819/1968355965/name/Drivers%2520of
%252Radicalisation%2520in%2520Afghanistan%2520Sep%252009.pdf+
&cd=1&hl=en&ct=c1nk&gl=us.

Lawrence, Lt. General George. *Reminiscences: Forty Three Years in India*. 2nd ed.
London: John Murray, 1875.

Le Messurier, Augustus. *Kandahar in 1879: The Diary of Major Le Messurier*. London: W. H. Allen and Company, 1880.

Liaison Office–Afghanistan (TLO). *District Assessment—Dand District, Kandahar
Province*. Kandahar, October 2010.

Lockhart, Clare, and Ashraf Ghani. *Fixing Failed States*. New York: Oxford University Press, 2009.

Martin, Frank A. *Under the Absolute Amir*. London: Harper and Brothers, 1907.

McChrystal, General Stanley. *My Share of the Task: A Memoir*. New York: Portfolio Penguin, 2013.

———, Commander NATO International Security Assistance Force, Afghanistan.
*Commander's Initial Assessment*. U.S. Forces Afghanistan, Kabul, August

30, 2009. http://www.dod.mil/pubs/foi/Reading_Room/Joint_Staff/10-f
-0025_Initial_United_States_Forces-Afghanistan_USFOR-A_Assessment
_08-30-2009.pdf.

Miller, T. Christian, Mark Hosenball, and Ron Moreau. "The Gang That
Couldn't Shoot Straight." *Newsweek*, March 19, 2010.

Norris, John. "The Crucible: Iraq, Afghanistan and the Future of USAID." *World
Politics Review*, November 19, 2013.

Obama, Barack. "Remarks by the President in Address to the Nation on the Way
Forward in Afghanistan and Pakistan." Office of the Press Secretary, the
White House, December 1, 2009. https://www.whitehouse.gov/the-press
-office/remarks-president-address-nation-way-forward-afghanistan-and
-pakistan.

———. "Text of President Obama's Speech on Afghanistan." Office of the Press
Secretary, the White House, June 22, 2011. https://www.whitehouse.gov/the
-press-office/2011/06/22/remarks-president-way-forward-afghanistan.

Office of the Special Inspector General for Afghanistan Reconstruction. *Quarterly Report to the United States Congress*. Washington DC, January 30, 2012.
https://www.sigar.mil/pdf/quarterlyreports/2012-01-30qr.pdf.

———. *Quarterly Report to the United States Congress*. Washington DC, April 30,
2015. https://www.sigar.mil/pdf/quarterlyreports/2015-04-30qr.pdf.

———. *Quarterly Report to the United States Congress*. Washington DC, January 30,
2016. https://www.sigar.mil/pdf/quarterlyreports/2016-01-30qr.pdf.

———. *SIGAR Alert Letter to the Secretary of Defense*. Washington DC, September
16, 2015. https://www.sigar.mil/pdf/alerts/SIGAR-15-86-al.pdf.

———. *U.S. Civilian Uplift in Afghanistan Is Progressing But Some Key Issues Merit
Further Examination as Implementation Continues*. Washington DC, October
26, 2010.

Recovery and Development Consortium, University of York. *A Strategic Conflict Assessment of Afghanistan, Final Report*. York, England, November
2008. https://www.york.ac.uk/media/prdu/documents/publications/pub
.Afghanistan%20Conflict%20Assessment%20Nov2008.pdf.

Robertson, Charles Gray. *Kurum, Kabul and Kandahar*. Edinburgh: David Douglas, 1881.

Sorley, Lewis. *A Better War*. New York: Harcourt, 1999.

Thornton, Thomas Henry. *Colonel Sir Robert Sandeman: His Life and Work on
Our Indian Frontier*. London: John Murray, 1895.

Tomsen, Peter. *The Wars of Afghanistan: Messianic Terrorism, Tribal Conflicts, and
the Failures of Great Powers*. New York: Public Affairs, 2011.

UK House of Commons. *Oral Evidence Taken before the Foreign Affairs Committee regarding the UK's Foreign Policy Approach to Afghanistan and Pakistan.* November 9, 2010. http://www.publications.parliament.uk/pa/cm201011 /cmselect/cmfaff/514/10110901.htm and http://www.publications .parliament.uk/pa/cm201011/cmselect/cmfaff/514/10110902.htm.

United Nations Office on Drugs and Crime and Islamic Republic of Afghanistan High Office of Oversight and Anti-Corruption. *Corruption in Afghanistan: Recent Patterns and Trends.* Kabul, December 2012. http://reliefweb.int /report/afghanistan/corruption-afghanistan-recent-patterns-and-trends -summary-findings.

U.S. Agency for International Development. "Education in Afghanistan." Washington DC. Accessed November 29, 2016. https://www.usaid.gov /Afghanistan/education.

——. *Results of USAID's Spending.* Washington DC. Accessed November 29, 2016. https://results.usaid.gov/afghanistan#fy2011.

——. *U.S. Foreign Aid by Country: Afghanistan.* Washington DC. Accessed February 28, 2017. https://explorer.usaid.gov/cd/AFG?measure=Obligations& fiscal_year=2011.

U.S. Department of Defense. *Report on Progress toward Security and Stability in Afghanistan.* Washington DC, December 2012. http://www.defense.gov /Portals/1/Documents/pubs/1230_Report_final.pdf.

U.S. Department of State. "Implementing a New Governance Orientation." Unclassified cable, U.S. Embassy, Kabul, February 8, 2010.

——. "Refining Our Governance Orientation in Light of Transition: Strengthening Afghan Capacity to Spend Resources Effectively and Accountably through Existing Systems and Institutions, at Three Key Levels of Government." Unclassified cable, U.S. Embassy, Kabul, December 16, 2010.

U.S. Senate Committee on Foreign Relations. *Evaluating U.S. Foreign Assistance to Afghanistan: A Majority Staff Report Prepared for the Use of the Committee on Foreign Relations.* Washington DC, June 8, 2011. http://www.foreign.senate .gov/imo/media/doc/SPRT%20112-21.pdf.

Waldman, Matt. *The Sun in the Sky: The Relationship between Pakistan's ISI and Afghan Insurgents.* Cambridge MA: Carr Center for Human Rights Policy, Kennedy School of Government, Harvard University, June 2010. http:// sshukla.tripod.com/lse.pdf.

World Bank. *Afghanistan Economic Update.* Washington DC, October 2011. http://siteresources.worldbank.org/AFGHANISTANEXTN/Resources /305984-1297184305854/AFGEconUpdate2011.pdf.

World Bank and Islamic Republic of Afghanistan Ministry of Finance. *Executive Summary, Transition to Afghanistan: Looking beyond 2014.* Washington DC, November 21, 2011. http://siteresources.worldbank.org /AFGHANISTANEXTN/Resources/305984-1297184305854/AFTransition .pdf.

———. *Transition in Afghanistan: Looking beyond 2014.* Kabul, November 21, 2011. http://www.washingtonpost.com/wp-srv/world/documents/presentation -transition-in-afghanistan.html.

# INDEX

Illustrations are indexed by figure numbers.

ANP (Afghan National Police) (*cont.*)
in Dand District, 33, 100, 159, 183;
equipment of, 91; impact on security, 153–54; in Maiwand District,
203–4, 208; outposts of, *fig. 12*;
problems of, 149–53, 219; relation
with U.S. military, 147–49, 152–53;
size of, 98, 159; supply shortages,
149–51, 152; taking over main base,
122; and the Taliban, 33, 147–48,
153–54; women in, 89; in Zabul
Province, 21

ANSF (Afghan National Security
Forces): in Band-i Timor, 206–8;
logistics problems, 151–52; in Maiwand District, 208; size of, 98;
tribal loyalties among, 30; U.S.
strategy with, 219–20

Arghandab District, 21

*Armed Forces Journal*, 151

armored vehicles, *fig. 5*, 82, 90–91

army (Afghan). *See* ANA (Afghan
National Army)

Asadullah (cluster leader), 89

Asia Foundation, 49, 139

assassinations, 88–90

auxiliary police, 203–4

AVIPA USAID (farm aid program), 51,
158

Baghtu (village), 41–42

Band-i Timor (Maiwand District),
202–8, 210

Barakzai tribe, 37

Battle of Maiwand, 199–200

bees project, 48

Bellanday (village), *xxii*, 86–87, 148

*A Better War* (Sorley), 160

Blaha, Sonia, 102–6, 108, 117

block grants, 215, 220, 223

border police, 97

British Empire, 199–200, 217–18

Buckles, Patti, 163–64

budget (district): funding gaps, 56–57,
61–63, 138, 215; lack of training in,
133, 184; in Maiwand District, 194;
O&M funds, 61, 130–37; problems
with, 101; proposed system, 62,
108, 121, 134

budget (national): block grants from,
215; development funds, 74, 124–25,
197–98; funding gaps, 128, 137–38,
183; O&M funds, 125–28; problems
with, 7, 48, 62, 73–74, 125–28, 132–
33, 215; proposed system, 48, 62,
108, 121, 134; road maintenance,
115; system reforms, 223

budget (provincial): block grants, 215;
for DOWA, 105; O&M funds, 125–28,
130–37; problems with, 62, 125–28,
215; proposed system, 62, 134

Burrows, George, 199–200

Campbell, George, 17, 55

Carl (cat), 87

CERP (Commander's Emergency
Response Program), 157

CHAMP USAID (farm aid program),
51, 158

Checchi (consulting company),
165–66

chicken farm projects, *fig. 13*, 48–49,
161–64, 214

cluster system, 42

COIN (counterinsurgency), 65–66, 70,
147, 218

*Colonel Sir Robert Sandeman* (Thornton), 217

community health workers, xiii, xiv
COP Ainsworth, 92–93
COP Edgerton, 13–14; background of, 20; Canadian withdrawal from, 87; facilities at, 20, 85; image of, *fig. 7*; living conditions at, 19–20, 87; U.S. military at, 24–25
corruption: among government officials, 77–78, 121, 193, 211; in the ANP, 151, 152, 204; and the drug industry, 209; extent of, 86; and financial controls, 65–66; forms of, 143; under Gul Agha Sherzai, 29, 39–40, 206; illegal tolls, 140–41, 144–46; in Kandahar Province, 83; in Maiwand District, 193, 204, 211; and nepotism, 143–44; in the NSP, 213–14; officially sanctioned types of, 142–43; and the women's programs, 117–20
counterinsurgency (COIN), 65–66, 70, 147, 218
Cowper-Coles, Sherard, 55
crony capitalism, 142, 144

DABS (power company), 180
Dahla Dam, 170
Daman District (Kandahar Province), *xxi*, 158
Dand District: base closures in, 122–23; compared to Maiwand District, 192–93; conservatism of, 105; DST at, 13–14; importance of irrigation, 49–50; map of, *xxii*; pacification under DG Nazak, 34, 42; security in, 81–82, 85, 95–99, 157–59; Taliban activity in, 24–25, 88–91, 153–54, 159, 184–85; tribes in, 37; unofficial status of, 40, 178; U.S. objectives in, 24–25, 26. *See also* Dand District Center (DDC); government (district)
Dand District Center (DDC), 20–21, 27–28; activity at, 70–71, 123; Canadian political advisor to, 18–19; corruption problems, 76–78; DG Nazak's impact on, 82–83, 128–29; DOWA trailer at, 103–4, 107; DST's removal from, 183–84; electricity needs, 130–31, 136, 179–81; empowering staff of, 71–72, 74–76, 78; images of, *fig. 1*, *fig. 2*; inadequate resources for, 56–57, 60–65, 67, 129, 132, 184, 185; issuing ID papers, 192; normal routine at, 24, 58–59, 79–81, 84–85; personnel of, 21, 22–23, 56, 58–60, 79–80; security at, 89, 100; sending funding requests, 126; staff salaries, xiv, 22, 59, 63; women seeking assistance at, 100–101. *See also* budget (district); government (district)
Davis, Daniel, 141
DCOP (district chief of police): in Dand District, 27–28, 153, 155, 159, 184–85; in Maiwand District, 191, 200–201, 204, 211. *See also* ANP (Afghan National Police)
DDA (district development assembly), 196–97, 215. *See also* maliks (village elders)
DDC (Dand District Center). *See* Dand District Center (DDC)
DDP (District Delivery Program), 47–48, 63, 128, 178, 220
Deh Bagh (village), *xxii*, 27–28, 30, 33
De Maiwand (village), *fig. 17*, *fig. 19*, 207

Department of Defense (DOD, U.S.), 4

Department of Women's Affairs (DOWA), 102, 103–9, 116, 117–21

DFID (Department for International Development) (United Kingdom), 29

District Delivery Program (DDP), 47–48, 63, 128, 178, 220

district government. *See* government (district)

district governors (DGs): acronyms, 27; armored cars for, 90; and political advisors, 18–19; types of, 141–42; work habits of, 21. *See also* Nazak, Hamdullah

district support team (DST). *See* DST (district support team)

DOD (Department of Defense, U.S.), 4

DOWA (Department of Women's Affairs), 102, 103–9, 116, 117–21

drug industry, 97, 154–56, 202, 209–13

DST (district support team): in Dand District, 13–14, 178–79; interpreters for, 19; limitations of, 138; in Maiwand District, 190–91, 193, 194–97; relations with Afghan staff, 190–91, 194–97; removal from Dand District, 183–84; removal from Maiwand District, 208, 214–16; responsibilities of, 64. *See also* field program officers (USAID)

Dupree, Louis, 113, 169

Durand Treaty (1896), 97

Durrani, Ahmad Shah Abdali, 23, 37

Durrani tribe, 37–39

economy: DG Nazak's plans for, 52–54, 57–58; funding DG Nazak's plan for, 66–67; GDP per capita, xv, 222; impact of funding on, 56–58, 174–75; impact of roads on, 139–40; impact on security, 44, 53; inequalities, 50; Keith Pratt's plan for, 49–50; political impacts of, 174; projects aimed at boosting, 161–64

Edgerton, COP (combat outpost). *See* COP Edgerton

education: building repairs needed, 126–28; challenges in, xvi–xvii, 61–62; current state of, 218; in Dand District, 22; in DG Nazak's system, 40; in Maiwand District, 193–94; progress in, xv; supply shortages, 59, 86, 127; training in agricultural techniques, 172; vocational training programs, 48, 76, 104–9, 113–14, 121, 124, 195–96, 214

education ministry: on book shortages, 86; in Dand District, 22–23, 59, 76, 86, 126–28; in Kandahar Province, 126–28; in Maiwand District, 191; and O&M funds, 126–28

electricity, 53, 83, 130–31, 136, 179–81

Elphinstone, Mountstuart, 35

embassy (U.S.): attitudes toward projects, 168; attitude toward projects, 46; and the DDP, 178; declining resources of, 6–7; district funding policies of, 63–66; grants for, 174–75; in Kabul, 8; at KAF, 10–11; plans for national budget, 124–25; predeployment training, 5–6

embroidery program, 106–9, 116–18, 119–20, 124

farming. *See* agriculture

field program officers (USAID): empowering district staff, 74–76;

limitations of, 47; living conditions, 19–20, 85, 87; normal routine, 79–81, 84–85; on patrols, 91–95; predeployment training, 3–8; qualities needed by, xvii–xviii; responsibilities of, 7, 26, 45–46, 47, 64; and the RSSA, 166–68; traveling to Afghanistan, 8; visiting villages, 85–87, 92–95; weekly planning meeting, 68–69, 84. *See also* DST (district support team); USAID (U.S. Agency for International Development)

Forsberg, Carl, 9, 27

Frere, Sir Bartle, 3, 88

FSI (Foreign Service Institute), 5–6

fuel allowances, xiv, 47, 60–61

funding: amount of, xvii, 50–51, 116, 189; from Canadian military, 42, 82; corruption, 117–20; of counternarcotics efforts, 209; District Delivery Program, 47–48, 63, 128, 178, 220; empowering Afghan staff through, 26; extreme gaps in, 198, 215; impact on villages, 34, 41–42; inefficient distribution of, 73–74; by international donors, 65; measuring results of, 70; objectives of, xvii, 26, 189; reductions in, 43–44, 53, 56, 78, 138, 158, 174–75, 178; for security, 50–51; subcontracting process, 46–47; U.S. failures in, 220; from U.S. military, 24, 51–52, 69–70, 103, 126, 157–58; for women's programs, 103, 104, 117–20. *See also* projects (development programs)

Gall, Sandy, 45, 189

Ghani, Ashraf, 223

Ghilzai tribe, 38–39

Gopal, Anand, 205

government (district): corruption in, 142–46; impact on security, 218; inadequate resources for, 64–65, 220–21; measuring support for, 70–71; relations with provincial, 72–73, 120–21, 126–28, 131–38; staff salaries, xiv, 59, 61, 192; system failures, 198, 213, 216, 219, 221; Taliban targeting, 89; U.S. failures in, 220–21; U.S. objectives for, 46, 64–66. *See also* budget (district)

government (national): corruption in, 29, 142–46; programs for women, 102; public support of, 29, 219; staff salaries, 61; system failures, 72–74, 125, 198, 213, 216, 221, 223; system reforms, 223–24; technocrats in, 22; and tribal rivalries, 38–39; U.S. failures in, xvi–xvii, 6, 219–20; U.S. objectives for, 46, 64–66, 197–98. *See also* budget (national)

government (provincial): corruption in, 142–46; relations with districts, 72–73, 120–21, 126–28, 131–38; staff salaries, 61; system failures, 125, 198, 213, 216, 219, 221; Taliban targeting, 89; U.S. policies for funding, 64–66. *See also* budget (provincial)

grants, 132–33, 215, 223

Haviland, Andrew, 133–36, 164, 195

Hayatullah, Haji, 158

healthcare system, xvi–xvii; clinics in Dand District, 71–72, 124; clinics in Maiwand District, 194; community health workers, xiii, xiv; current state of, 218–19

meeting with maliks, 92, 98, 123, 154–56, 159; meeting with VIPs, 55–57, 81, 82–83; mullah strategy, 156–57, 181; official position of, 225n1; and O&M funds, 126–28; political skills of, 23, 193; and the poppy industry, 154–56; project system of, 40–42, 56, 66, 95, 96; removing the Taliban, 28, 31–34; resignation of, 177, 178, 181; security *shuras* held by, 95–96; Taliban's imprisonment of, 35–37; Taliban targeting, 34, 89–90, 177–78; vacation to Germany, 175–76; and the vo-ed school, 113–14; on wastefulness, 49; and women's programs, 100–101, 104–7, 116–18; and the youth shura, 115

nepotism, 143–44

Neumann, Ronald, 6, 222–23

NGOs (nongovernmental organizations): chicken-farming projects run by, 214; in Dand District, 175; expense of, 106, 120; in subcontracting process, 46–47; and women's programs, 104, 106, 108

Nicholson, John, 217–18

*None So Blind* (Allen), 147, 160

NSP (National Solidarity Program), 62, 213

Obama, Barack, xvii, 88

Omar, Mullah Mohammad, 36, 38–39, 206

O&M (operations and maintenance) funds, 61, 125–28, 130–37

opium industry, 97, 154–56, 202, 209–13

Pain Kalay (village), 202–3

Pakistan, 29, 97–98, 174, 200

Panjpai Durrani tribe, 38–39

Panjwai District: Canadian military's shift to, 87; map of, *xxi*; security in, 43, 81, 87, 91, 92, 97; U.S. military's shift to, 69, 122–23

Pashtunistan, 97

Payne, Brian: background of, 24; funding projects, 25, 52, 75, 76, 103, 105, 114, 124, 126, 158; patrols of, 91–92, 147–49; relationship with DG Nazak, 52, 57–58; at security *shuras*, 96; at weekly staff meetings, 69–70; withdrawal from Dand District, 24–25, 122–23, 154, 157–58

Petersen, James, 46

police. *See* ANP (Afghan National Police)

political advisors (ISAF), 17, 18–19

Popalzai tribe, 37

poppy farming, 97, 154–56, 202, 204, 209–13, 215

Pratt, Keith, 13, 17, 19, 26, 30, 44, 49, 50, 52, 129

processing plants, 52–53, 173

projects (development programs): Afghan control over, 107–8, 196–97; agricultural, *fig. 3*, 161–64, 171–75, 210, 211; boosting employment, 214; Canadian-funded, 28, 34, 48–49, 60, 71, 74–75, 82, 86, 162; and corruption, 213–14; costs of, 106, 113–14, 120; decreased funding for, 43–44, 158, 159; in DG Nazak's system, 33, 34, 40–42; empowering Afghan staff through, 26, 74–76, 196–97; government funding for, 62, 124–25; limitations on, 45–47; in Maiwand District, 194–97, 203, 208;

projects (development programs) (*cont.*)
measuring results, 70, 85–87, 162, 166, 171, 182–83, 214; obstacles to, 54, 71–74, 126–28; political impacts of, 173, 183, 197; reduction in, 43–44, 178, 183; road improvements, 115; subcontracting process for, 46–47; successes, 34, 78, 124; U.S. failures in, 183, 220; U.S. military funding for, 24–25; vo-ed school, 76, 113–14; wastefulness in, 46–47, 49, 164–66; wells, 75–76, 84–85, 124; for women, 103–9, 115–21. *See also* USAID (U.S. Agency for International Development)

provincial government. *See* government (provincial)

PRT (provincial reconstruction team): and Checchi's training program, 165–66; and DDC's electricity issue, 180; and DG Nazak, 90, 136–37, 157; relaying problems to, 129–33; responsibilities of, 11, 64–65

Qayum, Mr., 22
*Quarterly Report* (SIGAR), 209, 217

radical Islam, 98
Rahmatullah, Major (DCOP), 155, 159, 184–85
railroads, 170–71
Rashid, Abdul, 48, 76, 77–78, 123–24, 162
Razziq, Abdul, 97
Reg Desert, *xxii*, 92
Regional Command South (KAF), 11
Regional Platform South (KAF), 10–11
*Reminiscences* (Lawrence), xv
Richards, David, 45, 189
ring road, 213, 218

road networks: in Band-i Timor, 206–7; deterioration of, 218; economic impact of, 139–40, 171; in economic planning, 52; impact on security, 140; improvements to, 115

Roberts, Frederick, 200
Roberts, Matthew, 91
Robertson, Charles Gray, 177
RRD (reconstruction and rural development) ministry, 59–60, 75–76
RSSA (regional south stability assessment tool), 166–68
Ruhabad (village), *xxii*, 107–8, 116–18

Sandeman, Robert, 217–18
Scaparrotti, Curtis, 152
schools. *See* education
Second Afghan War, 199–200
sheep projects, 48, 50, 86
Sherzai, Gul Agha, 29, 31, 36–37, 39–40, 181, 205–6
Sherzai family, 31
*shuras* (consultation councils): in Dand District, 42, 95–96, 104–5; image of, *fig. 17*; in Maiwand District, 200–201
SIGAR (Special Inspector General for Afghanistan Reconstruction), 5, 25, 150, 151, 209, 217
Sinclair, Jeffrey, 180–81
Sorley, Lewis, 160
Soviet Union, xiii, xvi, 30–31
Spin Boldak, *xxi*, 97
S-RAD (Southern Regional Agricultural Development Program), 158, 174–75, 196–97
State Department (U.S.). *See* embassy (U.S.)
Strongpoint Edgerton. *See* COP Edgerton

Strykers (armored vehicles), *fig. 5*, 82, 90
Sultan, Haji, 180

Taliban: and the ANP, 147–48, 150, 153–54; assassination campaign of, 88–90; attacks on KAF, 12; in Band-i Timor, 202–3, 205–8; and the Canadian military, 82; and corruption, 193; in Dand District, 28–34, 57, 184–85, 192–93; death tolls, xvi, 158–59, 218; DG Nazak's strategy against, 31–34, 40–42; and health workers, xiii; impact of paved roads on, 140; imprisoning DG Nazak, 35–37; increasing attacks of, 99, 220, 222; in Maiwand District, 192–94, 202, 205–8; origins of, 38–39; Pakistan's support of, 98; in Panjwai District, 92, 96; and the poppy industry, 155, 156, 210; popular opinion of, 219; recruiting young people, 49, 115; targeting DG Nazak, 177–78; targeting maliks, 41, 96; targeting mullahs, 42, 156–57; targeting teachers, 194; tribalism of, 38–39; use of IEDs, 28, 29, 82, 90–91, 184–85, 206–7; U.S. targeting, xvi; in Zabul Province, 21
*The Taliban's Campaign for Kandahar* (Forsberg), 9, 27
taxation, 57
"That Day" (Kipling), 199
Thornton, Thomas Henry, 217
Tomsen, Peter, 38–39
training (USAID): in countersurveillance, 7; driving techniques, 3–4; at FSI, 5–6; inadequacy of, 5, 45–46; National Guard camp, 6–7; in Washington DC, 4–5; in weapons, 7–8

training programs (vocational), 48, 76, 103–9, 113–14, 121, 124, 165–66, 195–96, 214
T-walls, 140, 222

*Under the Absolute Amir* (Martin), 79, 100, 122, 139, 169
USAID (U.S. Agency for International Development): agricultural programs of, 51, 60, 123–24, 158, 161–64, 171–75, 194; and Checchi's training program, 165–66; cooperation with military, 25; and DDC's electricity project, 179–80; decreasing funds from, 159, 174–75, 178; District Delivery Program, 47–48, 63, 128, 178, 220; effectiveness of, 47; funding economic plans, 66–67; limitations of programs, 76, 114, 116; predeployment training for, 3–8, 25, 45–46; problems with, 51, 84–85, 173; road network projects, 60, 115; sidewalk project, 214; spending amounts, 51; spending process, 125; S-RAD program, 158, 174–75, 196–97; staffing numbers, 46–47; subcontracting process, 46–47; wastefulness in, 46–47. *See also* field program officers (USAID)

vocational training programs, 48, 76, 104–9, 113–14, 121, 124, 195–96, 214

*The War against the Taliban* (Gall), 45, 189
wells: image of, *fig. 8*; need for, 92–94, 170, 208; programs digging new, 50, 84–85; repair projects, 75–76, 124; and water supply depletion, 210

Wesa, Tooryalai, 83, 142–43, 180
widows, 101–2, 104–5, 116
women: in Afghan society, 100, 101–2;
    attempting to see DG Nazak, 100–
    101; average life expectancy of, xiii;
    in chicken businesses, 119, 163, 214;
    embroidery program for, 106–9,
    116–18, 119–20; informal power of,
    113; marketing items produced by,
    119–20; projects for, *fig. 9*, 115–21,
    124, 165; Sonia Blaha's work with,
    102–6; widows, 101–2, 104–5, 116

Woodward, Billy, 136
World Bank, 73–74

youth shura, 115

Zabul Province, 21
Zahir, Mohammad, 19, 48, 79, 80, 91–
    95, 118, 145, 169–70
Zahoor (youth organizer), 115
Zia ul Haq, Mohammad, 98
Zirak Durrani tribe, 37–39